KEEPING THE SOUL
IN CHRISTIAN HIGHER EDUCATION

In our dreams the ancestors call to us: Finish our work! Finish our work!
All day and all night we come and go through your body.
Deep in your souls we continue the struggle.
Finish Our Work!

Nikos Kazantzakis, *Spiritual Exercises*

Keeping the Soul
in Christian Higher Education

A History of Roanoke College

Robert Benne

WILLIAM B. EERDMANS PUBLISHING COMPANY
GRAND RAPIDS, MICHIGAN

Wm. B. Eerdmans Publishing Co.
2140 Oak Industrial Drive NE, Grand Rapids, Michigan 49505
www.eerdmans.com

Published 2017
Printed in the United States of America

26 25 24 23 22 21 20 19 18 17   3 4 5 6 7 8 9 10 11

ISBN 978-0-8028-7517-4

Library of Congress Cataloging-in-Publication Data

Names: Benne, Robert, author.
Title: Keeping the soul in Christian higher education : a history of Roanoke
    College / Robert D. Benne.
Description: Grand Rapids : Eerdmans Publishing Co., 2017. | Includes
    bibliographical references and index.
Identifiers: LCCN 2017011332 | ISBN 9780802875174 (pbk. : alk. paper)
Subjects: LCSH: Roanoke College—History.
Classification: LCC LD4721.R32 B46 2017 | DDC 378.755/792—dc23 LC record available at
    https://lccn.loc.gov/2017011332

To Norm (1925–2017) and Jo Fintel
who cared for the soul of the college
and
To granddaughter Linnea Kremer
who was edified by it

Contents

CONTENTS

Acknowledgments

I am grateful to my colleagues at Roanoke College who read and offered feedback regarding the chapters I have written. Gerald McDermott (now at Beeson Divinity School, but at Roanoke for many years) unfailingly read and offered advice for each chapter. My wife, Joanna, read every chapter to keep the language from getting too technical or ponderous. I am particularly appreciative of those living Roanoke College presidents who read chapters about their administrations—replete with my critical remarks—without threats of legal action or even serious complaint. The current president of Roanoke, Michael Maxey, has been particularly supportive. I am indebted to the many persons I interviewed to gain first-hand insights into the workings of the college. I appreciate the help of the college archivist, Linda Miller, who dug out an ample supply of old manuscripts and letters for me to read. But, of course, the account I give of the college's long effort to "keep its soul" is my own, warts and all.

I also honor the writers who have challenged a generation of administrators, faculty, and students to grapple with the destiny of Christian higher education—James Burtchaell, Mark Noll, George Marsden, and many others. Because of those pioneers there is a burgeoning literature on the subject. I am even more indebted to those leaders who activated the concerns of those writers by actually reshaping colleges and universities. Among them is Don Schmeltekopf, who as provost at Baylor University helped that university strengthen its Christian identity while it rose to the level of a major research university. He established a leadership seminar (in which I had the honor of teaching) that helped a significant number of Baptist schools maintain and strengthen their "souls."

The organizers of the Lilly Network and the Lilly Fellows Program also helped to actualize the vision of the early writers, especially Mark Schwehn and Arlin Meyer. These leaders set in motion a movement that is helping colleges and universities with Christian heritages keep faith with them. The Christian moral and intellectual tradition that profoundly affected those schools throughout their histories has every reason to remain publicly relevant within them. That is the lesson those writers taught me and legions of others who care about Christian higher education.

Finally, I am obliged again to Eerdmans, who published my first major venture into Christian higher education, *Quality with Soul: How Six Premier Colleges and Universities Keep Faith with Their Christian Traditions* (2001). They have been stalwarts in publishing many works that have helped to keep Christian higher education alive as a real option. In the following pages I hope to tell the story of Roanoke College's efforts to "keep its soul" in such a way as to strengthen Christian higher education at Roanoke and at many church-related schools of a similar kind.

ROBERT BENNE
Roanoke College
December 2016

Introduction

When I arrived at Roanoke College in the fall of 1982, after five years of graduate school and seventeen years of teaching at a Lutheran seminary, I was in for a shock. I had expected Roanoke to be similar to the Midland College (now Midland University) I had attended in the late 1950s, a college that could accurately be called "Lutheran" and "Christian" because its Lutheran faculty unabashedly encouraged its heavily Lutheran student body to understand the Christian faith and live the Christian life. Surprisingly, Roanoke could no longer use the term "Christian," let alone "Lutheran," to describe itself. It had gathered a faculty whose leading voices would have bridled at the use of those words to identify the college. Some were self-consciously antireligious, while a larger number were apathetic, seeing no relationship between the Lutheran heritage of the college and its present incarnation as a liberal arts college. What did the former have to do with the latter? A small group saw that the two were related, but they worried that soon there would be so few Lutherans on the faculty and in the student body that the relationship would end by default.

Truth be told, most mainline Protestants would have had experiences similar to mine had they attended their church-related colleges in the 1950s and then turned up, Rip Van Winkle–like, to experience that same college in the 1980s. The processes of secularization were similar across the board in mainline Christian higher education.

However, my unsettling encounter with secularization at Roanoke was not the whole story. The president at the time of my arrival, Norman Fintel, wanted to strengthen the weakening connection between the sponsoring church and its college. And hiring me was part of his strategy. So I quietly started on my way by teaching courses in Christian theology and ethics and by slowly building a credible department of philosophy and religion. Another part of Fintel's strategy was to call an academic dean who was friendly to the project of strengthening the relationship between the college's Christian heritage and its current academic life. Small steps were taken; small gains were painfully made. And, over time, real progress was made, as I will document later in this volume.

However, a comprehensive understanding of what had happened to secularize Roanoke College over its long history and what strategy might be undertaken to mitigate that process was not available. I was puzzled by the distance a Lutheran-related college had come from the coziness with its sponsoring religious tradition in the late 1950s to the ambivalence, if not hostility, toward it in the early 1980s. What had happened? Why were we Lutherans and our concerns being eased out of the institution our Lutheran forebears had founded? What could we possibly do about it?

We were aided immensely in understanding what had happened by the appearance of a burgeoning literature on the secularization of Christian higher education. James Burtchaell fired the first bombshell, an article in the magazine *First Things* in April 1991, "The Decline and Fall of a Christian College," which analyzed the transition of Vanderbilt University from a robust Christian institution to a pervasively secular one. He documented each step in the movement. As our group of Roanoke faculty and administrators read it together, we had the eerie feeling that we could have substituted the name of our college for that of Vanderbilt in Burtchaell's account.

Burtchaell's pioneering article was followed seven years later by his massive *The Dying of the Light: The Disengagement of Colleges and Universities from Their Christian Churches* (Eerdmans, 1998), in which he traces the secularization process at seventeen different schools. Between Burtchaell's first article and his magnum opus, a number of very helpful books were published: a volume edited by George Marsden and Bradley Longfield, entitled *The Secularization of the Academy* (Oxford, 1992); Marsden's *The Soul of the American University: From Protestant Establishment to Established Nonbelief* (Oxford, 1994); Mark Schwehn's *Exiles from Eden: Religion and the Academic Vocation in America* (Oxford, 1993); Douglas Stone's *Faith and Knowledge: Mainline Protestantism and American Higher Education* (Westminster John Knox, 1994); and Philip Gleason's *Contending with Modernity: Catholic Higher Education in the Twentieth Century* (Oxford, 1996).

These books were insightful in their depiction of the secularization of church-related colleges and universities. While they helped us understand what had happened at Roanoke, they did not offer strategies either to stem the tide of secularization or to strengthen the relationship of the college to its sponsoring religious heritage. Moreover, Burtchaell's large volume is pessimistic throughout. Not only are all colleges likely to experience the same dismal fate as did Vanderbilt, says Burtchaell, but they are faced with a stark choice: to be a fully Christian college, pervasively shaped and governed by its sponsoring church, or to become a totally secularized, generic kind of college.

That grim scenario didn't seem right to me. I was quite sure that there were colleges and universities that had withstood the secularizing process and were vigorously committed to their Christian identity and mission. Moreover, I thought that there was more variety among Christian colleges than Burtchaell assumes. The stark choice he proposed had to be moderated by looking more carefully at different types of Christian colleges. Further, I thought, if we were to carefully analyze successful Christian colleges, we could get a more nuanced grasp of their variety and, most importantly, we could discover clues about how to maintain their character. For those colleges that had lost a good deal of their connection to their religious tradition, perhaps we could identify strategies to reconnect, as Roanoke has done, to a significant extent.

I soon had the chance to pay attention to the unanswered questions that the above studies had raised for me. I was able to spend a year (1999–2000) at Valparaiso University as the senior fellow in its Lilly Fellows program. The senior fellow was expected to undertake a major research project of his or her own and to share and discuss that research at a weekly seminar with the young Lilly fellows who were teaching at the university. There could not have been a better context in which to explore these issues surrounding Christian higher education: the Lilly Fellows program was dedicated to nurturing young faculty for work in church-related schools. The challenges of Christian higher education were at the center of its interest, as they were for many faculty members and administrators at Valparaiso University. Because I was right in the midst of the university, I chose to study Valparaiso as one of the schools that had kept faith with its Christian tradition.

I decided to examine six religiously affiliated colleges and universities that were not only recognized as quality liberal arts institutions but also had maintained a strong Christian identity: Wheaton College, Calvin College, Baylor University, Notre Dame University, St. Olaf College, along with Valparaiso University. I studied each school intensively and then spent about a week at five of the schools—but a whole year at Valparaiso. I spoke with all the constituencies I could. I digested the materials I had gathered, and then I tried to make sense of it all in a volume entitled *Quality with Soul: How Six Premier Colleges and Universities Keep Faith with Their Religious Traditions* (Eerdmans, 2001). In that book I analyzed each school in terms of three categories: vision, ethos, and the people who embodied the vision and ethos.

By "vision" I meant the theological/philosophical perspective that shaped the life of the college in all its facets. Such a perspective is articulated in the inaugural address of the school's president; it is distilled in the institution's mission or purpose statement; and it is embodied in its curriculum. The religious element in the school's mission is most clearly and systematically conceived by its religion department; but it is carried forward by many other professors as they relate their religious perspective to their secular field. This latter process is often called "faith and learning engagement."

By "ethos" I meant the way of life—expressed in practices—that is informed and guided by its vision. That includes the role of worship and Bible study on campus, the moral commitments that govern life together, the level of service and hospitality that ensue, and the subtle tones of "atmosphere" that characterize college life. By "people" I meant the personnel—faculty, staff, administrators, board—who know the guiding vision of the sponsoring religious tradition and unabashedly practice its ethos. The vision and ethos obviously have to be incarnated in real people; those people, along with other supporters, then carry the character and mission of the college. I was thus very interested in the hiring practices that brought the right personnel to the school so that the faith could be kept.

I found that, even among the six colleges and universities I selected, there were different types. I distinguished "orthodox" schools, in which all personnel had to be observant members of their Christian tradition, from "critical mass" schools, in which a majority of the personnel were either observant in or supportive of their sponsoring tradition. In either case, the Christian vision and ethos were paradigmatic for the school.

I also knew of many other colleges and universities that were not as robust in their Christian identities as the six I had selected, but still considered themselves to be church-related in a meaningful way. Roanoke College was a school of that sort. So I developed a category I called "intentional pluralist," in which the school guaranteed "a voice at the table" for its sponsoring tradition but did not privilege it beyond that.[1] The voice might be expressed in the president's inaugural address, and it might be represented in the reli-

---

1. The full typology is printed in the Appendix.

gion department and scattered around in other departments of the school. The president, some key administrators, and a number of the faculty members represented that tradition. Likewise, the ethos of the Christian body that sponsored the school was one honored subculture among a number of others. Usually a chaplain from that tradition was employed by the school. There are many church-related colleges and universities of this "intentional pluralist" kind.

By the word "soul" in *Quality with Soul*, I meant the discernible spirit (or *Geist*) of the school. It was expressed in a combination of its religious vision and ethos. This spirit animated the school and gave it character and shaped its mission. It was that special spirit that the school wanted to impart to its students. In my study I demonstrated that each school kept its vision and ethos—its soul—publicly relevant to the whole life of the school. But then I moved beyond the analysis of those six schools' Christian character to an attempt to discern the strategies they used to "keep their soul." These strategies were very important for those schools who wanted to keep and strengthen their soul, but they were also useful for those who wanted to regain their soul in some fashion. It was this latter use that was relevant to Roanoke College and likewise to those many colleges who wanted to maintain or regain a credible relationship with their religious heritage but could not likely achieve a thoroughly robust relationship. A section of my book, entitled "The Long Road Forward," offers just such strategies of "recovery."

Though I had written and lectured about the "soul" of Roanoke College over the thirty-some years I had been there, I knew that was only part of the whole story. I knew a lot about my time at the college, but what about the original definition of the soul of the college at its founding and its development over many years? What changes had it undergone? Was there any continuity between its soul at its founding and its life as a twenty-first-century liberal arts college? What is left of it, and does it still animate the life of the college?

Since the college was nearing the 175th anniversary of its founding, why not trace its quest for soul over that extended time? Not only would such a study illuminate the underlying meaning of the college over its long history, but it would also provide some broader lessons on how to define a school's soul, how to keep it, how to lose it, and how to recover it—at least partially.[2]

---

2. I must admit that I have a sense of obligation to those Roanoke College presidents and faculty who have gone before. Jaroslav Pelikan famously said: "Tradition is the living faith of the dead; traditionalism is the dead faith of the living." I feel part of the living faith of

This latter provision could be of great use to other colleges in their own struggle for soul.

After all, many other church-related schools have had similar challenges. I saw that the Lutheran-ness of Roanoke College was important to cherish insofar as it represented the college's connection to the Christian tradition in general. In this larger sense, the story of Roanoke College was the story of many American church-related colleges and universities. I saw that what has happened at this college has also happened to a legion of church-related schools across the country. This story is a microcosm of Christian higher education, at least for those schools of the Protestant mainline and perhaps even of the Catholic fold that have lost their earlier robust connections with their traditions. Perhaps, I thought, this story and what I learned from it could help other colleges and universities understand what had happened, and what might be done to reorient their institutions.

An additional impetus for telling the story is that the college's birthday coincides with the five hundredth anniversary of the Reformation, which has done so much to further higher education in the Western world. How has a Lutheran-related institution of long standing fulfilled the high aspirations of the Lutheran Reformation? Do the central Reformation themes—one of them to serve one's neighbor in one's worldly callings—still pulsate in the soul of the college? Finally, the story itself is intrinsically interesting, full of colorful characters, challenging situations, and heroic efforts to sustain the college and its mission. Simply telling the story has its own value.

While there have been three histories of the college, none has focused on the central question of meaning: What set of convictions has animated the college over its lifetime? William Eisenberg's magnificent history of the college, *The First Hundred Years: Roanoke College 1842–1942* (Shenandoah Publishing House, 1942), is a celebratory account of the college that covers most of the facets of its life. Full of affectionate portraits and indispensable facts, it refrains from critical interpretation and ends at 1942, before the great challenges of secularization had appeared. Mark Miller's *Dear Old Roanoke: A Sesquicentennial Portrait* (Mercer University Press, 1992) is an institutional account, illustrated with many pictures, that emphasizes the college's social history. However, it is uninterested in larger questions of meaning and

the Roanoke dead, those presidents and faculty who have gone before, many of whom have wholly devoted themselves to the cause of the college. I selected the quote from Kazantzakis as an epigraph for this book to challenge those who have the destiny of the college in their hands "to finish the work of their ancestors."

purpose, especially those of a philosophical or religious nature. A shorter volume by George Keller, *Prologue to Prominence: A Half Century at Roanoke College* (Lutheran University Press, 2005), covers the time from Roanoke's first application for a Phi Beta Kappa chapter in 1951 until it gained one in 2003. It attempts to be as comprehensive as possible in a brief eighty-six pages. Though I have a different intent than any of them, I owe much to their fine work, to which the many footnotes will attest.

In the following I trace the quest for soul at Roanoke College from its beginning to the present day. However, I want to enter a caveat here. I have not attempted a comprehensive history of the college, the kind a professional historian might accomplish. That task is beyond my training and ambition. The narrower focus on the "soul," the inner meaning and mission of the college, is closer to my training and vocation as a practical theologian. I pay little attention to many other important facets of college life—athletics, music, drama—and I treat but lightly finances, buildings, and campaigns. Among academic departments, I focus on the religion and philosophy department and, I am embarrassed to admit, ignore other great ones.

I will organize the chapters according to ten presidencies that extend from the college's origin in 1842 through 2016.[3] I analyze each administration by covering the categories I have explained above—vision, ethos, and people. I get at each of these categories in various ways since each includes many facets. One of the main ways I get at "vision" is to do a careful reading of the inaugural address of each Roanoke College president. I follow the example of Robert Bellah in his seminal 1967 article, entitled "The American Civil Religion,"[4] in which he analyzes the inaugural address of each American president to discern how each thought that he or she could amplify the spirit of America. I found that the presidents of Roanoke College revealed a number of important things in their inaugurals: what they were committed to as presidents; what they thought the college was committed to; and what they could contribute to that mission. The second revelation was very interesting. Except for the founding president, all succeeding ones sized up what they thought the college was committed to and then accommodated to that in noticeable ways. They shaped a good

3. There have actually been eleven presidents, but one (Thomas Dosh) lasted only one year and had little impact. I have devoted only a few paragraphs to him. Also, covering the current administration is problematic. Since the story of the present Maxey administration is incomplete, it seems wise to refrain from attempting a definitive assessment.

4. "The American Civil Religion," *Daedelus: Journal of the American Academy of Arts and Science* (Winter 1967): 1–21.

deal of their own vision according to what they thought the college was already committed to.

Each chapter begins with a depiction of the historical context in which the president held sway, and includes critical reflections on how the soul of the college fared under each one.[5] In the conclusion I take up the important task of elaborating the learnings we can glean from this long story: what went well and what didn't; what conserved and strengthened its soul and what diminished it; and, most importantly, what needs to be done to preserve its soul.

It is quite a story. I hope you, the reader, will find it as interesting and informative as I have.

---

5. It is important to convey a basic understanding of the society in which the president and the college carried on their mission. Chapter 1 includes a very extensive interpretation of the historical era in which the college was born. That era had a good deal of lasting influence on the first three presidents and on the character of the college. It could well be argued that the college was an evangelical college at least until the turn of the twentieth century, when it became more generically mainstream Protestant. However, it always defined itself broadly enough to encompass all sorts of Protestants, and later expanded the definition to include Catholics and Jews.

THE SURPRISING DAVID BITTLE (1853–1876)

The Formation of Roanoke College

"The most momentous duty of one generation to another is its education." That bold statement was uttered by David Bittle at the opening of his 1854 inaugural address as Roanoke College's first president.[1] The college continues to honor its first president by often quoting that remark. But it rarely delves into what Bittle meant by "education," which was distinctly and understandably different from what the current Roanoke College offers. Unpacking that meaning will not only reveal a rather surprising first president, but also the

---

1. His inaugural address was entitled "A Collegiate Education" and was published by the Roanoke College Board of Trustees in 1854 and printed in Gettysburg by H. C. Neinstedt. Roanoke College became a four-year degree-granting college in March 1853 by action of the Virginia House of Delegates. Prior to that, it was known as the Virginia Collegiate Institute, which was founded in 1842 by David Bittle in his parsonage in Augusta County, Virginia, where he was pastoring Mount Tabor Lutheran Church. The Institute was devoted to basic education for local young men. The Institute grew slowly at that location under Bittle and his friend and colleague, another Lutheran clergyman, Christopher Baughman, who served as principal. In 1845, Bittle departed for successful ministries in Maryland while Baughman carried on his duties with the Institute. Baughman and the supporters of the Institute decided to move it to Salem, Virginia, in 1847. Baughman oversaw that move and guided the Institute until he left in the spring of 1853 to become the first principal of Hagerstown Female Seminary, which David Bittle had also helped to found. It seems that Baughman disagreed with the Institute's board of trustees' decision to make the Institute into a full-fledged college; so when the position at Hagerstown came open, he took it. The board acted immediately in the summer of 1853 to fill the open position by calling David Bittle to become the first president of the newly chartered college. He accepted immediately and said, "I have laid myself out for work for Roanoke College" (quoted in W. A. Eisenberg, *The First Hundred Years: Roanoke College, 1842–1942* [Strasburg, VA: Shenandoah Publishing House, 1942], 73).

kind of college he formed in its years from 1853 to his death in 1876. The real Dr. Bittle is full of surprises. However, we cannot get to the full meaning of Bittle's statement without delving into the historical setting from which he came. That background includes not only the larger context of national and religious life in antebellum America but also the more specific context supplied by what is known as "Americanist Lutheranism," exemplified most dramatically by Bittle's mentor, Samuel Simon Schmucker.

Antebellum America

In 1835, Lyman Beecher, a well-known minister in New England, preached a sermon entitled "A Plea for the West," in which he observed that a vast new empire was opening in the American West and that Christians had to seize the opportunity to shape the "religious and political destiny of the nation."[2] Not only were Americans pouring into the West so fast that by midcentury over half the population was west of the Appalachians, but immigrants were coming in droves to both the East and West. The unchurched were not only a problem on the West's brawling frontier; only about 5 to 10 percent of the people in the East belonged to a church. The challenge seemed enormous, but the dominant strand of Christianity in the America at that time, evangelicalism, took it up with enthusiasm. Jonathan Edwards, a major figure in the First Great Awakening in the early eighteenth century, believed that after a considerable decline in the prospects of the church, the Spirit might generate a revival of the faith. This new revival certainly seemed to characterize the spirit of the times, fueled further by growing postmillennial expectations. Such hopes anticipated that the nation would be Christianized and would send forth missionaries to all the world, resulting in a thousand years of peace and harmony. After the final defeat of the devil, Jesus would come again. Postmillennialism was in the air.

American evangelicalism—typified by a high view of biblical authority, a fervent belief in Jesus as Savior, a conviction that one must be "born-again" to a disciplined Christian life, and a commitment to spread the gospel to everyone—had won the day among the denominations by the end of the eighteenth century, and it generated the Second Great Awakening. Specific denominations still persisted, but they all participated in the evangelical

2. As quoted in Bruce L. Shelley, *Church History in Plain Language*, 3rd ed. (Nashville: Thomas Nelson, 2008), 383.

surge. Even some Episcopalians and Presbyterians jumped on the band-wagon. And, as we shall see, Lutherans also were caught up in the enthusiasm. Many denominations gave up their theological distinctives, though a reconfessionalizing of the denominations took place in response to this surge, but that came later in the nineteenth century.[3]

Revivalism

Evangelicals took up the task of Christianizing America by using two major instruments: the revival and the voluntary society.[4] The new revivalism started long before Beecher made his speech in 1835. It was already going by 1800 among churches and colleges in the East, which provided much leadership for the western push. The western revivals began in the newly settled regions of Kentucky and Tennessee. Preachers conducted revivals in churches and then in lengthy camp meetings that sometimes lasted weeks. Vivid portrayals of heaven and hell brought forth many converts, many of whom became disciples of Jesus and members of churches. The revivals spread, waxed and waned, and then were given a whole new impetus by that master of the technique of revival, Charles Finney.

Finney (1792–1875), a "tempestuous son of Connecticut who found his vocation in the West," began as a lawyer but wound up as the father of modern revivalism. After he experienced a conversion in 1821, he refused formal training and immediately began a street-preaching mission in Adams, New York. He was spectacularly successful and moved his revivals to larger towns and cities in New York; he spent over a year conducting revivals in New York City.[5] He employed "new measures" in his revivals, which involved "the practice of praying for people by name, females praying in public meetings, the invasion of towns without an invitation of the local pastor, overfamiliarity with the deity in public prayer, protracted meetings, the use of the anxious seat, inquiry meetings, and immediate admission of converts into the churches."[6] Denying that these measures needed the work of the Holy Spirit, he declared

---

3. Mark Noll, *America's God: From Jonathan Edwards to Abraham Lincoln* (New York: Oxford University Press, 2002), 411.

4. Shelley, *Church History*, 384.

5. Sydney Ahlstrom, *A Religious History of the American People* (New Haven: Yale University Press, 1972), 461.

6. Mark Noll et al., eds., *Eerdmans' Handbook to Christianity in America* (Grand Rapids: Eerdmans, 1983), 176.

that a "revival is not a miracle, or dependent on a miracle in any sense. It is a purely philosophical (i.e., scientific) result of the right use of constituted means."[7] His revivals led him finally to Oberlin College, which he made into a center of revival in the West as well as a bastion of antislavery activism.

Though opposed by "old school" Presbyterians, Finney prevailed in his "new measures." He not only "produced" conversions, but also demanded "entire sanctification," which entailed visible and relevant social action following conversion. Holiness became a human possibility.[8] This vigorous new revivalism has reverberated even to the present day.

Revivalism in the Second Great Awakening was encouraged by a widespread belief that Christians at long last had a religious freedom that could really penetrate the people and the country. With the founding of the new nation came its Constitution and Amendments: the First Amendment guaranteed the free exercise of religion, and it prohibited an established national church. The evangelicals of the time had an "almost messianic belief in the benefits of liberty."[9] They believed that the entanglement of throne and altar throughout the ages had hampered both the state and church.[10] For the first time ever, the faith was free to experiment with new approaches to the evangelizing and Christianizing of the populace. The Spirit was now free to move through the churches to all the world.

Further, the government was no longer obligated to protect and privilege a fossilized, decrepit institution that was bound by the past. But government needed the virtue that lively religion could supply. This was the historical moment for free religion to contribute an essential ingredient to the new republic. The country required a *Christian republicanism* that would bring together personal morality and social well-being. The evangelical project was to supply that personal morality to the nation so that it could flourish. This Christian republicanism merged with a postrevolutionary liberal republicanism that placed "much more democratic trust in the people at large, much more attention to the protection of individual rights, much more concern for enhancing the economic opportunities for all white men, and even occasionally some concern for the participation of women in public life."[11]

7. Ahlstrom, *A Religious History*, 460.

8. Ahlstrom, *A Religious History*, 460.

9. Noll, *America's God*, 56.

10. Nearly every evangelical viewed the Catholic Church as an intractable foe of religious liberty; therefore, anti-Catholicism was pervasive. The heavy immigration of Catholics at this time added to evangelical alarm.

11. Noll, *America's God*, 55.

Moreover, the intellectual life of this era conspired to fuel both revivalism and Christian republicanism. It was dominated by the Scottish "common sense" philosophy stemming from Francis Hutcheson, Thomas Reid, and Adam Smith, which emphasized the innate capacity of the ordinary person to intuit truth in nature, religion, and ethics. All humans had faculties in their consciousness that could accurately perceive the nature of important dimensions of life. This philosophy was a constructive response to the skepticism of another Scottish philosopher, David Hume, as well as to what the intellectuals of the day thought was the corruption of traditional European ideas and practices. The revivalists, such as Charles Finney, needed no theological education or reliance on traditional thought (confessions or creeds) to interpret the Bible correctly. Furthermore, common people who heard the preaching could recognize the truth with their own faculties. Access to truth was being democratized.

In academic life this common sense philosophy was wedded to "faculty psychology," which posited three faculties in human nature—reason, passion, and will. The point of academic life was to appeal to common sense in matters of reason, which included ethics and the sciences, and to govern the passions with the newly educated ethical reason. The will, however, was another matter. Only true religion could break the will's selfishness and redirect it to the truth. So academic life always included a strong religious dimension that encouraged conversion. Therefore, the colleges of that time saw no disharmony between the Christian faith and the natural sciences or classical learning. All was held together by the confidence in common sense.[12]

Voluntary Societies

If revivalism was one potent instrument used by evangelicals in their great antebellum project to Christianize America, the second was the voluntary society. The former flowed seamlessly into the latter. What better way for born-again, energized Christians to show their discipleship than by joining one of the many voluntary associations that were being spawned by resurgent evangelicalism? Finney's doctrine of "entire sanctification" held that Christian perfection was attainable in this life and that signs of it were visible

12. Noll has a remarkable account spread throughout his book on these intellectual matters. See esp. *America's God*, 93–113.

in the actions of Christians, not only in private ones but also in public ones. He held that "politics are part of religion in a country such as this."[13] What better formula than to produce Christian citizens who would be ready to reform the country through voluntary societies?

These societies were interdenominational in character, gathering many kinds of Christians into their efforts. They were symptomatic of a movement among a number of denominations toward organic union. Among other denominations there was an effort to find the common doctrinal grounds upon which to go forward. But everyone agreed that there was enough agreement to form voluntary societies to help build a "righteous empire" in America. Among them were: the American Bible Society (1808), the American Board of Commissioners for Foreign Missions (1810), the American Educational Society (1813), the American Sunday School Union (1824), the American Tract Society (1825), the American Home Missionary Society (1826), the American Temperance Society (1826), the Lord's Day Observance Society (1831), the Anti-Slavery Society (1833), and other societies devoted to women's education, treatment of the mentally ill, and prison reform. This burst of energy was accompanied by fundraising of herculean proportions. These societies raised something like $2.8 million ($75 million in today's dollars) in thirteen years to further their goals, while the federal government spent only $3.6 million on infrastructure in the same span.[14]

The founding of educational institutions was part and parcel of this voluntary thrust. Between 1815 and 1861, approximately 150 colleges were founded in the American West to "provide an educated ministry and to propagate intellectual culture in these remote regions."[15] Many had academies attached to them to give young students a proper start. There were few public institutions in these areas, so the churches took up the challenge to educate the young. The great majority of the colleges were organized as private nonprofit corporations that were chartered by the states, with a board of directors drawn directly from the sponsoring denomination. Students and faculty were recruited from those churches. Faculties had little say in the governance of the colleges. This arrangement ensured that the religious purposes of the colleges remained front and center.

13. Quoted in Noll, *America's God*, 309.
14. Noll, *America's God*, 198.
15. Thomas Askew, "The Founding of Church Colleges," in Noll et al., *Eerdmans' Handbook*, 225.

The president's leadership capacities determined the destiny of the college. Typically, the president was a clergyman selected by the board of trustees to perform many functions, including teaching a capstone course on moral philosophy for all graduating students. That course provided an American Christian worldview for the students. Enterprising young clergymen, encouraged by their denomination and by the local leaders in churches they served, stepped forward to supply a wide array of educational opportunities for the common people of the frontier. Many of those colleges were weak and quickly expired, but a goodly number survived to provide a unifying force in American culture. Along with mathematics and the natural sciences, the curriculum of the old-style liberal arts college blended "the moral absolutes of biblical theism with the heritage of Western learning, especially emphasizing the classical languages of Greece and Rome."[16]

This antebellum period in American history was a bracing time. It is difficult not to admire the energy, enthusiasm, optimism, and activism of the era. American evangelicalism was indeed a species of "constructive Protestantism." The rupture of the Civil War is doubly sad when we realize how it sharply diminished those energies. Yet, even that catastrophe could not stop the evangelical efforts to shape the destiny of America.

Samuel Simon Schmucker, Americanist Lutheran

Without the preceding interpretation of the antebellum American religious scene, Samuel Schmucker would be impossible to understand. He is a vivid reflection of that era, indeed in some ways simply a carbon copy of its enthusiasms. But he was also a brilliant and innovative agent in his own right, though some of his innovations in time distanced himself sharply from confessional Lutheranism.

Samuel Simon Schmucker (1799–1873) was born in Hagerstown, Maryland, during the pastorate of his father, John George Schmucker, who himself was to become president of the Pennsylvania Ministerium, the oldest and strongest of the Lutheran synods.[17] The Schmucker family had been in America for several generations and had close connections to the great Muhlenberg family, which was deeply involved in the American Revolution

---

16. Askew, "The Founding of Church Colleges," 225.

17. William Eisenberg, *The Lutheran Church in Virginia: 1717–1962* (Lynchburg, VA: J. P. Bell, 1967), 153.

and the subsequent founding of the republic. The Schmuckers, in the portrayal of Frederick Wentz, were "birthright" Lutherans and Americans.[18] They grew up with the nation and had no sense of the feelings of isolation, powerlessness, and inferiority that many later immigrant groups experienced. Like the Muhlenbergs, they rubbed shoulders comfortably with the wealthy and influential. They also typified a strong strain of pietistic Lutheranism, which emphasized the religion of the heart.[19]

The young Schmucker, after attending York Academy in York, Pennsylvania, left for the University of Pennsylvania in Philadelphia to study under J. H. C. Hellmuth, the direct successor of Muhlenberg as America's Lutheran leader. Hellmuth was a moderate confessional Lutheran who resisted both the fashionably elite rationalism of his time, on the one hand, and the highly individualistic reading of the Bible by the evangelicals, on the other.[20] As a moderate confessionalist, he taught the young Schmucker to have an aversion to sharp theological distinctions.[21]

At eighteen, Schmucker returned to York to run the classical department of the academy, and he continued his theological study with his father. Then it was off to Princeton Seminary in 1818 to study with Archibald Alexander, who held to a moderate Presbyterian confessionalism but "seasoned [his] confessional loyalty with some alloy—[in his case] an interest in revival and Christian religious experience."[22] Schmucker's Princeton training encouraged in him a "broadmindedness and tolerance towards non-Lutherans that was destined to clash with the spirit of denominational exclusiveness that came to prevail about the middle of the century."[23] Thus, Schmucker, a "birthright Lutheran," began his ministry with the "best and broadest educational foundation that any native-born American Lutheran had received up to that time."[24]

18. Frederick Wentz, "Birthright Americans: The Shape of the Muhlenberg/Schmucker Tradition," *Seminary Ridge Review*, Lutheran Theological Seminary, Gettysburg, PA (Summer 1999): 12–13.

19. Abdel Ross Wentz, *The Lutheran Church in American History* (Philadelphia: United Lutheran Publication House, 1933), 169.

20. Noll, *America's God*, 410.

21. A. R. Wentz, *The Lutheran Church*, 169. "Confessionalism" means a strong adherence to the confessional documents of a religious tradition. Among Lutherans, it means taking the *Book of Concord* seriously as a crucial means of interpreting the Bible and articulating central convictions.

22. Noll, *America's God*, 300.

23. A. R. Wentz, *The Lutheran Church*, 169.

24. Eisenberg, *The Lutheran Church in Virginia*, 150.

Upon leaving Princeton, he determined to do three things: translate a worthy system of Lutheran theology, establish a Lutheran seminary, and found a Lutheran college.[25] Though his goals seemed grand, he realized each one in a relatively brief time. His translation of Storr's *Biblical Theology* appeared in 1826, the same year he was instrumental in founding Gettysburg Seminary. Gettysburg College followed in 1832. One could add to those worthy goals the rescue of the foundering General Synod in 1823, which he accomplished at the tender age of twenty-four. Samuel Schmucker was a phenomenon!

After his ordination in 1820, Schmucker became pastor in New Market, Virginia, in the lair of the Henkel family, who were far more ethnic and confessionalist in orientation. This led the young Schmucker to remark: "Henkel and sons persecute instinctively everything that bears the name Schmucker."[26] The tension between the two families anticipated the sharp divisions among Lutherans that were to take place later in the century. Schmucker was educating future Lutheran pastors in his parsonage; but in 1826, after six successful years in the New Market parish, he was called to establish—and become the first president and first professor of—the new seminary in Gettysburg.

Schmucker founded the seminary on fairly substantial Lutheran confessional grounds: the Augsburg Confession and Luther's catechisms. His seminary began to educate Lutheran ministers to answer the intense need for pastors in the expanding nation. But then he experienced a curious transition: he moved from his moderate Lutheran confessionalism to a vigorous embrace of the larger evangelical movement that was surging in America during the early decades of the nineteenth century, including many of the elements I have described above. There seem to have been several reasons for that fateful move. First, he had inherited a pietist "religion-of-the-heart" Lutheranism from his family, and that pietism had an affinity with American evangelicalism. Second, his study under Hellmuth had led him to fasten on basic Christian essentials and to avoid sharp theological distinctions that would lead to unnecessary division among Christians. The time and study he spent under Alexander at Princeton had opened him up to non-Lutherans and to a relatively positive assessment of revivalism. No doubt the general excitement attending the evangelical effort to Christianize the new nation was paramount. As a "birthright" Lutheran and American, he wanted to be

25. Eisenberg, *The Lutheran Church in Virginia*, 151.
26. Eisenberg, *The Lutheran Church in Virginia*, 151.

where the action was—where the shaping of the "righteous empire" was happening. He had no sense of being an outsider to the pulsating new energies
running through antebellum America; furthermore, he wanted to pull his
fellow Lutherans into the movement. Many of them were also "birthright"
Lutherans who could be called to arms. So he plunged in.

In 1838, Schmucker issued his "Fraternal Appeal to the American
Churches," calling for the reunion of the churches on "the apostolic basis."
It gained national attention. He also encouraged the General Synod, which
he rescued from collapse, to establish fraternal relations with many other
denominations and voluntary associations.[27] His commitment to the evangelical project was given increased urgency by the arrival of large numbers
of new Lutheran immigrants from Germany, many of whom were likely to
withdraw into ethnic enclaves of a much stricter confessional subscription.
Schmucker feared that the arriving Lutherans—especially those who would
later make up the Missouri Synod, whom he called "old Lutherans" or "ultra
Lutherans"—would not appreciate "our civil or religious institutions" and
hence would not contribute to the evangelization of America through revivalism and voluntary societies.[28] Rather, they would become impediments
by holding to their distinctives and creating division just when the churches
needed unity. This fear redoubled his efforts to Americanize the Lutherans
as quickly as possible.

It would be tedious to detail Schmucker's conformation with the general
evangelical tendencies of that era, but it is important to sketch out the main
points. He imbibed freely in the postmillennialist aspirations of the time:
America was to be the staging ground of the millennium. He believed that
the removal of government from religious jurisdiction was the triumph of
God's will. Not only was religion free, but the state took a republican form,
which he believed was right out of the New Testament. "God has placed His
people in circumstances most auspicious for the gradual perfecting of His
visible kingdom."[29] In order to further this millennial progress, an essential
step forward required that the church achieve as much unity as possible.
While this may not have meant organic union, it meant unity in basic Christian teaching and mission. This call to unity, of course, was to Protestants
only, for Schmucker, like all evangelicals of that period, considered Roman

---

27. Ahlstrom, *Religious History*, 521.

28. Paul Baglyos, "One Nation under God? Schmucker's Theology of the American
Republic," in *Seminary Ridge Review*, Lutheran Theological Seminary, Gettysburg, PA
(Summer, 1999): 31.

29. Baglyos, "One Nation under God?" 30.

Catholicism to be part of the corrupted past. But in order to bring Lutherans into unity with the evangelical consensus, Schmucker was willing to give up crucial Lutheran distinctives.

Schmucker avidly supported the ubiquitous voluntary societies during the Second Great Awakening; dearest to his heart was the Evangelical Alliance, which attempted to bring together all Protestants both in America and in Britain. He took an active role in the founding of the World Evangelical Alliance.[30] Furthermore, he became very involved in the Sunday School Union, believing that Christian education of the young was crucial to supplying virtue for the new republic. This led him to become an ardent proponent of Sabbath observance, going so far as to condemn the operations of railroads and canals on Sunday as "channels through which a regular stream of Sabbath desecration, week after week, flows through the length and breadth of our land."[31] Closely related to this crusade was the temperance movement, which he vigorously supported.

Of more importance to modern readers, Schmucker was heavily involved in antislavery activity, roundly condemning slavery in many of his writings. In 1840 the students at Gettysburg seminary asked him for an official seminary statement regarding slavery. He responded by developing fifteen propositions on the subject: the propositions, entitled "Of Slavery," are a thoroughgoing denunciation of slavery based on biblical and secular grounds, especially the Declaration of Independence.[32] He later presented the propositions to various synods.

This strong alliance with evangelicalism and his commitment to doctrinal unity led him into increased tension with traditional Lutheranism, a tension he had earlier experienced with the Henkels of Virginia. He sharpened the battle lines in 1846 by sending a "circular letter to Germany disparaging the Lutheran view of the Lord's Supper."[33] He favored the evangelical "religion of the spirit" over the Lutheran "religion of forms." He and his colleague, Benjamin Kurtz, who edited *The Lutheran Observer* in those crucial years, advocated the revival methods—the "new measures"—of Finney and emphasized personal piety above all else. They labeled those who opposed these emphases "head Christians" and "catechism Christians."

Schmucker adapted to the regnant anticonfessional interpretation of

30. Ahlstrom, *Religious History*, 521.
31. Baglyos, "One Nation under God?" 33.
32. "Schmucker," as introduced and edited by Mark Oldenburg, *Seminary Ridge Review* (Summer, 1999): 5–11.
33. A. R. Wentz, *The Lutheran Church*, 170.

the Bible. Theology was "to be governed entirely by the Word of God, interpreted according to the correct principles of common sense, which is the only true system of Historical Exegesis."[34] Furthermore, literal interpretation could be set aside only "when the passage literally interpreted *contradicts natural reason, common sense,* or the testimony of our senses."[35]

The Americanist movement in Lutheranism led by Schmucker gained a good deal of momentum during the thirties, forties, and early fifties of the nineteenth century, mainly via the leadership of Schmucker's students at Gettysburg Seminary. At least five leaders emerged from Gettysburg to promote the Americanist cause: Benjamin Kurtz, Ezra Keller, Samuel Sprecher, Theophilus Stork, and David Bittle. I have already mentioned Kurtz as a strong propagandist for the cause; those who founded colleges had even more impact. David Bittle founded the Virginia Institute—which was to become Roanoke College—in 1842. He was also instrumental in the founding of the Hagerstown Female Seminary in 1852. Ezra Keller, who came from the same congregation that Bittle did—in Middleton, Maryland—founded Wittenberg College in 1845 as an educational prong of the evangelical cause. He was followed by Samuel Sprecher, who was president of Wittenberg for twenty-five years and "exerted far reaching influence on behalf of the 'new measures' and a modified Lutheranism."[36] Theophilus Stork founded Newberry College in 1858 along the same lines.

But confessionalist forces gained considerable strength from the mid-1840s onward. The formidable confessionalist Charles Porterfield Krauth was more than an intellectual match for Schmucker. When Schmucker and Kurtz tried in 1850 to get the General Synod to adapt an Americanist doctrinal "abstract," it was defeated. Seemingly driven to more extreme measures by the strengthening numbers of his opponents, Schmucker wrote the infamous "Definite Synodical Platform" in 1855 to rally what he thought were his troops. This "Platform" revised the Augsburg Confession by excising significant Lutheran teachings: baptismal regeneration; the real presence of Christ and remission of sins in communion; and the two-kingdoms approach to public life. Further, he criticized the Augsburg Confession for its approval of the mass; private confession and absolution; and its laxity on the divine obligation of the Sabbath.[37] Except for several small synods under the

34. Quoted by Noll in *America's God*, 411.
35. Noll, *America's God*, 411.
36. A. R. Wentz, *The Lutheran Church*, 171.
37. A. R. Wentz, *The Lutheran Church*, 175.

influence of Sprecher, the rest of the church soundly defeated the "Definite Synodical Platform." Though there were a few more small skirmishes—a separate Melanchthon Synod was organized and existed for a short time—the vast majority of the synods of the Lutheran churches publicly repudiated the Americanist project. That defeat did not mean, of course, that its influence in many sectors of Lutheranism ceased.

Samuel Schmucker held on as president of Gettysburg Seminary until 1864, and he continued to attend every meeting of the General Synod until 1870. Sadly, he retained his hopes for the triumph of the Americanist project long after its prospects were dashed. He published a book entitled *The Church of Redeemer* in 1867, which reiterated all the themes he had pressed during his active theological and administrative life. Poignantly, he had prepared the text for a synod gathering in case the invited lecturer did not show up, which had happened the year before. Alas, the speaker did come, and Schmucker did not have the chance to give his lecture; he published it later in book form. In the end, his tenacity did not serve him well: "It alienated many of his former friends and clouded the evening of his days."[38]

The Surprising David Bittle

If Schmucker cannot be understood outside the context of the Second Great Awakening, that is doubly true of Bittle, whom we cannot understand without considering the influence of both the Second Great Awakening and Schmucker's mentoring. Doing so, however, produces a surprising portrait of David Bittle and the college he founded. Both were in many ways products of the historical context that shaped them (which I have sketched in some detail above). That portrait consists of a number of dimensions, and they are unexpected. First and foremost, Bittle was essentially an American evangelical with scarcely any traditional Lutheran content in his thinking or practice. The college he founded was an evangelical college meant to be an instrument in the Christianization of America and the world. Second, Bittle was a Christian republican of the first order: that is, he was engaged in the actions that evangelicals thought would supply virtue to the new republic. Third, Bittle had much more intellectual firepower than is usually expected of a man of action, which he was to an extreme degree. In short, Bittle was far more a creature of his time and a student of Schmucker than is generally

38. A. R. Wentz, *The Lutheran Church*, 170.

believed. That realization does not diminish his heroic stature at all, but it does get closer to explaining the convictions that drove him, and, in so doing, clarifies the vision he had for Roanoke College.

Bittle as an Evangelical

Identifying David Bittle as an evangelical does not mean that he had no loyalty to the Lutheran church of which he was a part. He was born a Lutheran, lived a Lutheran, and died a Lutheran. The Lutheran churches provided the religious setting in which he lived his life, and Lutherans were his people. Yet the Lutheranism of which he was a part was heavily conditioned by the Americanist version: it had little Lutheran content, though it had much Christian zeal. Bittle was self-consciously a part of that kind of Lutheranism.

Born on November 19, 1811, into a southern Maryland farming family that had been in America for several generations, Bittle grew up in a pietist congregation pastored by Abraham Reck, who was pioneering the "new measures." Bittle was inspired by Reck to pursue the ordained ministry, as was his friend Ezra Keller. In 1830 he attended the preparatory school in Gettysburg (soon to become Gettysburg College), graduating in 1835 along with his friends Keller and Theophilus Stork. Bittle then spent two years studying theology under the full sweep of Professor Samuel Schmucker's personality and teaching. During the last year of his seminary education, a wave of religious enthusiasm brought conversions among the Lutherans, even among the seminarians—perhaps even Bittle.[39] The young men were no doubt exhorted by their professor to move forcefully into the field of providing education, which to him was an essential instrument in the Christianization of America. They were also gathered into Schmucker's other evangelical enthusiasms (as we shall soon see). During his two years at the seminary, Bittle fell in love with—and in 1837 married—Louisa Krauth, the sister of the president of Gettysburg College, Charles Philip Krauth.[40]

---

39. George Diehl, *Sketch of the Life and Labors of Rev. David F. Bittle, D.D.* (Gettysburg, PA: Wible, 1877), 5.

40. Both Charles Philip Krauth (1797–1867) and his son, Charles Porterfield Krauth (1823–1883), were Lutheran confessionalists, especially the son. Louisa lived with her brother, Charles Philip Krauth, while he was president of Gettysburg College; but when her husband, David Bittle, died in Salem in 1876, she went to live in Philadelphia with her nephew, who had moved from Gettsyburg to the new seminary in Philadelphia, where he was a leading professor and proponent of the reconfessionalizing of Lutheranism. It is

Bittle was ordained in May 1839, along with Theophilus Stork. Bittle brought the ordination to a close with an "animating discourse on Joshua 24:15."[41] It is interesting that the gathering then concluded its session with a number of resolutions: all preachers should preach annually in favor of the sanctity of the Sabbath; all pastors should establish Sabbath schools, temperance societies, and prayer meetings in their congregations; and all pastors should hold communion services three times a year. If congregants were absent three consecutive times, they should be disciplined.[42] The first two of these recommendations were in line with evangelical initiatives, and the final one indicated a "low-church" tendency to offer communion infrequently.

However, even before they were ordained, Bittle and his friend Stork showed their strong evangelical commitments by doing some committee work given to them by the Virginia Synod: to ascertain whether candidates for ministry in the Virginia Synod who were from the Tennessee Synod should be approved. (The Tennessee Synod was strongly confessionalist and was influenced by the Henkel family of New Market.) In short, the two young committee heads emphatically said, "No!" But why such a cheeky response from candidates for ordination who were neophytes themselves? It was simply because they believed that the young men from the Tennessee Synod had not fully jumped on the evangelical bandwagon. Bittle and Stork said that the latter denied the necessity of regeneration by relying on external observance of church ordinances; were opposed to Bible, missionary, tract, and temperance societies, as well as Sabbath schools, prayer meetings, and revivals; and did not cooperate with evangelical Christians. Bittle and Stork pronounced sentence, denying "their claim to be Evangelical Lutherans."[43]

If these actions did not sufficiently show his colors, one of the first publications to come from David Bittle's hand certainly did. In 1839, two years after he had begun serving congregations in Augusta County, Virginia, he put out a tract entitled "On New Measures."[44] (The "New Measures" were the controversial techniques used by Charles Finney in his revivals.) It is astonishingly revealing that Bittle identified himself so clearly with Charles Finney, who had also influenced Bittle's mentor, Samuel Schmucker, so

---

interesting to speculate whether Louisa Bittle's sensibilities were more "Lutheran" than her husband David's, or whether her move there was just a matter of family loyalty or necessity.

41. Eisenberg, *The Lutheran Church in Virginia*, 168. This Bible passage includes the well-known declaration of Joshua: "As for me and my house, we shall serve the Lord."

42. Eisenberg, *The Lutheran Church in Virginia*, 169.

43. Eisenberg, *The Lutheran Church in Virginia*, 167.

44. David Bittle, *On New Measures* (Staunton, VA: Kenton Harper, 1839).

strongly. Finney was far from traditional Lutheranism on almost all important theological points—that repentance can be manipulated by technique and that the will is free to decide for Jesus, to name but two.

In this tract Bittle endorses all the techniques Finney used: protracted revivals and prayer meetings; calling out the names of those who needed to repent; and anxious benches. He emphasizes the need to experience conversion at a specific time; he warns people not to assume that they are fine with the Lord by simply going to church; he strongly supports the evangelical societies that were so necessary for the shaping of the culture; he extols the revival efforts of Finney and Jonathan Edwards and defends the "New Measures" against their detractors. Against those who worried about disturbing traditional practices, he argues that Luther, Edwards, and Wesley all did new things; and against those who worried that the "born-again" experience might be superficial, he retorts that with God all things are possible. Further, he argues that pastors should not dress in special garb, that they should preach in English, that they should not use the stipulated texts for the day (pericopes), and that they need not use unleavened bread in communion.[45]

The tract was not merely a theoretical exercise. Bittle put into practice his theories, with enormous success. During his first Virginia pastorate at St. John's (which was reorganized into Mount Tabor Lutheran Church), from 1837 to 1845, the church flourished.[46] He was a diligent pastor who visited his parishioners as well as the unchurched. Furthermore, he was a revival preacher who could connect readily with young people. He held preaching sessions for several days in succession, sometimes for a week. Awakenings and conversions followed. He did not confine his preaching to the church; he also went to schoolhouses and private homes to preach. His congregation blossomed: he reported confirmations of thirty-two and forty-five in successive years. And he was beloved by his congregation.[47]

In addition, in 1842, Bittle established the Virginia Collegiate Institute, a small preparatory school, in his parsonage. He wanted to offer an austere classical education to the young men of the area, which he hoped would produce some prospective pastors who would help assuage the dire lack of pastors among the Lutherans. Rev. Christopher Baughman, his friend and classmate at Gettysburg, joined him in the new educational endeavor. This

45. Bittle, *On New Measures*, 1–16. The emphasis on conducting ministry in English indicates Bittle's distance from ethnic Lutheranism. The institutions with which he was involved were all committed to the English language.

46. Mark Miller, *Dear Old Roanoke* (Macon, GA: Mercer University Press, 1992), 6.

47. Diehl, *Sketch of the Life*, 6.

institute was to become Roanoke College after it was moved to Salem in 1847, and Baughman presided over it there until Bittle's arrival in 1853.

In 1845, when Bittle was thirty-four, he was called to the Middletown parish in Maryland, close to his boyhood home. There he duplicated the success he had experienced in the St. John's parish in Virginia by significantly developing this new parish: confirmations of 121, 75, 40, 40, 32, 35, and 24 were celebrated over his seven years there. (The gradual decrease in the numbers of confimations in those years shows that he was evidently running short of prospects after educating so many confirmands.) In doing all this, he used the "New Measures": alarming calls to the sinner, faithful rebukes to the inconsistent, and earnest appeals to the young. The Middletown parish also flourished, and when he resigned, the local newspaper reported that "the love and respect of the people for [the] pastor knew no bounds, and would have stopped at no sacrifice to renew the relation."[48]

In 1852, Bittle took up residence in Hagerstown, Maryland, where he devoted himself for about eighteen months to raising funds for home missions and for the successful establishment of the Hagerstown Female Seminary. He had obviously impressed everyone with his zeal and persuasive ability. During his work in Hagerstown he wrote "A Plea for Female Education," a 111-page document comprising six lectures on the subject.[49] He admits in the introduction that he is more a compiler of wise opinions about female education than a creative author in his own right. Nevertheless, his convictions about education in general—and women's education in particular—are clearly evident, whether by his own hand or by the hand of those he quotes. These reflections are the first we have of his mature convictions about the nature of Christian higher education. They are pervaded throughout with the evangelical emphases of the time. Moreover, Bittle articulated these convictions just before he was to take up the presidency of Roanoke College in 1853.

The first chapter (or lecture) contains more of Bittle's own writing than do later chapters. Most of this has to do with his own commitment to republicanism (which I will examine below). But he emphasizes several other evangelical themes: he calls for unity among all Protestants, as did his mentor, Schmucker (12); he endorses strong moral training in education; but he says that training cannot be efficacious without "the power of the religion of our Lord and Savior, Jesus Christ." Only the "divine teaching of God's Word

48. Diehl, *Sketch of the Life*, 9.
49. David Bittle, *A Plea for Female Education* (Hagerstown, MD: McKee and Robertson, 1852). Hereafter, page references to this work appear in parentheses within the text.

and the influence of the Holy Spirit" can overcome the natural depravity of the human heart (16). The religious element is essential in all education, including public education. "These fountains of influence (public schools) can be kept pure and refreshing only by means of gospel truth" (20). All education should unite religious and secular knowledge, and faith and learning should be integrated.

Lecture 2 calls for the education of women so that they can be good Christian mothers who will bring up Christian children, especially young men who may become pastors and missionaries. He uses many biblical and historical examples to make his case. Lecture 3 explains that educated women can be the frontline troops in the various evangelical societies that were flourishing: overseas missions, tracts, and temperance. They can become major contributors in charitable organizations, teachers in Sabbath schools, and public and religious school teachers. Bittle's encouragement of women to participate in the life of voluntary associations in the public realm is one of the marks of the evangelical awakening, as is the effort to give "reborn" Christians opportunities beyond the home to live the obedient life. Lecture 4 contains a passionate argument that women are the equal of men when it comes to spiritual, moral, and intellectual capacities. He suggests that their capacities might even be superior to those of men, and thus all women should be educated (66). But lest one become too enthusiastic about perceiving Bittle as an early feminist, it should be noted that these female capacities are all to be expressed in fairly well-defined, "allotted stations." "We have no sympathy," he says, "with the infidel movements in some parts of the country under the designation of Women's Rights" (65).

Lecture 5 argues that the schools founded by the churches should be under the control of church leaders, who were to make sure that the students were taught by godly and devoted instructors, who would, in turn, "interest themselves in the conversion and religious welfare of their pupils" (87). This statement is certainly a harbinger of his *modus vivendi* as a president and instructor at Roanoke College. Bittle even calls for each congregation to have its own primary school, given that public schools are in "wretched condition" (84–85). Lecture 6 features Bittle's answers to objections to women's education, which gives him a chance to reiterate his earlier arguments.

Less than a year later, Bittle became the first president of the newly incorporated Roanoke College, as well as being designated professor of moral and mental science. He continued to elaborate his convictions about Christian higher education in his inaugural lecture, which he gave in the fall of 1854 at the Presbyterian Church, and in which his debt to Schmucker's evangelical reinterpretation of Lutheranism is evident. The first two-thirds of the address argues that the whole man must be educated: his intellectual faculties have to be honed and trained, his thinking sharpened. Hence he proposes a good deal of language study, mathematics, and immersion in the classics of Greece and Rome and the natural sciences of the day. The scheme was informed by the "faculty psychology" and commonsense assumptions of the dominant educational philosophy of the day (see p. 5 above.) All this conformed to the old-style liberal arts curriculum common in almost all colleges.

However, Bittle's rhetoric heats up as he develops his republican and moral themes in his conclusion. The "moral" is his window to the religious formation he expects to happen at the college. "The moral faculties need the same care and attention in their development as the intellectual."[50] The student's will must be regulated, his passions governed, and his affections cultivated. In short, the character of the student must be molded.

This, however, could not be done without biblical religion. "But for soundness of morals, purity of heart, and integrity of character, a higher agency than that of man is essential. The deep fountains of corruption of the human heart can only be removed by the Word of God, the atoning merits of Jesus Christ, and the renovating power of the Holy Spirit." "With this view of collegiate education, we believe those institutions are only upon a safe basis which embody a large amount of religious element in their plans of instruction, which have a large number of their students decidedly pious, which, among their graduates, send forth a proportional number who will become ministers of the gospel and missionaries in heathen lands." Only those colleges that send forth young men "who are consistent members of the church, well grounded in the evidences of Christianity, the doctrinal and practical precepts of the Bible, and whose hearts are regenerated by the Holy Ghost"—such schools "alone have the approbation of God, and can look to heaven for ultimate and permanent prosperity."[51]

He goes on to criticize those schools where "no special means are employed for the conversion of the students, and there are no revivals of religion to gather talented youth to the Lord." On the contrary, Roanoke should be a school "where that religion is made a primary object, that enlightens the mind, and renovates the heart by the Holy Ghost, and imparts that high

50. Bittle, *A Collegiate Education*, 28.
51. Bittle, *A Collegiate Education*, 29. Interestingly, Bittle is the last president to invoke the work of the Holy Spirit.

19

humanity that aims at bringing the whole world to God's heritage."[52] Some millennial hopes here!

This vision of education became incarnated in both the curriculum and the ethos of the school. The curriculum, informed by "common-sense" assumptions, emphasized just the things that Bittle envisioned in his address. It was an integrated curriculum that was built on the conviction that the natural sciences, the classics, and the moral and intellectual sciences all fit together with biblical religion. And there was, as Bittle anticipated, much religion in the curriculum: moral philosophy; evidences of Christianity (using the text written by Schmucker's teacher at Princeton, Archibald Alexander); natural theology; "analogy of religion" (after Bishop Butler's famous apologia for the faith); and geology and ethnology in their relationship to the Pentateuch. The curriculum that Roanoke began with in 1853 remained fairly stable right up to the time of Bittle's death in 1876. The Civil War did not shake the intellectual workings of the college.

Oddly enough, there was no direct study of the Bible in the curriculum. There was also no trace of a classical Lutheran approach to higher education—that is, no church history or Reformation history, no study of Luther or Lutheranism, and no Lutheran worship or hymnody. The ethos of the college certainly did express evangelical religion. There were strict rules governing personal life—management of time, socializing, and religious life. Temperance, missionary concerns, and Sabbath-keeping were front and center, resulting in organized societies for each of those causes. On Sunday students were required to go to church and to attend faculty recitations on the Bible.[53] Each day began and ended with chapel. In addition, there were frequent revivals and preaching sessions in the neighborhood, some of them performed by Bittle himself. He and the faculty were single-minded in their effort to convert students and then nurture them in their born-again faith.

Like the curriculum, this evangelical enthusiasm seemed to continue on throughout Bittle's presidency. In 1860, eight years into his presidency, he reported to the Virginia Synod that only three of the thirty graduates of Roanoke College up to that point were not members of churches. Indeed, eighteen of the thirty were in the ordained ministry or preparing for

---

52. Bittle, *A Collegiate Education*, 30.

53. At this point the Roanoke faculty was made up exclusively of Lutherans of a strongly evangelical bent. They were assembled by Baughman and Bittle during the school's earliest years in Augusta County, and later during the college's beginnings in Salem. The faculty members were handpicked by the president and had little influence in shaping the curriculum. Only pious Lutherans could form the students well.

it. "Every year we have a number of hopeful conversions among the students, and we endeavor to make religion the main characteristic of the college."[54] During the latter part of his presidency, in 1867, Roanoke formed the Student Christian Association, one of the first in the nation. A reminiscence of a student from that period recalled the faculty's aim to make the students Christians as well as scholars: "If a young man left College without becoming a Christian, no matter what his intellectual attainments were, they regarded their work, with regard to him, half undone." He said that the special revivals conducted by Dr. Bittle every evening for several weeks also buoyed up the religious ethos of the school. "He preached awakening sermons, and after the congregation was dismissed would talk to all who indicated a desire for a personal interview" (425). Some of the more classical Lutheran students (who believed in baptismal regeneration) complained about Bittle's unrelenting effort to convert them (128). Indeed, it could easily be said that Bittle blurred the line between college and church; appealing to the mind was simply not enough for him.

To the last he exhibited his hope that the college's efforts would produce more workers and leaders for the church. On the day of his death, September 25, 1876, he prayed fervently at a meeting of the Education and Missionary Society for "the Lord of the Harvest to raise up men to preach the everlasting Gospel." After making the rounds of the student quarters, he returned to the meeting, where he sat down and quietly expired (138).

Besides his duties at the college, David Bittle shepherded three Lutheran congregations from 1853 on, one of which became the namesake of the college, College Lutheran Church. He served it from 1853 to 1859, and then again from 1861 to 1869. He oversaw its first building project in 1858 (520). No doubt he used the same approach in those churches that he had with much success in his Augusta County and Maryland pastorates.

It is also clear that David Bittle remained Samuel Schmucker's student to the very end. Though he had little time to write books or tracts in his presidential years, his actions seem to indicate that the evangelical faith burned brightly in his heart and mind. This brings to mind an interesting question: How did he react to the strong currents of Lutheran re-confessionalizing that were flowing all around him from 1850 onward? In his early tracts or in his inaugural address, there is little indication that he was disturbed or altered by them. He simply does not mention those controversies. After the

54. Quoted by Eisenberg, *First Hundred Years*, 88. Hereafter, page references to this work appear in parentheses within the text.

Civil War he seems to have continued his evangelical practices and taken no notice of the theological controversies raging around him. It is likely that he put first things first, and the first thing was the survival and flourishing of Roanoke College. He was operating in a territory in which both parties in the intra-Lutheran controversies were well represented. Lutheran families were on both sides. The confessionalist Henkels were active up and down the Shenandoah Valley, and the conservative Tennessee Synod was close by. But many Lutherans were still part of the evangelical upsurge, albeit chastened no doubt by the ravages of the Civil War. It is likely that Bittle did not openly take sides in this controversy over the nature of Lutheranism. That would have involved him in serious conflict, which he did not want for Roanoke College. Therefore, he just continued to do what he always did, which meant that Roanoke College itself would follow Bittle's evangelical convictions and practices.

Bittle as a Republican

Another surprising feature of the full portrait of David Bittle was his vigorous republicanism, which must have been in some tension with the aristocratic strands of Southern society. This, too, was part of his inheritance from Schmucker and his involvement in the larger evangelicalism of his time. What enabled his republicanism was his sense of being a "birthright" American Lutheran. His family had been in America for generations, and he had little ethnic flavor or loyalty in him; that could have led to a sense of isolation and powerlessness. Like Schmucker, he not only wanted to be where the action was but also had the confidence to join it. He wanted to be part of the great effort to mold the religious and political destiny of the nation, which he was emphatically doing in his shaping of Roanoke College.

He was heavily involved in the two great evangelical instruments for the Christianization of America—revivals and voluntary societies. He used the "New Measures" in his parish ministries and at Roanoke College. He preached at many revivals beyond the churches. He founded a number of societies at Roanoke College that promoted temperance, Christian formation, home missions, and foreign missions. He participated in specifically Lutheran societies for those purposes. Early in his career he and Stork advised that several Lutheran candidates for the ministry be refused because they did not endorse nor participate in these voluntary societies. But above all he devoted his life to that one great voluntary society that formed young men and women—higher education. He helped to found and fund the Hagerstown Female Seminary and he gave the most productive years of his life to the survival and flourishing of Roanoke College.

Bittle saw both of these educational institutions within the larger republican project, which he articulates in both his tract on female education and in his inaugural address at Roanoke College. In the former, he outlines all the themes: the great gift of religious liberty; the chance to evangelize and educate the masses pouring into America; public and private schools guided by "our common Christianity"; the need for Protestant unity around the basics; the freedom from the corruption of Europe, typified most clearly by the Catholic church; a democratic government that resists tyranny; a great new chance for the common man; the progressive improvement of the age; and gratitude for the "Provident Hand" that is guiding our history.

What better example of the mutual work of both church and state in building up the populace than this exhortation: "How immensely important is it that the cause of self-government should suffer no damage by our example: that the great principles of civil and religious liberty, which are now spreading from our shores over the face of the whole earth, be kept healthy and sound at home: that we hold the doctrine, a free and open Bible, the watch-tower and lighthouse of American liberty—the government of written law! . . . And that we strive by all possible means to imbue the educated popular mind with the conservative and saving power of true religion."[55]

Bittle's inaugural address reiterates these same themes. When his rhetoric heats up toward the end of his address, he explicitly declares his conviction: "A leveling republicanism is one quality that will embody itself into our educational systems."[56] Here in America, he argues, Christianity is no longer hampered by state ordinances. It is free from the needless speculations—he makes fun of Saint Thomas in this regard—that characterized European Christianity and is set free for a practical Christianity that will stamp a republican character on a free people. He admires European universities—particularly the German ones—but criticizes them sharply for not educating the common man. In America it is different. One of his best lines in the inaugural is this: "This is the country where education must become popular, great men rise from obscure families, and men of great means and little minds, be forgotten forever."[57]

---

55. Bittle, *A Plea for Female Education*, 11.
56. Bittle, *Collegiate Education*, 25.
57. Bittle, *Collegiate Education*, 26.

He commends the study of the classics for the curriculum at Roanoke because both the Greeks and Romans practiced republicanism. The classical writers were "free and independent thinkers, sturdy and consistent republicans, who not only declaimed in favor of freedom, but when necessary, put on their armor and battled in her sacred cause. . . . Classical literature is the same as American literature."[58]

Bittle's "birthright" Lutheranism also gave him the courage to engage the great and the near great movers and shakers of republican America. He moved easily into the public sphere. I have already noted his fundraising abilities in Maryland on behalf of the female seminary. Then, toward the end of the Civil War, he negotiated with the Union forces to save Salem and the college from destruction. After the war, he quickly moved to recruit students and donors from North and South alike. He became acquainted with Southern men of wealth and convinced them to send their sons and dollars to Roanoke College. Indeed, he made it a point to get acquainted with men in influential positions. "There was scarcely a governor, or senator, or prominent judge in the south he did not know. In this way the fame of Roanoke was constantly extending."[59]

Bittle's movement among public figures put Roanoke's reputation right up there with the finest in Virginia—namely, Washington College and the University of Virginia. When he died, W. H. Ruffner, Virginia's superintendent of public instruction, gave a lengthy eulogy at the memorial service in Richmond. It is obvious from the intimate tone of the talk that the superintendent considered Bittle a personal colleague. He put Bittle in a class "among the great men and the successful men of the time," arguing that "in one respect the building up of Roanoke College was the most remarkable educational work ever done in Virginia."[60] (Take that, Thomas Jefferson! Seriously, the "one respect" is that the college was founded in Salem and did not have a supportive constituency.) As a civic figure in Salem, Bittle was so important and revered that the whole town closed down to observe his funeral. His funeral procession to East Hill Cemetery extended almost from the church to the cemetery, a good half mile away.[61]

There is one puzzling element in Bittle's republicanism, one in which he departed from his mentor, Samuel Schmucker. Schmucker was an avid

58. Bittle, *Collegiate Education*, 27–28.
59. Diehl, *Sketch of the Life*, 21.
60. Diehl, *Sketch of the Life*, 26–27. Hereafter, page references to this work appear in parentheses within the text.
61. *The Roanoke Collegian* (October 1876): 13.

antislavery advocate who participated in several antislavery societies and who wrote a set of propositions publicly denouncing slavery. But with his student, David Bittle, there seems to be an anomaly. While Schmucker openly included black people in the robust republicanism he embraced, it appears that Bittle never directly mentions black people or even their enslavement—or their need for emancipation—anywhere in his writings. There are some indirect but inconclusive hints about his attitude toward that awful institution.

The first incident came when *The Observer*, a widely read Lutheran journal published in Baltimore, openly espoused the Union cause in the run-up to the Civil War. Bittle, more than a bit intemperately, declared:

> It is a matter of life and death with us—our homes, the virtue of our wives and daughters, and our all is at stake in this terrible struggle, yet you send *The Observer* with its influence, as far as it goes, against us. Great God Almighty, do you wish to make our church paper an instrument to assist in our extermination? (Eisenberg, 214)

Furthermore, when the war began, Bittle served as a chaplain to the Confederate forces when time allowed (Eisenberg, 217). Though he "had entertained strong partialities for the Confederacy," however, he accepted the result of the war and quickly rekindled friendships among supporters in the North (Diehl, 20).

Even though he was a supporter of the Confederacy, why this silence on the issue of slavery? It is probably for the same reason that he avoided the confessionalist/Americanist controversy among his fellow Lutherans. He was concerned, above all, that Roanoke College survive, and he knew very well that there were important populations on both sides of the issue among the college's constituency. He knew many of the college's supporters in the North—and even in the South—who were against slavery. Yet he was surrounded by slaveholders. Nathaniel Burwell, a prominent Salem citizen and chairman of the Roanoke College board, was the largest slave-owner in Roanoke County (Eisenberg, 71)! So prudence would dictate circumspection, which he diligently practiced.

Bittle as a Scholarly President

Anyone with a mere passing acquaintance of the Roanoke College narrative knows about David Bittle as supremely a man of action. His herculean efforts brought the college into existence without a large supportive constituency. Earlier in his life, he had been a highly successful pastor and an instigator in the founding of a female seminary. While he was president of Roanoke, he was a determined fundraiser who traversed much of the American East and South to make sure that his beloved college would survive. He recruited prospective students from among the many acquaintances he had made, and he nurtured the young men who came. He was an administrator who was willing to take on many roles, even a steward's role (procuring food and drink for the students) in order to keep the college open during and after the Civil War. He taught the senior capstone course in moral philosophy, and he was a mentor and father figure to students who matriculated at Roanoke College, some of whom succeeded him as presidents and faculty members of the college.

Stories of his colorful and dramatic deeds abound. One of the most well-known of his exploits involved his role as steward of the college. When food ran short during the Civil War, he took a group of students and rode seventy miles southwest to procure fourteen head of cattle from Lutheran farmers. He had to drive them back through hazardous territory that was infested with marauding bands of both Union and Confederate soldiers. It took him several days of moving from one friendly farm to the next, but he eventually returned safely to Salem. Such heroics enabled Roanoke to be one of the few colleges in Virginia that remained open during the Civil War (Eisenberg, 102–3).

Considering all the actions that were required of him, it is difficult to see how he found any time for the life of the mind. But he was impressively learned and kept up a surprising amount of reading and intellectual activity throughout his life. After building a reputation as a diligent student in seminary, he opened a preparatory school at Mount Tabor, his first parish, where he taught mathematics and presided over debating societies (Eisenberg, 22). As a young pastor, he not only carried on his pastoral duties but also "set aside time for the systematic study of theology, the classics, and the general sciences" (Eisenberg, 18). He added books to his library whenever he could, and he read them thoroughly. He was an extemporaneous preacher, so he did not spend time composing written sermons. Rather, he mentally composed them while he was literally in the saddle, and that habit allowed him time for general study when he was in his parsonage (Diehl, 6).

Bittle wrote two lengthy treatises as a young pastor: his defense of Charles Finney's "New Measures" (1839) and his plea for female education (1852). The former required a broad knowledge of the revivalist movement of his time, to which he added his own spirited defense of it; the latter featured his acquaintance with the great debates over the education of women. He was privy to the major voices supporting women's education, and he scattered their arguments throughout his small book. He also tapped into the republican ideas surging in the country.

But his presidential inaugural address of 1854 is perhaps the most concentrated and complete account of his wide-ranging intellectual commitments. After that, it seems, he simply became too busy to write lengthy pieces. The address, however, is something of a full exercise of his thinking. Like the curriculum that followed from it, the address is organized around the "faculty psychology" and "common sense philosophy" of the day. Humans have the faculties of reason, passion, and will; each faculty must be properly trained and shaped by the education the college offers. The mind has reasoning powers that must be cultivated for reflection and abstraction. Languages and mathematics train those facets of the student's intellect. Good taste must be trained so that the works the student chooses will "mature his judgment, strengthen his memory, and elevate his imagination."[62] Students should read a few great works with great intensity rather than many lesser works; yet Bittle names a vast array of writers the students should admire. Indeed, the first section of the address exhibits an amazing erudition. If the president actually read these authors—and his library contained many books by those writers that were purportedly well-worn—he had educated himself rather impressively in those years when he set aside time every day for reading in the classics and sciences.

He shows great admiration for both German and English university education and lists the leading thinkers at their universities. Reading these thinkers "draws out minds from their apparently hidden resources."[63] His catalogue of great scholars, including many theologians, goes on for pages and pages, which must have taxed the attention spans of his listeners. Throughout the address, Bittle carries on a dialogue with the leading educational philosophers of the day, indicating that a Roanoke education will be indebted to them. As I have observed above, the last third of the address features a more exciting rhetoric. He argues that Roanoke's education should be American—that is, it should be shaped by America's republican tradition. He waxes polemical against the European countries that did not offer education to their common people. As we have already seen, he addresses the

62. Bittle, *Collegiate Education*, 8.
63. Bittle, *Collegiate Education*, 23.

faculties of the passion and will. The passions must be governed by a will that is informed by moral sense. Finally, however, the will must be transformed by conversion—through the work of the Holy Spirit. Therefore, religion is to play a central role in both the curriculum and the ethos of the school.

The curriculum (already discussed) was pretty much a reflection of Bittle's intellectual convictions, which were not at all unusual for leaders of the old-style liberal arts colleges of the day. All of the learning disciplines were assumed to be integrated by common sense, and all were compatible with biblical truth. Natural philosophy and natural science fit perfectly with biblical truth. Together they could stand against the intellectual threats—rationalist atheism and deism—that derived from the Enlightenment and came to prominence in America after the Revolution. Bittle himself kept up with the natural sciences of his day and put together one of the finest mineral collections in the region for the college, which led to a reputation boost for Roanoke College in science education (Eisenberg, 84).

After Bittle's death, an admirer remarked about "his deep thought, strong ideas, big conceptions, most varied knowledge" and quoted another admirer as saying that Bittle "knows everything. He is a perfect encyclopedia; open him where you will and you will always find what you want, and he does not seem to think it anything strange that he should know it either—that such was a matter of course."[64]

Perhaps witty humor is also an indication of an intellectual bent in a person. Though seemingly possessing a very serious personal style, Bittle also had a good sense of humor. The most erudite example occurred on the occasion of that herding of cattle to Roanoke College in the midst of the Civil War. There were Union forces nearby, and when one of his accompanying students cried, "Yankees!" it was reported that "the Doctor said he thought of an aeronaut in a thunderstorm, and then Kant's psychological question came into his mind, 'Are synthetic propositions *a priori* possible?'" (Eisenberg, 102). The students must have been impressed as they hurriedly herded the cattle away from the Yankees.

Two further examples of humor came from Bittle's experiences during the war. After negotiating the surrender of the Confederates to the Union forces in order to save Salem from the destruction of serious fighting, the Union commander sent an underling back to the city from the outskirts. As Bittle walked back to town with the young soldier in tow, he quipped to the large number of bystanders watching this little parade: "Ladies, you see I

---

64. Attributed to "Monitor," *The Roanoke Collegian* (October 1876): 14.

have taken one prisoner." But, it was reported, the ladies would not smile in return. "Their feelings were too sore for a joke" (Diehl, 19).

When the Bittles had assembled a significant portion of meat to feed their family at the close of the war, Bittle's wife, Louisa, wanted to conceal it. Bittle told her not to, since he had fervently engaged in prayer with the Union captain who was in charge of occupying Salem. He assumed that the Yankees would not take the meat after such prayerful collegiality, so he put it in their own smokehouse. Sadly, he was wrong: the Bittles lost all their meat. "The Doctor declared he would never attempt faith again without works, nor set the example to his friends" (Diehl, 20). Finally, toward the end of his long life of fundraising for the college, he offered this thought: "When I die, I hope my funeral sermon will be preached from the text (in Luke 16:22), 'And it came to pass that the beggar died'" (Diehl, 25).

Conclusion

Three major features of David Bittle were surprising to me: his evangelicalism, his republicanism, and his intellectual firepower. What was not surprising were his personal strength, determination, and perseverance—and, on top of that, his indefatigability. All these traits combined in him to give sharp definition to his own life but also to the formation of Roanoke College. That is why I have focused so intently on him. The presidents of the old-style liberal arts colleges had the power to impose their vision on the colleges they founded and led. David Bittle certainly did. The college was a vibrant evangelical school that aimed at producing thoughtful Christian gentlemen who would play their part in shaping the religious and political destiny of the nation. While the millenarian optimism of the antebellum period faded after the Civil War, Bittle never wavered in his continuing commitment to the college—seeing it as an instrument for the furtherance of the churches and the country. He and the college were committed to Christian republicanism. Furthermore, he had enormous influence on the next two presidents of Roanoke College, who were his students and, in many ways, his "sons." In the next chapters we shall see how far that influence extended.

2

JULIUS DREHER (1878–1903)

Roanoke's Cosmopolitan Champion of Benevolence

Before Julius Dreher died, in Florida in 1937, he provided in his will that his remains be interred in David Bittle's square in Salem's East Hill Cemetery even though his wife of thirty-one years, who had died earlier that same year, had her remains sent to her family's vault in Pennsylvania.[1] This extraordinary gesture of filial piety was not out of character for Dreher. When Bittle died unexpectedly on September 25, 1876, Dreher poured out his admiration for his mentor in the *Roanoke Collegian*:

> Our leader has been taken away! Our friend and father has been called away! . . . The character of that devoted servant of God rises before my mind clothed in a majestic dignity and grandeur before which the fame of the Caesars and the wealth of the Rothchilds sink into insignificance.[2]

Dreher even planned for his inauguration and the dedication of the new Bittle Hall to be on the third anniversary of Bittle's death, September 25, 1879. There was great affinity between the two men, not only in their commitment to each other and the college they loved but also in their basic vision of the college's mission. But there were also significant differences, not only in their personal styles but also in their theological-religious perspectives and in the scope of their concerns.

1. W. A. Eisenberg, *The First Hundred Years: Roanoke College, 1842–1942* (Strasburg, VA: Shenandoah Publishing House, 1942), 377.

2. Julius Dreher, "Our Loss—Our Legacy—Our Duty," *The Roanoke Collegian* (Salem, VA) 3, no. 2: 1.

Dreher was actually the third president of the college. He followed the very brief tenure of Rev. Thomas Dosh, who resigned after an unpleasant interlude in which he tried to tighten the scholarly and disciplinary requirements of the college. The students rebelled and made life miserable for the president, who quickly accepted the invitation to become the second professor of theology at the Lutheran seminary in South Carolina. Dreher was already a rising young star in the administrative and academic endeavors of the college and was an obvious candidate to succeed Dosh. Dreher was also a favorite of Bittle, who recognized his promise. When Bittle sent Dreher on a mission for the college, he intimated his hopes for Dreher to succeed him: "God bless you in your undertaking; begin with faith in the Lord, and if things do not go as you think, let not faith falter."[3]

In the following pages I will probe both the continuities and the discontinuities between these remarkable men. First, though, I think it will be helpful to sketch the historical context that conditioned the lives of the American people and institutions during the last quarter of the nineteenth century.

Historical Background

The great evangelical thrust to Christianize America and the world did not end with the debacle of the Civil War. The South as a region experienced a period of trauma after the war, but the major Southern churches—the Methodists and Baptists—soon recovered and continued their revivalist efforts, along with the formation of the population in rather legalistic moral precepts. They made great gains in membership while they sealed themselves off from the religious and social dynamics of the North, including the latter's efforts to come to terms with urbanization and immigration, of which the South experienced little. But the emancipation of the slaves did not mean that the South ceased its racist policies. Segregation and Jim Crow laws sprung up all around. Education was generally offered only to the white upper classes, thus retarding the economic and social development of freed slaves and the South in general. Lutherans were a very small group, and at the leadership level of their seminaries and synods, they were "involved in a confessional movement that was leading them toward a larger awareness of Lutheran unity."[4]

---

3. Quoted in Eisenberg, *The First Hundred Years*, 149.
4. Sidney Ahstrom, *A Religious History of the American People* (New Haven: Yale University Press, 1979), 727.

Conditions in the North were sharply different. It experienced great economic expansion and affluence, prompting historians to call the period from 1865 to 1900 the "Gilded Age." Many old-line Protestants made fortunes and contributed them to the cause of Christianizing America. Virtue seemed to be rewarded by wealth, so one major way to make everyone in the country wealthy was to increase their virtue, and evangelical Protestantism continued to see itself as the supplier of virtue for the republic. Though revivalism waned to some degree in the North, there were still highly visible evangelists plying their trade. The most renowned was Dwight Moody, who became a sensation first in England and then in the United States. Other Protestant clergy with real "star power" were perhaps even more prominent in the North than was Moody. Henry Ward Beecher, Phillips Brooks, and Josiah Strong became household names and wielded immense influence in the postwar North.[5] These influential pastors downplayed doctrine while they emphasized the ethics of uplift, the American middle-class virtues of hard work, thrift, temperance, patriotism, and especially benevolence (good will toward others). These virtues would enable ordinary people to prosper in the world, much like the older wealthy WASPs had done. And Christianity—minus its Calvinist baggage of sin and depravity—was precisely the religion that would produce those virtues. Indeed, this unabashed belief in the salience of "Christian civilization" was shared even by the Unitarians, who had become competitors with evangelicals in the Northeast, especially around Boston.

This amalgamation of American virtues into the Christian faith helped to establish a new version of Christendom: the Protestant empire. This "Christian America" was successful—at least on the surface—and highly energetic. Major Protestant groups tripled their membership between 1860 and 1900.[6] The leading families of the nation were old-line Protestants—Methodists, Presbyterians, Congregationalists, Episcopalians—of an evangelical hue, and they offered their considerable largesse to support evangelical initiatives. Out of this continuing movement to Christianize the country and the world came many new initiatives: the YMCA to Christianize the youth, many of them immigrants, in the new urban centers of America; the Student Volunteer Movement for Foreign Missions that aimed to "evangelize the world in

---

5. George Marsden, "Did Success Spoil American Protestantism (1865–1890)?" in *Eerdmans' Handbook to Christianity in America,* ed. Mark Noll et al. (Grand Rapids: Eerdmans, 1983), 277–95.

6. Marsden, "Did Success Spoil American Protestantism?" 283.

this generation"; the foreign-missions movement in almost all the churches; institutions to improve the lot of African Americans; women's movements that emphasized women's education and suffrage; and temperance, Sabbatarianism, and Sunday school. This era also featured the founding and development of many charitable organizations, including rescue missions, the Salvation Army, hospitals, orphanages, and homes for the elderly and indigent. In addition, this period saw the beginnings of the "social gospel" movement under the early leadership of Washington Gladden, who called the churches to address the underlying economic dynamics of the society and to ameliorate them on the basis of the teachings of Jesus.

Lutherans in the North were occupied with gathering large numbers of immigrants from Germany and Scandinavia into churches generally organized along ethnic lines. They founded their own colleges, charities, and missionary societies. Most were quite confessional and insular, though the "birthright" Lutherans of the East did participate vigorously in the continuing evangelical efforts to Christianize America and evangelize the world.[7] Efforts toward Lutheran unity—especially among the older Lutheran churches—flourished.

But these aforementioned Protestant "triumphs" masked some deeper challenges that were emerging. The immigration of millions of Catholics was perhaps the foremost challenge to the Protestant empire. The urbanization of the North was a second challenge, where masses of immigrants from abroad clustered. Secularization was an underlying current in which many sectors of life, including—and perhaps especially—education, were being freed from the constraints of Christian moral and intellectual guidance. The old-time liberal arts college, with its synthesis of science, philosophy, classics, and biblical religion, was being challenged by new models of education. The practical needs of the country called for more practical programs in the colleges so that students could be trained for technical and commercial work in the world. Furthermore, the German research university, with its emphasis on the unfettered search for truth in every facet of education, specialized learning in a new way and undercut the old synthesis.

The newly emerging public and private research universities began looking disdainfully on the old Christian liberal arts colleges. The leaders of those institutions were particularly skeptical of establishing colleges or universities on confessional grounds. "President [Charles] Eliot of Harvard

---

7. Abdel Ross Wentz, *The Lutheran Church in American History* (Philadelphia: United Lutheran Publication House, 1933), 233–44.

proclaimed in 1891 that it 'was impossible to found a university on the basis of a sect,' and that the great universities taught religious tolerance, in
contrast to many small, narrow, church colleges that presumably did not."
Moreover, the church colleges, compared to these new research ventures,
were "antiquated, inferior, belated, arrested, and starved," according to President Jordan of Stanford.[8]

The North was also where the great intellectual challenges to the Christian worldview were emerging and had to be confronted. Higher criticism of
the Bible called into question its status as the Word of God. Darwinism challenged the Genesis accounts of the creation of nature and man. It seemed to
reduce man to random processes and made God's role in nature and history
superfluous. Marxism undermined all inherited intellectual and moral norms
by attributing them to the machinations of those with economic and political
power. In addition, European refugees from the failed revolutions of 1848
fled to the United States and brought with them revolutionary thinking and
practices. Hence, in spite of the great successes of evangelical Protestantism
during this period, a good many challenges were operating just below the
surface, setting the stage for great conflicts.[9]

This bifurcated world—the traumatized and insular South and the affluent and expansive North—was the one in which Roanoke College and its
third president, Julius Daniel Dreher (1846–1937), found themselves after the
death of David Bittle in 1876. The college, located firmly in the decimated
South, was dependent on students and patrons from the North. Its third
president (actually second in terms of significance) was a son of the South
who nonetheless quickly became a cosmopolitan leader—well acquainted
with and in the North—upon his assuming the presidency of the college.
A devoted disciple of his mentor, David Bittle, he reaffirmed—and yet revised—his mentor's vision of the college in important ways. We shall explore
them in our reflections on the era of President Julius Dreher.

---

8. William Ringenberg, *The Christian College* (Grand Rapids: Baker Academic, 2006),
129.

9. I am indebted, in this historical background, to a number of historical accounts of
that period: a series of authors in the *Eerdmans' Handbook to Christianity in America*, already
cited; Sidney Ahlstrom, *A Religious History of the American People*, already cited; William
Ringenberg, *The Christian College—A History of Protestant Higher Education in America*,
already cited; James Hastings Nichols, *History of Christianity—1650–1850* (New York: Ronald Press, 1956); Jerald Brauer, *Protestantism in America* (Philadelphia: Westminster Press,
1963); and A. R. Wentz, *The Lutheran Church in American History*, already cited.

Dreher's Early Life: A Son of the South

Julius Daniel Dreher was born on October 28, 1846, in Lexington County
in South Carolina, the oldest of eleven children of John Jacob and Martha
Dreher. A devoted and influential Lutheran layman, the elder Dreher, who
owned a large plantation and a mill, was a prominent figure in the county.[10]
His family had been in South Carolina for at least a hundred years by the
time Julius was born, having migrated from Pennsylvania. As a youth, Julius
worked on the family plantation but was also enthralled with study, so much
so that he "had to be restrained for fear of injury to his health."[11] At seventeen,
he enlisted in the Confederate army, served honorably, and rose to the rank
of second lieutenant in his company. But upon returning to his home at the
end of the war, he found only devastation. The Dreher plantation had been
directly in the path of General Sherman's drive through the South. All the
animals, food, and buildings were either seized or destroyed. The family was
in such dire straits that "for many days his mother had no food for her children except corn scraped from the ground where Sherman's horses had been
fed. This was washed, dried, and parched, then pounded into coarse meal."[12]

Julius worked for four years to earn enough money to go to college,
and in 1869 he entered Roanoke, where he came under the teaching and
influence of David Bittle. It took him only two years to be awarded an AB
with honors. Bittle and the other professors recognized young Dreher's great
promise and offered him a subordinate position on the faculty, which he accepted for the next year. During the interim he studied law with a professor
from the University of Virginia, as well as theology at the Lutheran seminary
then located in Salem. After he entered full-time work at Roanoke College,
he rose quickly: from assistant professor of ancient languages to professor
of English language and literature (from which position he developed a department of English along more modern lines); then he became secretary
of the faculty; and a bit later (1875) was named the financial secretary of the
college.[13] After Bittle's death, Dreher also successfully adopted his mentor's

10. This made Dreher a "birthright American Lutheran," much like his mentor, Bittle,
and Bittle's mentor, Samuel Simon Schmucker. All three were members of families who
had been in America for generations. They had no sense of being "ethnic outsiders" who
were distant from American institutional life. They participated in American life with ease
and confidence.

11. Eisenberg, *First Hundred Years*, 372.

12. Eisenberg, *First Hundred Years*, 373.

13. Eisenberg, "A Heritage of Personalities," in *First Hundred Years*, 374.

peripatetic role of visiting many cities in the North—especially New York and Boston—and the South to gather patrons, donations, and students.

But what really caught everyone's eye was his organization of the gala twenty-fifth anniversary of the college during nearly a week of celebration in the spring of 1878. Twelve prominent speakers, including politicians and jurists from all over the country, but especially from the Northeast, offered congratulatory addresses during that week of celebration. And the Marine Band played twenty-two selections on commencement day itself. Dreher was quickly taking advantage of the many contacts he had made in his travels. He had so impressed his hosts during those visits that when he invited them to Roanoke College, they came. That, in turn, impressed Roanoke's faculty, board, and community.[14]

Therefore, when the unfortunate Thomas Dosh resigned in the spring of 1878, after only a year as president, Dreher was the obvious choice to succeed him. No one even hesitated, and Julius Dreher became president of Roanoke College at the tender age of thirty-two. And he came on with the wind at his back.

Two remarkable things stand out in Dreher's life up to this point. First, given his miserable experiences as a soldier—and afterwards as a civilian—on the losing side of the Civil War, one might think he would have become an embittered Southern sectionalist with a hostile attitude toward the North. But nothing could have been further from the truth. Like Bittle before him, he turned his attention toward the North immediately after he was employed by Roanoke College. He moved easily among the Northern "victors," who, in turn, influenced his religious and philosophical vision. During those years he came to know Theodore Roosevelt and Charles Eliot, the president of Harvard University. In time he became one of the North's favorite Southerners.

Second, though he was short on formal education, Dreher seems to have been something of an intellectual prodigy. His writing indicates wide knowledge and exhibits persuasive rhetoric. He picked up much of this erudition on his own, no doubt, but the education he received at Roanoke must have been exceedingly fruitful. His association with Bittle and some of the learned faculty certainly helped as well, along with his brief studies in law and theology. At any rate, he conversed with and obviously impressed many highly educated elites in Northern cities. In 1881, a mere three years into Dreher's presidency, Williams College conferred a PhD on him (which was considered both an honorary degree and an earned degree at that time). This kind of recognition was remarkable for a poor boy from the South with little formal education.

14. Eisenberg, *First Hundred Years*, 147.

Julius Dreher as President of Roanoke College

Moral Formation in the Service of Christian Republicanism

The crucial continuity between Dreher and the mentor he admired was in their shared vision of the central mission of the college: the moral formation of young men from ordinary circumstances who would then go on to contribute to the churches, the young republic, and the world. This vision was anchored in the Christian republicanism that had emerged in the antebellum period and had survived the trauma of the Civil War. Colleges were one of the main domestic vehicles of that project. Moreover, Christian republicanism not only survived but increased its scope. The *world* was to be Christianized by missionaries bearing "Christian civilization" to the pagan globe.

Dreher's inaugural address in 1879 firmly struck the theme of moral formation in the service of Christian republicanism. Even its title, "Education for Useful Living," is evocative of the theme. After approvingly quoting Bittle's famous dictum that "the most momentous duty of one generation to another is its education," Dreher strikes a robust and expanded republican theme when he says that Roanoke will offer an education "which is destined to exert a mighty influence on the fortunes of the Republic and the Christian civilization of the world."[15] Dreher then goes on to offer his version of what a Roanoke education is all about:

> By education, we understand not merely the acquisition of sufficient knowledge for the discharge of the ordinary affairs of life; but also such a discipline and drawing out of the intellectual powers, training of the moral character, and cultivation of the religious affections, as shall fit a man for the faithful and efficient performance of his duties to his country and humanity, to himself and his God. (26)

He then proceeds to lay out the importance of studies involved in *intellectual, moral,* and *religious* education. Intellectually, the student at Roanoke must draw out, develop, and strengthen the mental faculties by studying English language and literature; ancient and modern languages (especially German); mental, moral, and social sciences; and mathematics and natural sciences.

---

15. Julius Dreher, "Address," in *Addresses at the Inauguration of Julius D. Dreher as President of Roanoke College* (Board of Trustees of Roanoke College, 1879), 24. Hereafter, page references to this work appear in paretheses within the text.

This studying should be done in an unhurried fashion that imparts a breadth of learning that prepares the student not merely for work but for all of life. It should not end with formal education but continue through life.

Then comes the centerpiece: the drawing out, development, and training of the *moral* faculty. Without moral education and the training of character, intellectual knowledge cannot "save nations and individuals from vice and ruin" (41). Knowledge must be wedded to virtue. The moral virtues, Dreher argues in good Aristotelian fashion, are gained by developing good habits, which over time become settled dispositions toward duty, obedience, self-denial, truthfulness, courage, and industry. He laments the lax discipline in many families that fails to instill those virtues (44).

"Character above all" is a section in which Dreher argues that good character is a man's greatest possession. Good character includes the classic virtues listed above but is crowned by active benevolence, "the pure devotion to the welfare of mankind" (46). Training in these grand virtues will be done in textbooks in moral science, but also in many types of classic literature that hold up human achievement. Above all, they will be garnered by following the models that faculty and his companions offer. And they can only be achieved by a discipline that leads to self-governance (47–48). The moral education of its students by Roanoke College would contribute to the health of the nation, whose guarantee of permanence and progress is anchored in "the moral worth of its individuals." "The character of a nation is nothing more than the aggregate character of its individual citizens" (49).

Further, Roanoke will offer this moral training to "young men of slender means" in order to diffuse the blessings of education to the "right education of all classes." "In no country in the world is general intelligence so necessary as in ours for the maintenance of free government." In offering such education to all kinds of students, Roanoke would produce citizens who would do their part in the world's work—"to aid in carrying forward human progress in another stadium toward its final consummation" (55–56).

The Religious Element

While Dreher shows a nearly complete concurrence with Bittle in his emphasis on Christian republicanism as the central mission of the college, that is less true of the two leaders' assessment of the place of religion in higher education. Dreher certainly agrees with Bittle that religion is essential in higher education—as well as in society. Though he devotes a much briefer section in his inaugural on the essential role of religion in personal and social life than Bittle did, he waxes eloquent and passionate about its importance for Roanoke College.

> Christianity is a great living, personal power—the sun around which the moral virtues revolve. . . . It is an important element in conserving the welfare of society, because it enters as a personal force, a controlling principle, into the lives of individuals. It brings the affections into harmony with the will of heaven, fosters the spirit of universal benevolence, and animates man, amidst the activities of this life, and ennobling aspirations for the life to come. The holy precepts of the Christian religion do more than all else to purify and vitalize the fountains of thought, to sanctify the uses of learning, to inspire true greatness of character, and to prepare man for the highest realization of useful living. (50)

This is eloquent testimony to the importance of the Christian religion in higher education, but it views religion's value primarily in terms of its usefulness and power in moral formation. There is little talk of salvation, truth, conversion, discipleship—or of the church and its gospel. Indeed, it is striking that the address does not mention Jesus or the Holy Spirit. Rather, it conveys a kind of protoliberal, Unitarian version of the faith. The main utility of the faith is to generate universal benevolence. This contrasts sharply with the robust revivalist thrust of Bittle's evangelicalism, in which he constantly calls on the Holy Spirit to effect conversion to Christ and holy living. In Dreher we have moral living without the need for conversion; we have the serious moral formation Bittle was so concerned about without his conviction that it could happen only through the work of the Holy Spirit. Dreher's vision of Christianity focuses on the human moral efforts rather than the works of God that enable them.

Where did this different version of the faith come from? Perhaps a reason for Dreher's distancing himself from revivalism was his status as a layman. He simply did not feel comfortable with, or capable of, the kind of evangelism that Bittle found to be second nature. Or perhaps it can be accounted for by his temperament. He was a very earnest and moral man without the robust, overt religious vitalities of Bittle. But, more likely than these reasons, he was much influenced by the religious milieu of the North, especially that of Boston, which he visited and engaged so often in his years as president.

From the beginning of his presidency, Dreher was expected to travel widely to acquire students, gifts, and patrons for the college. He certainly did that: "In a typical year he would depart from Salem by the end of September and not return until the close of term. . . . Armed with letters of introduction and soliciting newspaper endorsements, Dreher entered the social worlds of Philadelphia, New York, Hartford, Newport, and Boston."[16]

His favorite destination was Boston, where he took Roanoke College into "the hearts and homes of Boston aristocracy."[17] Indeed, one could argue that the apex of Roanoke's—and Dreher's—stature in the North featured a grand gathering in the home of a Mrs. Fiske in Boston during the autumn of 1882. An incredible array of influential people—judges, mayors, ex-governors, senators (Henry Cabot Lodge!), and academics—gathered to hear Dreher speak about the challenges and potential of Roanoke College. President Eliot of Harvard opined that Roanoke was now what Harvard had been one hundred years before, and that it could be expected to improve greatly in its mission of liberal education. Several clergy of note, including Washington Gladden of "social gospel" fame, offered their endorsements of the college. Gladden visited Roanoke College as its commencement speaker in 1882, and Dreher and Charles Eliot became lifelong friends.[18]

I emphasize this Boston connection because it most likely influenced Dreher's religious vision and how it worked its way into the college. Boston was home to the patrician Protestants who were influenced by that star of an Episcopal pastor, Phillips Brooks, "a master at integrating modern thought and Christianity into an optimistic, though socially and politically conservative, 'American' message."[19] Furthermore, Eliot, a Unitarian, had helped to make Harvard a bastion of Unitarian thinking. He despised narrow sectarianism (confessionalism) and had contempt for education built on such foundations. Yet he profusely complimented Roanoke as a liberal arts college.

If Dreher moved easily in that world, one can surmise that he broadened his notion of a common Christian base from the strong and well-defined evangelicalism of a Bittle to include the protoliberal thinking of a Brooks and the Unitarianism of an Eliot. All agreed that Christianity in its American Protestant construal had great civilizational potential. It could morally form the young of the nation for both domestic and foreign purposes. Such was the tendency of

16. Mark Miller, *Dear Old Roanoke—A Sesquicentennial Portait* (Macon, GA: Mercer University Press, 1992), 75.

17. Eisenberg, *First Hundred Years*, 162.

18. Eisenberg, *First Hundred Years*, 163.

19. Marsden, "Did Success Spoil American Protestantism?" 291.

the progressive thinking of the day, a well from which Dreher drank deeply. And he brought that thinking to Roanoke College: "Roanoke became known far and wide as a sane, thorough, liberal, progressive, Christian small college."[20]

This "broadening the base" did not mean Dreher overtly rejected the more vigorous evangelicalism of Bittle or of the surrounding religious culture of the South. He continued to revere Bittle throughout his life. He was for many years a vice president of the Evangelical Alliance of the United States, and he always took a strong interest in the work of the YMCA, the strongest religious organization on the Roanoke campus. He encouraged the Student Volunteer Movement for Foreign Missions at Roanoke. Yet his own vision and rhetoric were closer to a Unitarian construal of the faith than an evangelical one. Religion was a grounding and a utilitarian instrument for the moral life. If his religious vision was evangelical in any sense, it was a highly "enlightened" evangelicalism. His views were not "sectarian" enough to offend his Unitarian friend Charles Eliot. His religious views "were equally broad [as his political ones], though he was a member of the church of his ancestors."[21] It is worth noting that, in 1901, Dreher's "broad" religious approach led to the first non-Lutheran being elected to the permanent faculty, which led to some consternation among the college's Lutheran constituency. However, Dreher knew that the college could not exist without a broadly Protestant student body and set of donors and supporters. There simply weren't enough Lutherans in the region to sustain it in those crucial categories. The same was true of the faculty. Besides, the Lutherans on the faculty were part of the same evangelical spirit as other Protestants, and including non-Lutheran Christians was not a radical leap for them.

A noteworthy feature—and one that Dreher shared with Bittle—was a complete lack of Lutheran language and themes in his writing: themes such as the pervasiveness of sin, the extravagant grace of God in Christ, justification, vocation, and the two ways that God reigns in the world are absent from his constructive thinking, as they are from the curriculum of his day (which I will examine below). This is all the more noteworthy since Lutherans at the national and synodical level were focusing more on their confessional unity as Lutheran Christians.[22]

Why does Roanoke College seem so impervious to this "Lutheranizing" of the Lutheranism of his day? It seems probable that at the congregational

20. Eisenberg, *First Hundred Years*, 201.
21. Eisenberg, *First Hundred Years*, 376.
22. A. R. Wentz, *The Lutheran Church*, 216.

level, and thus at the college level, the effects of the Americanist movement in American Lutheranism were far from extinguished after Schmuckerism's demise in the 1850s.[23] The broad-based commitment to Christian moral formation that could embrace both Southern evangelicalism and Northern Unitarianism persisted in the colleges founded by Americanists such as Bittle (Roanoke), Keller (Wittenberg), and Schmucker (Gettysburg). Many of the surrounding congregations were no doubt embedded in the broad evangelicalism of the Protestant empire.[24] Roanoke College persisted along its path of Americanist Lutheranism.

The Curriculum

While Bittle was able to impress his convictions directly on the faculty as well as on the curricular and extracurricular life of the college, Dreher was less able to do so. A good deal of that was because he spent so much time traveling as an ambassador and fundraiser for the college. "At least it [his travel] tended to rob his office of the authority of its influence."[25] He could no longer serve as chairman of the faculty, and his title was changed from professor of moral and political science during his first years as president to simply "President" in 1887.

Nevertheless, some of the changes in higher education that I have referred to above began to seep into the college's curriculum, partly due to

23. This was a movement initiated in the 1830s and 1840s by Samuel Simon Schmucker of Gettysburg Lutheran Seminary, which emphasized Christian unity concerning American evangelical principles and at the same time relinquished distinctive Lutheran teachings and practices in favor of evangelical unity. Bittle followed his mentor, Schmucker, in this Americanist direction (see chap. 1 for more details).

24. One of the most puzzling addresses given at Dreher's inauguration was offered by Charles Porterfield Krauth, the leading figure in the re-confessionalizing of American Lutheranism in the postwar period. In his congratulatory address, Krauth praises Roanoke College for its education of men of discernment and intelligence, for its training of laymen and clergy for the church, and for its efforts to reconcile North and South. But the word "Lutheran" does not appear in his address, let alone an exhortation to the college to appropriate its Lutheran heritage more fully. One would think that a leader in the confessionalist movement against the Americanizers would take the occasion to strike a blow for his side of the struggle. But not a word. Perhaps it was simply a case of good etiquette—one does not antagonize one's host at a celebratory event—or perhaps he thought it was a lost cause. At any rate, the great confessionalist says nothing about Lutheran identity or belief in the life of the college.

25. Eisenberg, First Hundred Years, 170.

Dreher's familiarity with the larger educational world of the North. For instance, the college inaugurated a "scientific course" in 1880, which meant that students could forgo more studies in the classical languages after the junior year and take more courses in science, leading to a B.S. degree. A department of history and political science began in 1882, and courses in Western civilization were introduced. From 1883 on, students had to pass exams in English language and literature.[26] Other courses of a more practical nature—in teaching and business—were also added.

The only real change in religion and philosophy courses was the introduction of a course in English Bible: it was requested by students and faculty in 1888, but did not find its way into the curriculum until 1893. It was not as though study of the Bible had not been present in the earlier life of the college; but that took place mostly in the numerous extracurricular practices. Now it was in the curriculum. But none of the great challenges to the Christian worldview in Northern intellectual life that I have referred to above seemed to be taken account of and examined in courses in the curriculum. Nor were there any courses one might expect from the re-confessionalization of Lutheranism—such as church history, Reformation history, and Martin Luther himself. The classic courses of the old-style liberal arts college seemed to hold sway from the time of Bittle to the end of Dreher's tenure: mental philosophy, moral philosophy, philosophy of religion, history of philosophy, and Christian evidences. Only Butler's *Analogy* (an apologia for Christianity) and natural theology had been dropped. "Faculty psychology"—the belief, deriving from Scottish "common sense" philosophy, that ordinary humans have faculties to recognize the True and Good when they are presented to them—was still the organizing principle of the curriculum.

Though Dreher was quite aware of the new challenges arising—in his inaugural address he mentions the conflict between religion and science, as well as the rise of materialism and communism—he seems to avoid taking up any of these new challenges in the curriculum. The faculty whom Dreher sent off to various Northern and European universities for advanced degrees were certainly aware of Darwinism, Marxism, higher criticism of the Bible, and free thought. Yet Dreher seems to mollify any of his hearers' worries by declaring later in his address that there is no real conflict between religion and science. He affirms the unity of learning that was so assumed in the old-style synthesis of science, history, the classics, and biblical religion: "All

26. Mark Miller, *Dear Old Roanoke*, 73.

branches of knowledge are but so many avenues of approach to the Source of all truth."[27]

Was this a failure of nerve to take up the challenges with which modern schools in the North were wrestling? Or an excuse not to bring in new courses that touted the college's Lutheran heritage? Possibly. But a more likely answer is that Dreher and the faculty did not want to upset their clientele unduly. After all, they were located in the South. The college was continually scraping for students and money in those difficult postwar years, and it would have been foolhardy to offend that clientele by immersing itself in controversy or by narrowing its religious base. It was more prudent to continue the curriculum of the old-style college in religion and philosophy and to tinker with other less threatening innovations.

So, though the curriculum was evolving slowly in more practical and flexible directions, there was a good deal of continuity with the college of the antebellum years—especially with regard to religion and philosophy. No doubt the more highly educated faculty took up some of the emerging intellectual challenges within their courses, but the courses themselves remained pretty much the same. Dreher, who had less influence on academic matters than did Bittle, did not press for radical changes either.

Extracurricular Life

Religious and moral formation continued to be a strong focus of the extracurricular life of the college. Morning and evening chapel, obligatory Sunday church attendance, and required presence at weekly faculty recitations on portions of the Bible continued during the Dreher years, though Bittle's revivalist fervor receded. Lutheran pastors, however, thought that formation was not as strong as it should be. Though the Lutheran synods never came up with much monetary support, they evidently thought the college should be preparing more pious laymen and pastors for the church. Dreher, in response, agreed that "more attention should be given to the religious and moral welfare of the students, and more personal interest taken in them by the Faculty. My own efforts to secure these ends have failed for lack of cooperation."[28]

27. Dreher, *Addresses*, 35.
28. Eisenberg, *First Hundred Years*, 183. Perhaps an unintended effect of Dreher's upgrading of the faculty was that their attention was drawn more to their own intellectual

A member of the board of trustees, D. B. Strouse, agreed with Dreher and put the college mission in more explicitly Christian terms than the president had: "Roanoke College is a religious institution . . . and the Board earnestly desires and expects the Faculty by individual effort, by earnest exhortation in Chapel, and by religious services, to win the students to Christ and to build them up in the most holy faith of our Lord."[29] The old evangelical enthusiasm of Bittle may have diminished in Dreher's rhetoric but not in that of the board's leadership.

This Christian fervor was also borne by the Young Men's Christian Association, which held prayer meetings, sponsored Bible study, invited speakers, conducted services at a mission in town, and even had its members teach in African-American Sunday schools in the community. It also spawned Clericus, an organization for pretheological students, as well as the Missionary Band, which was Roanoke's version of the Student Volunteer Movement.[30]

The Student Volunteer Movement (SVM) for Foreign Missions arose in 1886 under the inspiration of the great evangelist Dwight Moody, and it brought college students into the ranks of missionary work as never before. Thousands signed the pledge to become foreign missionaries, and they dispersed to China, India, Japan, and Africa. Roanoke's Missionary Band sent delegates to the SVM gatherings; in fact, in December 1886, five of the six Roanoke College delegates to an SVM conference at the University of Virginia signed the pledge to become missionaries. Among them were J. A. B. Scherer and R. B. Peery, who became pioneer missionaries to Japan.[31] At least a dozen other collegians followed them in bringing the gospel to foreign lands.

There was a fascinating domestic dimension to this missionary thrust at Roanoke College, which was engineered by Julius Dreher. It had to do not only with the great missionary movement occurring during the last decades of the nineteenth century, but also with Dreher's particular notion

---

nurture and production than the earlier faculty had been. Dreher collected a number of academic stars who did a good deal of publishing, the most prolific among them being F. V. N. Painter. And Dreher recruited other strong faculty members who had perhaps not published as much but had studied at an astonishing array of elite American and European universities.

29. Eisenberg, *First Hundred Years*, 183.

30. Eisenberg, *First Hundred Years,* 426.

31. Scherer not only was a founder of churches, schools, and a seminary in Japan, but he also became a major commentator on Japan's political propensities. After returning to the United States, he became the president of California Technical Institute, where he gathered an array of Nobel Prize–winning scientists.

of mission work. The missionary movement is very clear: it is continuous with Bittle's effort to form men and women for proclaiming the gospel to the world. The SVM further built on that endeavor. But Dreher's notion of missionary work was more about bringing Christian civilization to benighted pagan cultures than it was about proclaiming the gospel to perishing souls, though he certainly did not reject the latter endeavor.[32] In his lectures on higher education, Dreher would preface his remarks with his rationale for bringing education to the masses.[33]

> The benevolent spirit is so intimately connected with religious sentiment, that the interest manifested in Christian education and mission may be taken as the measure of the benevolent spirit of any people. . . . The highest attainment of the race is expressed in the term Christian civilization. How to improve and perpetuate this civilization where already established, and how to extend it over the world, are the great questions pressing upon the attention of the benevolent. Fundamental, then, to any successful effort to extend our civilization, is the higher education to fit men for the work of exposing the rottenness of existing pagan systems, and of planting on the ruins of these the fair fabric of Christian society—the foundation of permanent civilization.[34]

32. It is a huge irony that theological liberals of Dreher's era were so enthusiastic about linking Christian missions with the vigorous spread of American Protestant culture that they were unabashed about proclaiming it during that epoch. But toward the latter part of the twentieth century they became extremely squeamish, if not derisive, about the "cultural imperialism" that attended Christian missions. Some churches, such as the Evangelical Lutheran Church in America, were so remorseful about that "imperialism" that in 1999 they decided to give up sending missionaries of the gospel to those who hadn't heard it in favor of "accompaniment," i.e., aiding already-established churches throughout the world who asked for their help.

33. Dreher became a well-known lecturer around the country on higher education. As a son of the South who also was familiar with education in the North, he often compared the affluence of Northern education with the poverty of Southern. He repeatedly called for more "benevolence" to strengthen education in the South and West, including the education of Native Americans and African Americans. For example, he gave a speech, entitled "The Benevolent Spirit and the Higher Education," to the Educational Association of Virginia in 1881 and "Colleges—North and South" to the Department of Higher Education of the National Education Association in Topeka, Kansas, in 1886. In each lecture he connects benevolence with Christianity and exhorts his hearers to channel that benevolence into higher education for all citizens. He also argues for a strong religious component in higher education, even in public ventures. American destiny would be at risk without schools imparting virtue to their students.

34. Julius Dreher, "The Benevolent Spirit and the Higher Education," an address before

46

American missionaries brought such civilization to foreign lands and peoples, but Dreher thought that another mission strategy would be to bring foreign students—and Native Americans—to Roanoke College to expose them and acculturate them to the Christian culture that the college was communicating to its own students. No doubt part of his motivation was to "foster international and intercultural understanding," but far more was going on.[35] He was bringing pagans to enjoy and learn from the "fair fabric of Christian society." And pagans he brought—young men from the Choctaw tribe, from Mexico, Japan, Korea, Canada, Puerto Rico, and the West Indies. The total came to 128 during Dreher's presidency. The college paper boasted that "Roanoke College has had more foreign students than any other college in Virginia."[36]

These students were obligated to perform the regular curricular and extracurricular duties required of their American counterparts, including attendance at chapel, church, and biblical study. Their immersion in Roanoke College's "Christian republicanism" paid dividends to them and their countries. Many became political leaders, professors, physicians, and pastors. The second wave, which came toward the end of the century, were Christian students sent back by Roanoke College missionaries.[37] Perhaps the most distinguished of the foreign students was Kimm Kuisic, who became one of the democratic leaders of Korea before the Korean War. He was captured and imprisoned (until his death) by North Koreans after they invaded South Korea in 1950.

Two other major initiatives of the latter part of the nineteenth century deserve mention. Earlier I observed that many new charitable institutions emerged during that period—hospitals, orphanages, homes for the elderly, and other ministries of mercy. While the aftermath of the Civil War prevented the impoverished South from building up as many of these institutions as the North was able to, the Lutherans of the South did organize an "Orphan Asylum" in the Roanoke Valley, of which President Dreher was

---

the Educational Association of Virginia at Norfolk, Virginia, July 8, 1881, in the *Educational Journal of Virginia*, 4–5.

35. Mark Miller, *Dear Old Roanoke*, 73. Miller notes that Dreher and Roanoke College were expanding the horizons of the students by establishing a department of history and political science, as well as exposure to international issues in various courses. No doubt bringing foreign students to Roanoke was part of that expansion of horizons, but it seems the education of those students in Christian faith and morals was even more important.

36. Eisenberg, *First Hundred Years*, 202.

37. Eisenberg, *First Hundred Years*, 202–17.

an incorporator and board member.[38] The 1870s and onward also saw the emergence of intercollegiate sports among colleges and universities. Roanoke College was no different: the students became particularly enthused about baseball and football. However, the soberly earnest Dreher was not so enthralled: "Even in an age run mad over athletic contests, we venture to advocate gymnastics as a prescribed part of educational training."[39] He did not view participation in organized sports as a character-building activity.

Life after Roanoke

After twenty-five years of giving his heart and soul to Roanoke, Dreher, who was a bit provoked by criticism from the church, decided to leave while he was still relatively young and move on to new things. His departure in 1903 coincided with the fiftieth anniversary celebration of the college's founding, which he generously helped to organize. It was as grand as the twenty-fifth had been at the time of his inauguration. Soon after he left, he finally found time for marriage—to Emeline Richmond of Scranton, Pennsylvania. Immediately after their marriage, the couple set off for Tahiti, of the Society Islands, where Dreher became President Theodore Roosevelt's consul. Later on, Dreher, at the behest of his friend Roosevelt, served a number of consulates. He wrote extensive reports on the people he served and the work he accomplished. After his retirement, in 1924, he settled in Florida, where one of his dearest friends, Charles Eliot, emeritus president of Harvard, lived nearby. He died in 1937 at eighty-nine.[40]

Conclusion

Both David Bittle and his devoted successor, Julius Dreher, worked intensively to keep Roanoke alive in difficult times. Both had amusing quips about their lives as fundraisers for the ever-voracious Roanoke College. Bittle mused: "When I die I hope my funeral sermon will be preached from the

---

38. Eisenberg, *The Lutheran Church in Virginia, 1717–1962* (Lynchburg, VA: J. P. Bell Company, 1967), 387.

39. Dreher, *Addresses*, 54.

40. Eisenberg, *First Hundred Years*, 376–77.

text, 'And it came to pass that the beggar died,' Luke 16:22."[41] In 1928, Dreher opined in a commencement address at the college: "During that entire period of twenty-five years I played the role of a peripatetic college president in perennial search of a deficit extinguisher; but that deficit proved to be sort of an *ignis fatuus*, always a little ahead, and never quite overtaken."[42]

However, both men devoted themselves to far more than the college's mere survival. They aimed at excellence within the confines of the old-style liberal arts college, which had a fully integrated—though by this time nearly obsolete—approach to teaching and learning. Moreover, they were deadly serious about the religious and moral formation they thought was the essence of Christian higher education, and they assembled a faculty to carry out that important function. Dreher began the great Roanoke tradition of sending promising students and current faculty off for graduate study to the best universities of America and Europe. Some of the faculty published widely. The whole enterprise was held together by a passionate commitment to Christian republicanism, the evangelical belief that colleges should supply virtue for church and society.

It could be argued that Dreher's was a golden era of education at Roanoke College, in spite of its financial neediness. The curriculum and co-curriculum were integrated by a coherent vision of Christian education, and students were powerfully formed by it. The faculty was excellent and supported that coherent vision. The student body, though small, was intellectually formed by a highly disciplined method of recitation and critique. An incredible number of students went on to be pastors (about a third of the graduates right up to 1900), teachers, college administrators, lawyers, and doctors. Most were Christian men of conviction who did indeed take up their callings with seriousness. Studying this era closely makes one shun the easy notion that contemporary versions of higher education are always superior.

Dreher was not the revivalist or evangelist in the way that Bittle was, but his other strengths compensated for that lack. His extensive contacts with the great and near-great, especially in the North, gave Roanoke an excellent reputation far and wide, and provided Dreher with a cosmopolitan sophistication that opened the college to wider horizons. Though Dreher was drawn to a liberalized version of the Christian faith, he did not reject the

41. George Diehl, *Sketch of the Life and Labors of Rev. David F. Bittle, D.D.* (Gettysburg, PA: Wible, 1877), 25.

42. Eisenberg, *First Hundred Years*, 152.

more robust evangelical fervor of the college's normative culture. The college produced more missionaries during his tenure than it ever would again; it gathered in and "Christianized" many foreign students. Yet he was himself of a much "cooler" religious temperament and belief. Christianity was essentially about ethics, especially the benevolent spirit, which he seemed to possess in excess.

The college went on in the Americanist Lutheran tradition, which meant that it upheld few Lutheran distinctives. Because it always needed more students and money than the Lutherans of Virginia could or would supply, the college continued in a broadly American evangelical direction in order to draw widely and deeply from its Southern and Northern constituencies. It lived in both worlds with ease, led by a president who was himself able not only to survive in both worlds but to live usefully in them.

3

JOHN MOREHEAD (1903–1920)

Roanoke as Prelude to Greatness

Serving as president of Roanoke College was not John Morehead's (1867–1936) greatest contribution to the church or the world—or his greatest claim to fame. "The best known and best loved Lutheran of his time" did such heroic relief and refugee work in Europe following World I that he was nominated by four nations for the Nobel Peace Prize. (He died before that nomination could be acted upon or awarded.) Shortly after the war, in 1923, he called the Lutheran churches of the world together for the First Lutheran World Convention in Eisenach, and then served as its president. He received honorary degrees from a host of European universities and honors from the president of Germany and the kings of Denmark and Finland.[1] While David Bittle and Julius Dreher put Roanoke College on America's map and themselves basked in some fame, neither of them made an impact on church and world as massive as did their successor. Indeed, it could be argued that no Roanoke president before or after achieved such an impact.

In this chapter, however, I do not focus on the period after he resigned from Roanoke College, which he did in a letter that he sent to the board in April 1920 from a hotel in Warsaw, where he was deeply involved in relief and refugee work on behalf of the National Lutheran Council. Rather, I am primarily concerned with his presidency of Roanoke from the fall of 1903 to the time of his resignation. During that seventeen years he served the college and the church effectively and nobly. Before we embark on that story,

---

1. W. A. Eisenberg, *The First Hundred Years: Roanoke College 1842–1942* (Strasburg, VA: Shenandoah Publishing House, 1942), 395.

however, it would be helpful to sketch briefly the national milieu that was the backdrop of his life and times, as well as an account of his upbringing in that context.

America, 1900–1920

The North and Midwest

Many of the trends that emerged in the period between the Civil War and the turn of the twentieth century continued up to the beginning of World War I. The North experienced surging population and economic growth, a good deal of it fueled by continuing immigration. Urbanization increased while populations also moved west. Big business got bigger, along with the challenge of administering large organizations effectively. Labor continued to organize, and the period featured frequent strikes. Bigger business organizations begat bigger government—to counter the power of business—and as the country expanded and consolidated, a new national spirit emerged.

From the turn of the century onward, "a tide of moral earnestness began to swell in American political life."[2] Aggressive young reformers such as Theodore Roosevelt began to appear in public life. The Progressive movement was afoot, bringing forth many reforms that not only tamed monopolistic tendencies but also headed off any serious socialist movement. It enlisted the surging evangelical churches—especially the Methodists—so fully that the Progressive Party's 1912 campaign theme song was "Onward Christian Soldiers."[3] The same churches, joined by many other Protestant denominations, pressed forward their central agendas: prohibition of alcoholic beverages at home and foreign missions abroad.

Yet, beneath the surface, secularization in many sectors of life continued apace, especially in education, freeing the schools from Christian moral and intellectual guidance. The old-time liberal arts college, with its synthesis of science, philosophy, classics, and biblical religion, was further eroded by new models of education. The country's practical needs called for more practical college programs that would train students for technical, professional,

---

2. Abdel Ross Wentz, *The Lutheran Church in American History* (Philadelphia: United Lutheran Publication House, 1923), 209.

3. Grant Wacker, "The Social Gospel," in *Eerdmans' Handbook to Christianity in America,* ed. Mark Noll et al. (Grand Rapids: Eerdmans, 1983), 319.

and commercial work. The methods and models of the German research university took over in the great private and public universities and filtered down to the more advanced liberal arts colleges; the fully prescribed curriculum made way for a proliferation of electives; lecturing by faculty replaced recitation by students. An unfettered search for truth was the order of the day, and education shifted from learning inherited wisdom to discovering new truths, and that could indeed become unsettling.

The historical-critical method was applied to the Bible, which led to doubts about authorship and historical veracity. Darwinism challenged the Genesis accounts of creation and seemed to reduce man to random processes without any need of God's guidance. Marxism undermined inherited intellectual and moral norms by attributing them to the manipulations of those with economic and political power. These challenges led to great unease and division in the country, its churches, and their educational institutions.

Some theologians in the Northern universities and seminaries fully accepted the modern challenges and revised the faith to accommodate them. Others did not embrace this liberal theology so fully but followed instead the earlier protoliberal approach of emphasizing Christian ethics and de-emphasizing theological claims. One wing of this approach became the full-blown Social Gospel movement, which emphasized the application of Christian ethics to economic and political concerns. Others reacted with strong affirmations of biblical inerrancy. Between 1910 and 1915, a twelve-volume series entitled *The Fundamentals* was widely distributed, spawning fundamentalism in America.

In spite of all this upheaval, the churches gained many members, including those who joined new Pentecostal and Holiness churches.[4] The many ethnic Lutheran churches in the Midwest were growing rapidly on the strength of continuing immigration from Germany and the Scandinavian countries. The strongly ethnic Lutheran churches of the Midwest tended to maintain their confessional identity as part of their ethnic set-apartness. They constructed their own set of institutions—seminaries, colleges, mission societies, social service organizations, etc. Along with the ethnically insulated churches, however, were those established and pastored by Eastern Lu-

4. This historical background is indebted to a number of historical accounts of the period: a series of authors in *Eerdmans' Handbook to American Christianity*, already cited; Sidney Ahlstrom's *A Religious History of the American People* (New Haven: Yale University Press, 1972); Abdel Ross Wentz's *The Lutheran Church,* already cited; and William Ringenberg's *The Christian College: A History of Protestant Higher Education in America* (Grand Rapids: Baker Academic, 2006).

therans, who were much more Americanized than their ethnic counterparts. These churches—one in which I grew up—were often generically Protestant, influenced a great deal by frontier churches such as the Methodist Church. Nevertheless, most were held together liturgically by the *Common Service Book and Hymnal*.

As churches grew, they imitated large commercial organizations. "Systematic and business-like organization was one of the outstanding characteristics of the church."[5] While a stronger sense of denominational identity prevailed, there was also a vigorous move toward interdenominational cooperation, including the formation of the Federal Council of Churches in 1908 and many mission societies.

The South

In the South, Methodist and Baptist churches grew rapidly, not much bothered by the controversies raging in the North. Revivalism in the church continued as strongly as it had in the antebellum period, though segregation and Jim Crow laws held sway in society and culture. Lutherans made strong moves toward unity: the United Synod of the South, organized during the Civil War (1861) and later led by John Morehead (1910–14), merged with the General Synod and the General Council to become the United Lutheran Church in America in 1918. Elite Southern Lutherans participated in a reconfessionalization that was consonant with the new sharper sense of denominational identity in the country; but at the local level the Americanist Lutheran characteristics persisted, not least in the ongoing life of Roanoke College.

The Americanist movement of 1820–50 was an effort to blend Lutheranism into the regnant evangelicalism of the day,[6] and it had lingering effects on many churches. The movement was resisted by Lutherans who defended and promoted the distinctive teachings and practices of Lutheranism. A sign of this continuing conflict came in the 1890s, when an early version of the Common Service (including a set Lutheran liturgy) was promoted at College Lutheran Church in Salem, Virginia. That initiative was vigorously opposed by a prominent Lutheran member of the Roanoke College faculty, F. V. N. Painter, who wrote an attack on the Common Service in a book he wrote

5. Wentz, *The Lutheran Church*, 213.
6. See chap. 1 for a full explication.

with Gettysburg Seminary professor J. W. Richard, entitled *Christian Worship: Its Principles and Forms* (1892). Painter lost the battle over the Common Service in the long run, which led to his departure from the Lutheran ministry and move to the Presbyterian Church.[7]

The relatively consistent trajectory from the close of the Civil War to the onset of World War I was sharply broken by that war. Roanoke College was not exempt from the effects of the "Great War," not least of which was the abrupt departure of its president, John Morehead, to do relief and refugee work in Europe immediately after the war.

The Formation of John Alfred Morehead

Since the Civil War had ended only two years before Morehead's birth in 1867, times were hard in southwestern Virginia. Families had to work diligently to survive, especially if the family was the size of James and Katherine Yonce Morehead's—eight children (five boys and three girls). James was of Scottish Presbyterian heritage, while Katherine was German Lutheran; both of them were from families who had long been in America. Katherine's Lutheranism won out, and the brood was brought up in a devout Lutheran home. John grew up and was catechized in a church pastored by a confessionalist Lutheran, Alexander Phillippi, who was sympathetic to the conservative Lutheranism of the Henkels of New Market and the Tennessee Synod. Because elementary education was fairly sporadic, John—known in the family as "Fred"—compensated for it by much reading and home study.

One of his older brothers, Wythe, had worked hard to get the money to go to Roanoke College and then to become a professor of English there. He paved the financial way for John to enter the college in 1886 as a sophomore. One could say that John Morehead was immersed in Roanoke College's orbit before he even knew about other schools. There was not only the influence of Wythe, but also the encouragement of his uncle, W. B. Yonce, who likewise was already a professor there (in the field of ancient languages). Indeed, Morehead mentions in his inaugural address that it was his "privilege as a child to behold the form of the sainted Dr. David F. Bittle, founder of the institution." He also mentions his debt as a student to Roanoke professors, such as his uncle and Samuel Wells, both of whom molded his views of life.

7. Noted in Eisenberg, *The Lutheran Church in Virginia, 1717–1962* (Lynchburg, VA: J. P. Bell, 1966), 519.

In addition, Morehead said, "I have sustained relations of personal friendship with my predecessor, Dr. Julius Dreher, so that altogether it seems just to claim that I am no stranger to the institution."[8]

Morehead graduated from Roanoke with honors in 1889 and was asked to stay on to teach at the college, which had become something of a pattern at Roanoke at that time. The president and faculty recognized highly promising students and proceeded to invite them to teach, then often sponsored their higher education at elite universities before their return to Roanoke. As I have mentioned above, they had done the same thing with Julius Dreher, Morehead's predecessor. Morehead taught math and science for a year, then went off on his first excursion to the North to attend seminary at the Lutheran seminary in Philadelphia, itself a bastion of confessional Lutheranism. While there, he took philosophy courses at the University of Pennsylvania.

Morehead was ordained in 1892 to serve several country parishes in Burke's Garden, Virginia, where he also "took to wife" Virginia Fisher, the daughter of a poor widower whose family had earlier been taken in by the Moreheads. He followed that with a highly successful stint in an urban parish in Richmond, Virginia. In 1898 he was called to be the president and professor of systematic theology at the Lutheran seminary near Charleston, South Carolina, where he worked effectively for four years, though he spent the last one in theological study at Leipzig. His alma mater, Roanoke College, conferred on him the D.D. degree in 1902.[9]

During his successful ministry in Richmond, Morehead received a number of calls to other congregations, one of them, in 1897, from College Lutheran in Salem, Virginia, where he was later to become a member during his years as president of Roanoke College. He regretfully declined that call, but mentioned how interested he was in Christian higher education, the students of Roanoke College, the people of Salem, and College Lutheran Church. The next year he would be in Charleston at the Lutheran seminary, and six years later he would be back at the college in Salem.

When Julius Dreher resigned from Roanoke in the spring of 1903, Morehead was unanimously elected to succeed him in the fall of the same year. After all, he was one of Roanoke College's own, and the board and faculty

8. John Morehead, "The Mission of the Christian College," *The Roanoke Collegian*, Salem, VA (June–July 1904): 99.

9. These details of Morehead's early life are drawn from Eisenberg's *First Hundred Years*, 392–93, and from Samuel Trexler's *John A. Morehead: A Biography* (New York: G. P. Putnam's Sons, 1938), 30–52.

had followed his considerable successes over the twelve years since he had graduated. At thirty-six, he was four years older than was his predecessor, Dreher, when he became president.

Why did Morehead leave the presidency of a seminary—and a professorship in theology—to become the president of an undergraduate Christian liberal arts college? It was a difficult decision for him, but he believed that God had called him to guide "Roanoke College to larger and higher usefulness to the Church and to the world in the work of Christian education." While the theological education of pastors was an extremely important task, that education rested on a prior foundation: "the adequate development of the institutions of the Church for Christian education." Without being supplied with students with excellent undergraduate education, seminaries were at a severe disadvantage in performing their calling. Morehead thought that the general state of Christian education in the South left much to be desired, and he believed that his leadership could make Roanoke a leader in that noble task.[10]

Morehead as President of Roanoke College

The Vision

John Morehead's inauguration at Roanoke took place during the college's commencement celebration in the spring of 1904. His address was organized around "one central theme: The Mission of the Christian College." He articulates the content of that mission in that address and in his other writings and talks at Roanoke College. That content has remarkable continuity with what Bittle and Dreher had identified as the mission of the college, though his articulation of the mission also has some important and intriguing differences from that of David Bittle.

Morehead begins his inaugural address by noting the gravity of the task to which he has "been constrained by providential indication." He calls upon the "abiding presence and blessing of Almighty God for the strength to perform the duties of this office."[11] He then pays great tribute to his predecessors, Bittle and Dreher, and affirms the continuing commitment of the college to

10. Trexler, *John Morehead*, 52–53.
11. Morehead, "The Mission of the Christian College," 99. Hereafter, page references to this address appear in parentheses within the text.

goals set by them. Bittle's distinctive contribution to those goals was "the religious element in education." Morehead commits himself to continuing the "conscious maintenance of the Christian element in education" (101).

What he means by this "Christian element" was that the "spiritual powers" of the student must be developed along with the physical and intellectual. "Moral and religious influences are more directly effective than any other means as character forming agencies." The college should educate the "entire man—the end being the attainment of well-rounded culture or character or manhood, ready for the work of life" (101).

Noting that public colleges and universities cannot directly use these moral and religious influences, he affirms that Christian colleges play a particularly important role because they are, on the contrary, permeated by the Christian spirit. While devoted to the cause of truth in its broadest sense, their "atmosphere is harmonious with the Bible and favorable to Christian faith" (101). Those influences are reinforced by the Roanoke faculty, the student body, and the town of Salem. Altogether, they collaborate in the development of manly character, fulfilling the work of Christian education.

Morehead goes on to praise his immediate predecessor, Julius Dreher, for enabling the college to make important material and financial advances. Dreher's distinctive contribution, he says, was the "development of the efficiency of the college as a teaching force" (102). This efficiency enabled the college to continue to educate in the broadest and best sense of the word: learning useful knowledge, developing thinking power, promoting the ends of culture and practical life, forming appreciative sympathy for all things human, focusing on service to humanity and, above all, forming manly character.

Only small colleges can do this well, he observes, and proceeds to quote studies done by a Professor Dexter of Illinois University that confirm this. The faculty, for its part, must make a "specialty of every student," promoting the method of "personal interest, aid, and influence in all the college's work." That will carry the work of the college on—"widening and deepening its own life, blessing and uplifting mankind, serving and accomplishing the will of God, like the mighty river in its progress to the sea." By active consecration to this cause, Roanoke College would be in the "field of highest service of Church and State, of the Kingdom of God and the kingdom of humanity" (104).

The continuity of Morehead's view of the mission of the college with the views communicated so enthusiastically by Bittle and Dreher—the Christian republicanism spawned in the antebellum period—is powerfully clear. And the formation of Christian character is central. That means that young men must be imbued with the spirit of service to church and world. (Dreher called that spirit the virtue of "benevolence.") In serving both, they contribute virtue to the ongoing life of the republic as well as further the advance of Christian civilization in the world. True, the college must educate the whole person—intellectual, physical, and spiritual—but what makes the college special is its emphasis on the "religious element," a phrase that is used persistently in the inaugural addresses of all three men.

For Morehead and Dreher, religion is prized primarily for its use in forming the moral character of the students. Both presidents retreat from the full-blooded Trinitarian thinking of Bittle, whose inaugural address emphasized not only Christian truth claims, but also held firm to the conviction that only the Holy Spirit could break the human bondage to sin. Students had to be converted. Dreher and Morehead, on the other hand, showed a more optimistic view of human nature and a more limited view of the role of the college. The moral virtues can be formed in young men without unrelenting efforts to convert them. Religion is essential, but mostly for its moral impact. Neither Dreher nor Morehead mention Jesus or the Holy Spirit in their inaugural addresses.[12] Yet all three presidents view the moral formation of students as the primary mission of the college. That formation should be aimed at their becoming "manly Christians," which conforms to the "muscular Christianity" of the regnant evangelicalism of the day. (This shared value of Christian manliness held by Dreher and his friend, Theodore Roosevelt, had no doubt cemented their friendship.[13]) Further, though Christian character can be nurtured in the classroom (more about that later), the presidents see formation in virtue as a function of the "Christian atmosphere" of the college as it is fashioned by the faculty, staff, fellow students, and even the town of Salem.

12. A bit of caution must be exercised in the case of Morehead, whose inaugural address comes to us in only extracted form. Oddly, there seems to be no extant copy of the full address in the college or ELCA archives. One possible reason for this puzzling absence is that William Eisenberg might have acquired the full address from the college when he did his history of the college. His literary estate is held in the archives of Grace Lutheran Church in Winchester, VA. But up until now, no one has worked through his collected literary artifacts to find out whether the full manuscript is there. The note of caution should be observed with regard to other generalizations about Morehead's address.

13. See chap. 2 above, entitled "Julius Dreher—Roanoke College's Cosmopolitan Champion of Benevolence," which records his work for Roosevelt in a number of consulates after the conclusion of his presidency at Roanoke College in 1903.

This utilitarian approach to the "religious element" of the college enabled Dreher and Morehead to appeal to the many kinds of Christians who came to the college as students and/or those who supported the college financially. It also enabled them to embrace both the "enlightened evangelicalism"—sometimes bordering on Unitarianism—of their Northern constituency along with the more traditional evangelicalism of the South.

Dreher learned how to speak the liberal religious language of the patricians in the Northeast, while simultaneously remaining active in the Evangelical Alliance and the YMCA. He seems to have suffered no cognitive dissonance from such strained commitments. He was a layman who naturally—perhaps unconsciously—embraced a broad variety of religious traditions to fuel the college's commitment to the Christian republican project. A discriminating theological sophistication was neither his gift nor his desire.

Morehead must have made a conscious decision to follow the pattern of his immediate predecessor rather than that of the founder. How else to explain the absence of a more developed theological rationale for Christian education at Roanoke? How can we account for the absence of any trace of Lutheran rationale for Christian higher education on the part of the well-educated former professor of systematic theology at Southern Lutheran Seminary who would later go on to found the Lutheran World Convention? Morehead was certainly prepared well enough intellectually to interject those themes into his inaugural address and into the intellectual life of the college. But he refrains. This is just as puzzling as the decision of Charles Porterfield Krauth (a leading Lutheran confessional theologian of the post–Civil War period) not to articulate any Lutheran themes in his address at the inauguration of Julius Dreher in 1878.

The likely answer to these puzzlements is that the generic Christian republicanism of the college was so embedded that it provided the best available religious rationale for a high-quality, coherent education at Roanoke. What's more, its gentle utilitarian approach to religion allowed the college to encourage many Christian traditions to flow into its republican project. Theological distinctions were not as important as moral intensity, which was the main aim of a community devoted to Christian virtue.[14]

14. Christian virtue included strong emphasis on temperance, another cause to which all three early Roanoke presidents were committed, and to which the surging Methodists and Baptists were likewise dedicated. President Morehead joined other citizens of Salem in a common effort to prevent the establishment of beer-and-pool halls in Salem. See Norwood Middleton, *Salem: A Virginia Chronicle* (Salem, VA: Salem Historical Society, 1986), 182.

Morehead decided to work with the extant tradition rather than try to change it.

This broad approach to Christian doctrine may well have protected Roanoke College from some of the sharp controversies that were shaking colleges and universities in the North. Higher criticism, evolution, Marxism, and versions of the Social Gospel did not seem to either take root or provoke major conflicts in the college's intellectual life. There seemed to be a protective cocoon around the college, due partly to its Southern location but also because of the broad religious base it expressed and cultivated. Young men of a "muscular Christian" kind could be formed without too much theological specificity.

The "Elson Affair"

This Southern cocoon did not, however, protect Morehead and the college from a horrendous local conflict that almost destroyed the school in the spring of 1911—and going into the following year. A young professor at the college used a textbook in a course on American history whose treatment of the Civil War enraged a local judge whose daughter was in that course. (It is still known as the "Elson" controversy, named after the author of the American history textbook.) The judge rallied a whole coterie of angry Confederates, who demanded not only that the book be banned but that the professor be fired. Local and regional newspapers piled on. Threats were made against the professor, President Morehead, and the college. Though the college did quit using the textbook, Morehead and the faculty and board staunchly defended the academic freedom of the professor, who they thought used the text responsibly. The college took major losses in enrollment and financial support, but held firm. Morehead showed great courage in one of the most painful and harrowing episodes in the history of Roanoke College. The conflict, which began as a very local affair, was later played out on a national stage, in which the college received great approbation, but also encountered denunciation.[15]

Morehead, like Bittle and Dreher before him, was a son of the South. He believed that "the antebellum civilization of the South was unique among the civilizations of the world." Also like his predecessors, he called for a "broader

---

15. Eisenberg devotes a whole chapter to this dramatic story (Eisenberg, *First Hundred Years*, 259–89).

patriotism" after the bitter fight was over. He quoted General Robert E. Lee, who pronounced after the war: "Abandon all local animosities and make your sons American."[16]

Morehead's opting for the broadly American Christian republican tradition is evident in many other writings that he offered later in his presidency. Here are several statements that could well have been uttered by his predecessor, Julius Dreher: "The practical aim of the college is to develop cultured Christian manhood, which holds to the ideal of usefulness in living. In order to accomplish this aim, the spirit of unselfish service in the college is indispensable." "In serving the cause of Christian education, Roanoke College represents the most direct activity for the weal of humanity, the progress of the Church, the safety of the nation, and the strengthening of the forces of Christian civilization." "By the development of Roanoke College and the extension of its usefulness, can be made our notable contribution to the progress of Christianity and our most patriotic gift to the welfare of our country." "If the church is to prosper, if Christianity is to spread, if Christian civilization is to persist, if our free institutions are to be preserved, we must have a trained leadership of cultured, Christian men. Such training is the mission of the College."[17]

One of the striking features of Morehead's inaugural address is his repeated use of the word "efficiency." He compliments his two predecessors for their efficiency—Bittle for bringing his "remarkable efficiency to the tasks of the college," and Dreher for the "development of the efficiency of the college as a teaching force" (99, 102). Furthermore, the college must cultivate the "highest ideals of efficiency in the matter of giving a liberal education." In its striving for future growth, "efficiency is to be the watchword!" The Christian man developed by the college is to be "efficient," as well as broad-minded and filled with the spirit of service (103, 104).

16. Eisenberg, *First Hundred Years*, 287. Morehead's paean to the South was an attempt to show his detractors in the Elson controversy that he, too, appreciated the South's gentility and agrarian values.

17. Morehead, in his 1912 report to the board of the college, as quoted by Eisenberg, *First Hundred Years*, 231–32. He exhibits this Christian republicanism in public lectures he gave to various audiences: "The Place of the Church School in the Educational Work of the Republic" and "The Protestant Reformation and the Democratic Spirit," the latter given to the Virginia Synod on the occasion of the Reformation Jubilee of 1917. In spite of such vigorous Americanism, President Morehead was tailed by a federal secret agent when the onset of World War I coincided with a celebration of the college's Lutheran heritage (Eisenberg, *Lutheran Church in Virginia*, 257).

Added to Morehead's focus on efficiency might be Dreher's preoccupation with usefulness. Dreher entitled his inaugural address "Education as Preparation for Useful Living" and refers to "usefulness" repeatedly throughout the address.[18] It seems that both presidents were caught up in the broad utilitarianism of Christian republicanism. For them, American education had to be practical, and what is most practical is the formation of solid virtue in young men for the benefit of church and society. Moreover, such practical moral education had to be offered to a whole range of income levels so that the nation could advance. This was especially necessary in the South, where education for all had been underappreciated and underfunded.

While Morehead endorses such usefulness, he also adds the notion of efficiency, which seems to have had high currency in an era in which organizations—business and church alike—were growing in size and complexity. Efficiency was a buzzword of the era, and Morehead certainly brought that concern to Roanoke College.[19]

Such an emphasis was utterly necessary for the college, which had great dreams but, as usual, few resources. Roanoke had to be efficient. Nevertheless, Morehead achieved much. The endowment was doubled during his tenure, the student body enlarged, the faculty expanded from eleven to twenty members, their pay increased, and a number of major building projects were completed. Indeed, Morehead raised the reputation of the college so high that its AB degree was classified by the national Bureau of Education as next in value to that of the University of Virginia.[20] Paying for all this necessitated that he, too, like his predecessors, had to spend an inordinate amount of time traveling—recruiting students and seeking financial support. In addition to the well-worn paths established by his predecessors in the South and North, Morehead expanded his travel to the West, turning up students and donors as far west as Chicago.[21] His efforts had to be redoubled because of the loss of local support in the "Elson controversy" over academic freedom and the turbulence caused by the onset of World War I.

---

18. Julius Dreher, "Education as Preparation for Useful Living," in *Addresses at the Inauguration of Julius D. Dreher* (published by order of the trustees of the college, 1879).

19. Mark Miller, *Dear Old Roanoke—A Sesquicentennial Portrait, 1842–1992* (Macon, GA: Mercer University Press, 1992), 132, notes that "system" was also a buzzword in the 1910s, which fits neatly into Morehead's emphasis on efficiency and usefulness.

20. Eisenberg, *First Hundred Years*, 238.

21. Eisenberg, *First Hundred Years,* 225.

The Curriculum

Morehead worked with the generically Protestant republican tradition of Roanoke College rather than trying to alter it toward a more confessional Lutheran direction.[22] The same is true of the curriculum of the college, which pretty much persisted along the lines of the old-style liberal arts approach that reached back to the foundation of the college. Again, rather than bringing Lutheran themes and sensibilities to bear on its curriculum, Morehead stuck with the founding tradition. Not only was the tradition strong, but he was so busy traveling that there was little time for him to pay attention to serious revision. Like Dreher, Morehead had far less chance to put his imprint on the college's vision and curriculum—its intellectual life—than did Bittle. Both Dreher and Morehead were often absentee presidents and did not teach crucial courses in the curriculum, especially its important senior course on moral philosophy, or ethics. The faculty determined the curriculum.

The curriculum was evolving slowly during Morehead's time, from 1903 to 1920. Classical languages and literature were getting less attention: Greek was gone by 1915, and Latin was down to one course. English language, rhetoric, and literature got more. Modern languages—especially German and French—were emphasized. The natural sciences were strengthened, practical courses in commerce and education were offered, and students were allowed more electives, though the curriculum was still heavy with prescribed courses.

The teaching of religion and philosophy showed some evolution, too. The three courses in English Bible that had been introduced during the Dreher era were expanded to four, including the specific study of Old Testament history, the life of Christ, and the apostolic church. Mental and moral philosophy morphed into a history of civilization and ethics. Toward the end of Morehead's tenure, three philosophy courses—which seem to have been deeply imbued with religious concerns—were introduced. A course called "Christian Evidences" was a constant throughout the era: it examined the arguments for a future life summed up copiously in a text written by the

---

22. Additional evidence that Roanoke persisted in its generic Protestant republicanism is indicated by the endorsement of Charles Eliot, the great enemy of confessional education and friend of the Unitarian base for higher education. The president of Harvard, who had praised Roanoke during the Dreher era, continued his support of Roanoke in 1906 by calling its education "liberalizing" and "uplifting" (Eisenberg, *First Hundred Years*, 163).

long-tenured Roanoke professor of philosophy Luther Augustine Fox.[23] Indeed, nearly all the courses in religion and philosophy were taught by Fox from the time of his arrival in 1882 until his death in 1925.

Fox, a remarkable professor (1843–1925), also a son of the South, graduated with an AB from Roanoke College in 1868. He had no formal theological training but rather studied under his father, Dr. Alfred Fox. He had outstanding success as a pastor and was awarded a DD by Roanoke in 1881, right before it called him to a professorship. His self-acquired theological and philosophical knowledge enabled him to serve on theological adjudication boards of the church as well as to write the text *Evidence of a Future Life from Reason and Revelation* (Philadelphia: Lutheran Publication House, 1890), which is impressively erudite as it surveys many arguments for and intuitions of a future life.[24] (He mentions Martin Luther only once.) He was offered many chances during his long tenure to take positions that would have advanced his career, but he demurred, saying at the end of his life that "regardless of what I might have done elsewhere, I am glad my life has been devoted to Roanoke." Eisenberg says that "no other Roanoke professor has been more influential or more loved."[25]

As noted above, Morehead cooperated with and promoted the Christian republican rationale for the mission of the college rather than reshaping it along Lutheran lines. Likewise, he made little effort to "Lutheranize" the religion and philosophy courses of the college. Luther Fox had already staked out his dominant role in religion and philosophy twenty years before Morehead arrived, and he continued that dominance after Morehead departed. The religion and philosophy offerings were untainted by Lutheran themes or concerns: no courses on Luther, Lutheran teachings, or Reformation history, and Morehead evidently made little effort to interject them. Again, like the traditional rationale for the mission of the college, the persisting approach to the teaching of religion and philosophy was well established, and Morehead decided to leave well enough alone. Luther Augustine Fox reigned. Besides, the president had little time for working out major changes.

The old-style liberal arts college continued at Roanoke throughout Morehead's era even though it had unraveled in many colleges in the North. The old-style assumptions—based on common sense philosophy and faculty

---

23. These depictions come from working through the Roanoke College catalogues (of the curriculum) from the Morehead era.

24. *Evidence of a Future Life from Reason and Revelation* (Philadelphia: Lutheran Publication House, 1890).

25. Eisenberg, *First Hundred Years,* 383.

psychology—that the natural and social sciences, classical learning, philosophy, and biblical religion fit together coherently and reinforced each other still reigned at Roanoke. All the courses were taught by believing Christian—overwhelmingly Southern Lutheran—professors who experienced scarcely any controversy over the challenges to the faith that were so bothersome in the North.

Ethos

As I have indicated above, Morehead thought that the formation of manly Christian men of character was more efficiently carried on by the example and mentoring of the Christian men of the faculty and fellow students than by classroom work, though that was obviously important as well. The most difficult responsibility of his position, he thought, was to "assemble an adequately trained faculty who were also properly qualified in the direction of character. . . . To get both a scholar and a Christian gentleman is a task that matches the difficulty of finding ministers for our churches."[26]

In good Aristotelian fashion, he believed that a virtuous community is necessary for the inculcation of virtue in the individual. The faculty was extremely important in this process: "What a student becomes at college is largely the result of what he acquires from the personal influence of his professors, and therefore it is hoped that the members of the faculty will use every effort to extend personal influence." In contrast to his predecessor, Dreher, Morehead believed that the faculty was doing a good job in this vein. He was able to report this to the board in 1913: "The relations between the students and faculty have been unusually wholesome. The faculty has made decided progress toward the efficient [!] social, moral, and religious development of the body of students."[27]

Taking such a strong *in loco parentis* role entailed a lot of required activities. Students had to attend daily chapel at 9:30 in the morning, often presided over by President Morehead himself (required evening chapel had gone by the wayside). They were required to go to Sunday church services and were encouraged to attend Bible studies at the churches' Sunday

26. Trexler, *John Morehead*, 55.
27. Eisenberg, *First Hundred Years*, 240 (exclamation point added). The process of formation was made a bit easier by the fact that the high-water mark for student enrollment during the Morehead era was 218.

schools. Tuesday evenings were given over to Bible study led by members of the Roanoke chapter of the YMCA, which continued as the strongest religious association on campus. In accordance with the evangelical temperance agenda of the time, the consumption of alcohol by students and faculty alike was strongly prohibited, not only on campus but also in the town and home. Smoking was frowned on. Student life was regulated by a whole raft of regulations that were spelled out in the college's catalogues. Needless to say, such regulation of young men brought out some rebellious behavior by the students.[28]

Rebellious behavior was unlikely to happen in front of the tall and handsome president because of his natural dignity. While unfailingly courteous to everyone—he always tipped his hat even to students—Morehead "was never the back-slapping type of official." Further, "he did not mix with students in such matters as athletics, dramatics, or literary or social activities." Though affectionately known as "Big Doc" by the students—behind his back, no doubt—his politeness "was not to be interpreted as a softening of the brain or a willingness to compromise." "He could take the hide off without gloves and scare the wits out of them."[29]

Conclusion

John Morehead's presidency of Roanoke College seems to have had a strong paradoxical element. In those areas where one would have thought that a well-trained Lutheran systematic theologian would have had great influence—developing a theological rationale for the mission of the college and interjecting Lutheran themes into the curriculum—Morehead did little. On the other hand, in areas where one would have thought he might have been inept—building the institutional structure of the college and lifting the faculty quality to new heights—he excelled. Roanoke continued along its antebellum Christian republican mission without much Lutheran influence, even as it rose to the level of the University of Virginia in its perceived quality of education. Morehead left little of his own intellectual imprint on the college, but he made it more "efficient," as he claimed he would do in his inaugural address.

---

28. Miller, in *Dear Old Roanoke*, has a rich account of student and institutional life in his chapters on Morehead's era.

29. Trexler, *John Morehead*, 55–58.

His time at Roanoke ended on something of a melancholy note. The bitterness engendered by the Elson controversy continued to fall on Morehead long after the conflict flared in the spring of 1911. "The home communities [of Salem and Roanoke College] never forgot that he defended Elson's history, and he never forgot the indignities that were threatened. He suffered. His work suffered." And the beginning of World War I in 1914 made one of the "most deservedly popular college administrators in the land flounder and fumble." The college struggled badly in the last years of his tenure, which was publicly recognized by his successor, Charles Smith, when he became president of the college in 1920. "Through it all John A. Morehead kept his head and held his purpose high. He did his best, but the zest had gone out of his work."[30] No doubt, when the newly organized National Lutheran Council asked him to become one of the commissioners to go to Europe to supervise the administration of Lutheran relief and refugee efforts, he was ready for a new and different challenge.

One could easily devote an entire book to Morehead's heroic work in that new challenge. He coordinated efforts that saved or ameliorated the lives of millions of victims of the catastrophe of World War I, as well as of the fallout of the Bolshevik Revolution, which especially oppressed the lives of the Volga Germans. The account of his work by Samuel Trexler in his biography of Morehead both impresses and moves the reader. There are compelling reasons for his being nominated by at least four countries—Germany, Finland, Sweden, and Denmark—for the Nobel Peace Prize, why he received honorary doctorates from great universities in Europe, why he was knighted by Great Britain, and why he was honored in other ways by many countries. And that was not the end of this greatness. He used the occasion of the suffering caused by World War I to facilitate a call to the world's 80,000,000 Lutherans to a new solidarity by organizing the first Lutheran World Assembly in 1923 in Eisenach, Germany. At that assembly he was elected president, and in that office he presided over further conventions at Copenhagen (1929) and Paris (1935), when he was made honorary president.

In addition to his heavy churchly duties, Morehead continued relief and refugee work in many places in Europe, bringing him into contact with many secular authorities and officials, including the future US President Herbert Hoover. He continued to travel and work in both the United States and Europe from his National Lutheran Council office in New York.[31] Finally, in the

---

30. Eisenberg, *First Hundred Years*; all quotes are from page 236.

31. During the years that he led the world's Lutherans he delivered many sermons and

spring of 1936, exhausted by his work and in bad health, he returned to Salem with his wife, who was also seriously ill. Since he had no home of his own in Salem, he and his wife stayed with her brother's family, who ministered to them with tender care. Their only child, a daughter, came from California to visit them.

Morehead's last days and hours took a sad turn, but one that was soon transformed into Christian hope. His wife, Virginia, died on May 29, 1936. He was too sick and weak himself to attend her funeral and burial on June 1. "From his sickbed at the time of his wife's burial, he summoned the nurse. 'Will you kindly ask my physician how long before I shall join my Nellie?' We do not know the reply he received, but three hours after asking the question he had joined her."[32]

Morehead's funeral took place on June 4, 1936, at College Lutheran Church in Salem. A great number of Lutheran dignitaries from church and academia attended the grand service. He was then buried next to the fresh grave of his wife in nearby Sherwood Cemetery.[33] Trexler pays tribute: "After he had touched the whole world he finally was laid to rest amid the simple surroundings of his own native Virginia."[34]

---

wrote many letters and articles that exhibit the kind of theological acumen he did not employ in his time at Roanoke College. The Evangelical Lutheran Church in America archives hold his writings from that period of his life.

32. Trexler, *John Morehead*, 161. Trexler has a detailed account of his organizational work for the Lutheran World Convention as well as his other work with the National Lutheran Council. He also provides much detail about Morehead's family life.

33. Morehead was not buried in East Hill Cemetery alongside his revered predecessors, Bittle and Dreher. Perhaps the area around their graves was already taken, but another explanation might be offered. Right next to the graves of Bittle and Dreher is the grave of Judge Moffett, the judge who gave Morehead and the college such a bad time by instigating the Elson controversy. Morehead may well have decided he did not want to be near his nemesis, even in death.

34. Trexler, *John Morehead*, 162.

4

CHARLES SMITH (1920–1949)

Continuity in Tumultuous Times

The longest-serving president in Roanoke College's history certainly lived in interesting times, mainly because such a lengthy tenure (1920–49) is bound to involve more than one daunting challenge. The times he faced were so distinctive that they have well-known tags: the Roaring Twenties; the Great Depression; World War II; and the "baby boom" of the immediate postwar period.

The Eras of Charles Smith

The 1920s were a decade of contradictions. Called the "Roaring Twenties" because of its wide-open "revolution in morals," it was also the time of Prohibition, the crown of evangelical Protestantism's temperance agenda. The nationalistic fervor that had accompanied World War I subsided, but strong nativist movements flourished. The Ku Klux Klan reached its zenith in 1925. Religious liberalism—though chastened by the Great War—continued to gain strength in the North, while fundamentalism emerged as a strong, organized movement throughout the country. The conflict between them was epitomized in the Scopes Trial in Tennessee (1925), pitting the secular liberal Clarence Darrow against the evangelical populist hero William Jennings Bryan. Immigration was closed off legally, but the newly arrived immigrants consolidated their strength in relatively insulated ethnic churches, with their own educational institutions and confessional theologies—Catholic, Dutch Reformed, and Lutheran. With high birth rates, they kept up with the multiplying Baptists. The denominations in the North were particularly strained over the debates provoked by Darwinism. In the South, evangelicals and fundamentalists dominated and, after the Scopes debacle, separated themselves further from the urban North and from national public life.

By 1930 the number of college-age students had multiplied by twenty-one times from their number in 1870; during that same period the population of the country merely tripled. Expanding industry and commercial life demanded that education become more "practical." Universities expanded their facilities and student bodies, often supported by wealthy entrepreneurs who had little interest in the religious dimension of academic life. The German-style research university became the model for large universities. The ensuing specialization and professionalization of knowledge doomed the old-style liberal arts college, with its synthesis of science, classical languages and literature, mental and moral science, and biblical religion. Church-founded colleges and universities often dropped their Christian distinctives as they competed with numerous newly founded public colleges and universities. As Mark Noll mordantly notes: "Universities named professional academics rather than ministers as presidents. Businessmen replaced clergy as trustees. In the hiring of faculty, specialization (represented best by the new PhD degree) became more important than Victorian morality or Christian beliefs."[1]

In October 1929, the exuberance of the Roaring Twenties came to a screeching halt. Economic life collapsed, causing widespread unemployment and hardship. Institutions dependent on voluntary giving struggled greatly. "From 1931 to 1936 more immigrants returned to the lands from which they had come than arrived on American shores."[2] The loose lifestyle of the 1920s reverted to a much more disciplined and austere morality to cope with hard times, which lasted throughout the 1930s. The Depression impressed a sober worldview on the lifetimes of all those who experienced it.

Roosevelt ushered in the New Deal, which pleased Protestant liberals, blacks, and most Catholics, but which excited all the worst fears of conservative white Protestants. Prohibition failed in 1933, after which the churches diminished their engagement with political life, though theologians such as Reinhold Niebuhr began to gain influence as major "public intellectuals." Niebuhr struggled with the dominant pacifism of the mainline denomina-

1. Mark Noll, "Christianity and Higher Education," in *Eerdmans' Handbook to Christianity in America,* ed. Noll et al. (Grand Rapids: Eerdmans, 1983), 389.
2. "From the Great Depression to the War," in Noll et al., *Eerdmans' Handbook,* 404.

tions—Presbyterian, Episcopalian, Northern Methodist, Congregational-ist—which had a difficult decade. Oddly enough, the immigrant churches, especially Catholics, along with Southern Baptists, fundamentalists, and the "new" churches—Pentecostal, Holiness, Nazarene—actually grew. By 1935, Catholics had overtaken the total combined membership of the four largest Protestant denominations.[3]

Niebuhr was one among a number of religious intellectuals who cas-tigated the liberalism that had dominated American intellectual life in the North. Along with the rise of neo-orthodox theologians in Europe, a number of American theologians recovered some of the classic doctrines that had been neglected or rejected by liberals: original sin; the radicality and neces-sity of the gospel; the unique mission of the church; and the judgment and sovereignty of God. Theological education took a distinctively *theological* turn, emphasizing Christian belief as well as Christian ethics.

This theological realism helped prepare the churches and the nation for the great challenge that lay at the end of the 1930s—World War II. After huge debates in the United States over whether to enter the war, the decision to join the Allies in the war was clarified by the Japanese attack on Pearl Har-bor on December 7, 1941. World War II finally brought America out of the Depression. Its economy was mobilized for war, and the country enlisted every able-bodied person into the workforce, which was required because sixteen million Americans were serving under arms, including nearly twelve million who were sent overseas. Blacks and women were brought into the expanding economy. Millions of young men left their campuses and jobs to enlist in the armed services. Dissent against the war was rare. The disloca-tions caused by the war were immense: economic, social, familial, churchly, governmental, and civic. Voluntary associations of all sorts were all deeply affected. Everyone's efforts were directed to winning the war, which finally was brought to a horrific conclusion with the dropping of atomic bombs on Hiroshima and Nagasaki, a presidential action that was supported by 85 percent of the American population.[4]

After the conclusion of the war, America experienced a major boom. Men returned from the war to marry and begin families, and many went to college on the GI Bill. The economy expanded, the suburbs grew, and as consumers were finally liberated from rationing, churches began a vigorous membership growth that continued until the mid-1960s. Life returned to a lively normal.

3. "Religious Membership and Affiliations," in Noll et al., *Eerdmans' Handbook*, 408.
4. "World War II and Postwar Revival," in Noll et al., *Eerdmans' Handbook*, 423.

But the bright skies did not last long. Soon after the Allies' defeat of Germany and Japan, the Cold War began: Berlin was blockaded; the Iron Curtain rolled down on Central and Eastern Europe; and the nuclear arms race began in earnest. Soviet totalitarianism filled the vacuum left by the fall of Nazi Germany and imperial Japan. The middle of the twentieth century brought a coherent and unified culture at home, but new threats abroad. Such were the times during which Charles Smith was president of Roanoke College.

The Formation of Charles Jacob Smith

"His was a private Roanoke College tradition all its own," writes William Eisenberg, the historian of the college's first one hundred years.[5] Indeed, there were many links between Charles Smith and Roanoke College. His father, Luther Smith, was persuaded by David Bittle, the first president of Roanoke College, to enter the ordained ministry after his graduation from the college. While at Roanoke, Luther Smith courted the sister-in-law of the Rev. T. W. Dosh, who briefly succeeded Bittle as president of Roanoke. After marriage and seminary, Luther Smith's first call was to Mount Tabor Church in Augusta County, where Bittle and his friend Baughman had in 1842 founded the Virginia Institute, which was to become Roanoke College in 1853. If it had not been for Luther Smith's refusal to live in the rundown parsonage of that parish, Charles Smith's birth in 1882 would have been in precisely the same house where Bittle had begun his educational venture forty years earlier.

Charles Smith attended Roanoke College (beginning in 1898 as a sophomore at the tender age of sixteen) and came under the tutelage of its president, Julius Dreher. He was an excellent student who also participated avidly in baseball—as a third baseman—and in literary societies. He graduated in 1901 and gave the commencement address on "The Renaissance of Southern Literature." Smith later observed that John Morehead "directed my thought to the Christian ministry and became my trusted colleague, counselor and friend."[6] He was given an honorary Doctor of Divinity degree by the college in 1915 and became its fifth president in 1920. It is difficult to imagine a person more connected in so many ways to Roanoke College. Indeed, he joked in

---

5. Eisenberg, *First Hundred Years*, 290.
6. Eisenberg, *First Hundred Years*, 299.

his inaugural address that he took up the presidency of Roanoke College "for sentimental reasons."

He did, however, have a life independent of Roanoke College before and after his student days there. Soon after his birth at Mt. Tabor, the family moved to Strasburg, Virginia, where his father shepherded congregations in the Shenandoah Valley. Charles was schooled at home by his mother until he was ten, after which he attended several preparatory academies. Then it was off to Roanoke College. Following the Roanoke tradition of arranging graduate education for its best students, Julius Dreher used his connections to get Smith into Princeton University immediately after his graduation in 1901. At Princeton, Smith studied political science under Woodrow Wilson and English literature under Henry Van Dyke. He received his master's degree in 1902, and then went on to study theology at Mount Airy Lutheran Seminary in Philadelphia. He received his bachelor of divinity degree in 1905 and then pastored a congregation in Lancaster, Pennsylvania, for three years. During that short pastorate in Lancaster, Smith was offered the chairmanship of the history department at Roanoke, but declined. His reputation as a preacher and orator led to a call from Holy Trinity Lutheran Church in New York City, a prestigious pulpit. During his twelve fruitful years (1908–20) at Trinity, he was much sought after as a university preacher and platform lecturer. During that sojourn he married Mary Eleanor Price of New Market, Virginia.

Charles Smith as President of Roanoke College

Only days after the resignation of John Morehead in April 1920, the Roanoke College board urgently and unanimously invited Charles Smith to be president. Elaborating their view of the duties of the president of a Christian college, the board emphasized that "it is especially desired that the internal affairs of the college shall be so conducted as to assure the patrons of the institution that their sons shall receive at Roanoke College such instruction and culture, in body, mind, and soul, as will develop manly Christian men."[7]

---

7. Eisenberg, *First Hundred Years*, 257. It is astonishing how often the Roanoke College presidents use the notion of "Christian manhood." This concept is still widely used in evangelical Christianity, from whence it originally sprung. It seems to denote a masculinity that can embrace service and moral conduct without seeming effeminate or weak. "Muscular Christianity" emphasized the strong and manly characteristics of Jesus, who was also the model of a servant. Such an emphasis was an attempt to counter the widespread prejudice that religion is a woman's thing.

The board had had its eye on Smith ever since Morehead had taken a leave of absence in 1919. It prepared the way by inviting Smith to give a series of lectures at the college in the spring of 1920, providing an occasion for mutual sizing up. In May they called him; he took a month to accept.

Upon accepting the presidency, Smith affirmed the ongoing mission of the college by offering "my best talents to the cause of Christian education as conceived by Roanoke College in her past traditions, and in the present aspirations of her leaders and friends. All things are possible for those who are on God's side in this great work."[8]

The incoming president certainly had a lot of work before him. The difficult last years of Morehead's tenure, his leave of absence to serve in Europe after World War I, and the trauma of that war itself had taken their toll on the college. In his first report to the board in the fall of 1920, Smith enumerated the severe problems of the school, pledged strong efforts to strengthen the financial status of the school (especially the establishing of an endowment whose absence threatened the accreditation of the school), and reaffirmed its mission as a small liberal arts college. He mentioned that the college student body was less than one-third Lutheran and that it needed to continue to enlist a broad base of Christian presence and support. The college certainly had to continue to serve the church, but its education and culture "belong to the wholeness of society."

Smith's formal inauguration was held in conjunction with the college's commencement in the spring of 1921. He was charged by the presiding officer "to keep in mind the last words of admonition from the pen of President Bittle: 'Let not your faith fail.'"[9] Smith spelled out his vision for the college on that occasion. After giving due tribute to his illustrious predecessors and to his personal connection with each of them—he likened his link to them as "apostolic succession"—he launched into a restatement of the Christian republican tradition of the college. "As long as personality and character are living values, just so long will schools live magnificently for the inculcation of those values. Education and character are inalienably associated in the divine plan of the ages, and what God has joined together neither false leadership nor human apathy may tear asunder."[10] When schools put the two together

8. Eisenberg, *First Hundred*, 291.

9. Eisenberg, *First Hundred*, 298.

10. The following quotes on this and the next page are from his inaugural. Roanoke presidents from Bittle through Smith repeatedly use the word "personality" as a noun with positive connotations. It seems to have come from the Kantian tradition and means "moral excellence."

in their students, he declared, they would send out their "finished product into the engagements of life, saying to the world, 'Behold, a man.'"

Roanoke College has performed this task of educating the whole man nobly, he said, for "her sons are scattered over America and into many foreign lands. Through them the spirit of Roanoke College is being woven into the fabric of the workmanship of the world." This "spirit" is a product of taking Jesus's teaching seriously:

> He lifted them [people] out of their disconsolate atmosphere by teaching them that their lives were investments in love and that a sure exit from present distress lies through the open gate of finely cultured personality by which men learn to act justly, to love mercy, and to walk humbly with their God. Roanoke College has been committed to these ideals through all her history. She shall not desert them now. . . . She shall thus produce men who shall serve not only our own America; but who, through America, shall serve the world.

Smith, like all his predecessors in the office, saw the Christian religion as the primary vehicle of this moral formation. "Religion cannot be separated from education. . . . It is crucial in the education of the whole man, thus preparing him to meet with balance and with poise the wholeness of present-day challenge to true manhood." Speaking soon after the horrific sacrifice of life in World War I, Smith affirms the necessity and indestructibility of worthwhile faith: "This matter of God is a mighty important thing today. We breathe the air of a world's tragedy. We are unsettled. An atmosphere of futility envelops the whole earth. There is no way out until we find God."

What kind of Christianity is he talking about? Again, like earlier Roanoke presidents, Smith maintains that the college's formative religion must be a broad and tolerant Christianity.

> The college cannot be intolerant. . . . The narrowing of college service to any interest which is partial, however good it may be, would be a denial of the spirit of the nation, destructive of all true educational foundations, and a perverting of the will of Him who hath made of one blood all nations that dwell on the face of the earth. Personally, I would have no part in any college without religion, and, by the same token, I would have no part in one that recognizes only one type of religion as being essentially valid in the experience of mankind.

Further, he said, the college must

> stand for a real religious life, conceived narrowly enough to meet the needs of the particular religious faith to which the college owes allegiance, and at the same time, broadly enough to care for spiritual convictions of those who belong to other faiths and creeds. In a word, it must give itself unsparingly to the education of the whole man, thus preparing him to meet with balance and poise the great present-day challenge to true manhood.

As in earlier presidential inaugurals, Smith affirms a generic American mainline Protestantism as the ground for the moral formation of the students: not too broad as to deny Christian essentials, but not too narrow as to construe it according to Lutheran distinctives. Again, as with the earlier presidents, a well-educated Lutheran refrains from using any special Lutheran categories: justification, law and gospel, or vocation. Rather, his rhetoric, which could easily have been articulated by Presidents Julius Dreher or John Morehead, follows the pattern of Christian republicanism that runs deep in the Roanoke College tradition.

In 1924, Smith got involved in a national fracas when his talk to the National Lutheran Educational Association, entitled "The Social Life of Our College Students," was reported by the *New York Times*. Reflecting on the changes in social life in the "Roaring Twenties," Smith lamented that "the postwar breakdown in morals produced a class of women who played fast and loose with all decent social amenities, and who constituted a general menace to college social life throughout the country." He got in deeper when the newspaper reported his condemnation of cigarette-smoking, hard drinking, and scantily clothed women who were likely to engage in "violent petting parties in the luxurious retreat of a big limousine."

Quite a controversy ensued. Smith walked his statements back somewhat, but he stuck by his argument that the postwar culture had devolved to a "lower moral level," which colleges like Roanoke had to address seriously. Smith was obviously no social liberal, and this time the *Roanoke Times*, which had been so merciless in its condemnation of President Morehead during the college's controversy over a textbook's interpretation of the Civil War, sided with Smith. Trying to comfort him as well as correct him with a bit of wry criticism, retired President Dreher wrote to Smith: "I sympathize with you in the annoyance of having your remarks misunderstood and misrepresented. You have a wonderful facility in the use of language, and

I suppose you have to be on your guard often not to let it become a 'fatal facility,' as I once heard it described."[11]

Smith survived the national notoriety and moved on. He worked tirelessly to raise a sufficient endowment to enable the college to be accredited in 1927 as a full member of the Association of Colleges and Secondary Schools of the Southern States. The long-sought-after endowment—and its attendant accreditation—came at last.

In 1930 a controversy arose about "radical economic theories" that were taught by a professor in the college. Smith's response to this attempt to limit academic freedom was interesting, not least for what it revealed about the college's hiring policy for faculty. "Roanoke College employs teachers for their departmental abilities rather than for their political affiliations, religious adherence, or social theories. We demand that they be honorable men, good citizens, and upright in their moral standards of living. But, we cannot demand that they belong to a given church or a stated political party."[12]

These remarks reveal that the college did not insist, even at that early date, on hiring Christians, let alone Lutherans, though no doubt that selection by affinity produced a nearly unanimous Christian faculty. But that came about by an informal process, not by explicit intention. Rather, the college sought morally upright men who were expert in their fields. The Christian composition of the faculty was assumed, not managed. By the end of Smith's tenure, as it turned out, there were few Lutherans left on the faculty.[13] In 1939 the board rescinded its 1927 requirement that three-fifths of the board be members of congregations of the Virginia Synod. Rather, it directed that all candidates for trustee be approved by the synod and that the president be a Lutheran of some branch of Lutheranism.[14] By the end of Smith's tenure, there were only two clergymen on the board who were there "by tradition," not by requirement. The board majority was now made up of distinguished and wealthy business executives. This diminishment of churchly presence indicated a cooler institutional relationship between college and church.

In the fall of 1940, several hundred luminaries gathered at the Hotel Roanoke to honor Smith upon the completion of twenty years of his pres-

11. This whole episode is recounted in detail by Eisenberg in his *First Hundred Years*, 312–15.

12. Eisenberg, *First Hundred Years*, 348.

13. In the assessment of Dr. Robert Ayers ('47), the Lutherans were few in number—perhaps no more than five—and were outnumbered by Presbyterians, Episcopalians, and Methodists. Lutheran students were also outnumbered by Baptists and Presbyterians.

14. Eisenberg, *First Hundred Years*, 352.

idency. On that occasion he gave a report to the board that reiterated his convictions about the nature and mission of the college. He began by reciting the famous statement of the founding president, David Bittle, that "the momentous duty of one generation to another is its education. . . . It remains for us to determine before we close the career of life, whether we will educate our successors to be better men than we are, better qualified to incur the responsibilities of life, to possess superior wisdom, and a more refined humanity." Smith noted that the world—at that point well into the hostilities of World War II—needed even more such men as Roanoke had produced.

Then he looked toward the future. Besides a decent physical plant, the college, he said, needed faculty who were willing to guide youth toward an "articulate philosophy of life" that blended and unified the knowledge the student accrues at Roanoke. It needed a curriculum with a purpose. The curriculum should move students toward integrating knowledge so that everyone who graduates should be an "intelligent, moral, energetic, and benevolent person who knows how to think clearly, live nobly, and profoundly influence for good both the social order and the body politic."

Then, like all the presidents before him, Smith vigorously maintained that such purposes can only be grounded in the Christian faith, which, he noted, had been lost in many colleges that once had Christian foundations. The aim of the college is to build "a manhood and womanhood [women had been admitted to college as full students since 1930] which is essentially Christian." Smith argued that

Christian belief is a necessary part of the educational process. . . . It enlarges and enriches its service to those who must carry the world's burdens in the future. Paganism has about wrecked our world. Only an acceptance in thought and practice of the Christian way of life can restore it to sound foundations and point the way for all peoples to a better life in a better world.

But those Christian foundations need not be distinctively Lutheran. "We must make our College Christian in the broadest possible sense. The limitations of a narrow sectarian appeal must be avoided." Rather, this broad, dynamic Christianity must "through instruction and example produce qualities of unselfishness, kindliness, and upright living." "These moral assets, added to clear thinking, are the hope of the world of tomorrow."

Anticipating the darkness of World War II, Smith concluded that the college must preserve a "program of education which best serves both God and our fellowmen, and, above all else, carrying the burdens, which today weigh heavily upon all mankind, with high courage and a sincere faith that righteousness must ultimately overcome the forces of evil now arrayed against it."[15]

Smith's first twenty years as president of the college were bookended by two great world wars. World War I was followed by a period of struggle that the college endured in order to recover and become viable again. The mid-1920s featured the moral challenges of the Roaring Twenties, which were soon reshaped by the Great Depression, an era that Smith and the college weathered with considerable skill. But the last years of Smith's first two decades were framed by the darkening clouds of the rise of Nazism, of which Smith was very cognizant. All three moments in those first twenty years—the Roaring Twenties, the Great Depression, and the rise of Nazism—added urgency to the college's mission of Christian republicanism. Citizens of virtue were needed in each moment, and the college was there to provide them.

The need for virtuous citizens did not end with the defeat of Nazism. Soon Communism rose up as a threat to the West. The task of Christian republicanism seemed to be never-ending. In one of his last postwar columns in the *Roanoke Collegian* on the topic of the ideal college president, he writes: "In these critical hours for humanity when the destiny of all mankind lies in the balance, our great nation must be furnished with men and women of insight who combine great faith with great courage. Whence shall come the good citizens who will keep our country great unless the colleges? In a faulty way this has been my own guiding star."[16]

Smith had one last chance publicly to reflect on the mission of the college when he retired in 1949—amid the postwar expansion. He was invited to give the commencement address in that year, after he was affectionately commemorated in the 1949 edition of the college yearbook. There were no departures from his earlier articulations as he addressed ninety-two graduates, the most ever to graduate from Roanoke College. The title of his speech is "A Portrait of an Educated Person." At the outset he endorses his stewardship of Roanoke and its mission by claiming that he "would follow the same course and arrive at the same end" if he had it to do over. After he reaffirms the general values of classical liberal arts education, he argues that such an

15. The quotes from Smith's 1940 reflections are from Eisenberg's account in *First Hundred Years*, 357–59.

16. Charles Smith on the "President's Page," *Roanoke College Collegian* (December 1948).

education will form noble character, which is essential for a self-governing citizenry.[17]

And, to no one's surprise, Smith asserts that good character derives its insights and practice from religion: "It is scarcely possible for a truly educated person to be an atheist, to deny the existence of values beyond the material or secular, or to claim no citizenship in a spiritual kingdom which is within him, about him, and ever revealing itself in life's daily circumstance." An educated person will pursue the highest good, and that good is intrinsically associated with God. "They can never be divorced. The good life is one which is lived in the conscious recognition of God's directing presence. God alone can give poise and patience and precision to what would otherwise be only the darkest chaos. The educated person not only 'seems to be religious' but is religious, for he has learned that only by being a 'co-worker with God' may he make his life worthy, only thus may he learn the truth, the truth that sets men free. The educated man knows that his life is lived not alone in time but in eternity beyond time."[18]

The constant thread that runs through Smith's rhetoric from the beginning of his tenure at Roanoke to its end—one that extends back to Bittle through Dreher and Morehead—is that of Christian republicanism. The high calling of Roanoke College is to form men (and women after 1930) from all walks of life into moral agents who will supply virtue to the republic. That task is sharply accentuated in Smith's long tenure by the challenges that three wars—two hot and one cold—presented to the republic, challenges of which he is keenly aware. Internally, he also saw the threat that the morally unmoored Roaring Twenties presented.

Like all of his predecessors, Smith believed firmly that the Christian faith provided the necessary groundwork for the republican task of moral formation. Indeed, he seems to go beyond the more utilitarian view of reli-

17. Smith's address is permeated with concern about collectivist thought and practice, especially that practiced by the Soviet Union. This again demonstrates to him the need for a free and virtuous citizenry. Parenthetically, Smith uses Luther's address on "The Liberty of the Christian Man" erroneously to defend academic freedom. Luther's "liberty" in that tract refers to the freedom Christians have in Christ, not to political or academic freedom ("A Portrait of an Educated Person," *Roanoke College Bulletin* 32, no.1 [commencement issue, July 1949]: 12).

18. Smith, "A Portrait of an Educated Person," 13. It is interesting that Smith goes beyond the functional role of religion in shaping the moral person. Perhaps his appreciation for the more profound heights and depths of the Christian view of reality was due to the tragedies of the two massive wars he experienced, followed by the Cold War. In all those instances the moral function of religion seems to have faltered before the human propensity for war.

gion promoted by his immediate two predecessors, Dreher and Morehead. Christian men and women of character provide the needed commitment to service and upright living that society so badly needs, but religion gives to them the needed coherence for a meaningful life. The Christian faith is not only useful; it is true.

There are other continuities. The commitment to "nonsectarian" Christianity is a note sounded from Bittle through Smith. In Bittle's time it was a born-again robust evangelicalism that was widespread in the Second Great Awakening. In Dreher's time the evangelicalism was broadened to include the liberal, enlightened evangelicalism of the North, though the more robust evangelicalism of the South was never rejected. In Morehead's time, as in Smith's, the broad-based Christianity was a generic American Protestantism.

This "nonsectarian" Christianity protected the college from hard fundamentalism on the right as well as from Social Gospel liberalism on the left. The college was never damaged by the fundamentalist/modernist conflict over the authority of the Bible. Furthermore, Luther Fox, longtime professor of religion, had found Darwinian evolution compatible with Christianity before the turn of the century.[19] Even so, the college did not jump on the bandwagon of a Social Gospel activism that embraced pacifism, socialism, and the labor movement. It steered a more moderate path of commitment to the personal formation of its students through Christian example and instruction. Roanoke was characterized by moderation in all things.

Also continuous with earlier presidents was the avoidance of specifically Lutheran rhetoric in their appeal to a nonsectarian Protestantism as the grounds for the college's Christian republicanism. Martin Luther's name is mentioned only once in the three of Smith's major articulations of the mission of the college that we have available. Nowhere are distinctive Lutheran teachings or doctrines mentioned, save for the one Smith got wrong when he appealed to Luther's teaching on the "freedom of the Christian," which confused academic freedom with the ultimate freedom in Christ. It is noteworthy that after Bittle, the presidents rarely mention Jesus and never appeal to the Holy Spirit in their inaugurals. In fact, Dreher's inaugural address in 1878 does not even mention God—but rather "Christian civilization." (Morehead followed in much the same vein in 1903.) So it seems that the appeal to "nonsectarian" Christianity tends toward a quasi-Unitarian emphasis on God, the Creator and ground of morality. Though Smith went beyond a

19. Luther Fox, *Evidences of a Future Life from Reason and Revelation* (Philadelphia: Lutheran Publication House, 1890), 351.

utilitarian interpretation of the faith, he did not employ Lutheran themes in his college rhetoric. He opted for a generic Protestant construal of the faith.

If there are important strands of continuity with earlier presidential articulations of the nature and mission of the college, there are also some interesting divergences. All the presidents after Bittle left behind the conversionist emphasis that was so dear to him: that is, that the college was not only an instrument of the church but *was* the church. The point of education at Roanoke was to make born-again Christians out of the students. No president after Bittle expressed the same emphasis. Also muted in Smith's perspective, in comparison to all the earlier presidents, is the emphasis on raising young men for the ordained ministry. Furthermore, the zeal for training missionaries for work abroad seems to have waned in Smith's vision, perhaps because the disruptions of war were so much a part of his tenure.[20] Similarly, Smith does not talk about the onward march of Christian civilization that Roanoke College would contribute to mightily. No doubt warfare between Christians themselves in both world wars, and the shattering of Christian civilizations in Germany and the Soviet Union, dampened any kind of optimism about the triumph of Christian civilization in the world. Rather, the college's task, like America's, was to affirm and protect the republic and its democratic values.

Another interesting disappearance is the emphasis on classical civilization as a major source of Christian republicanism. Earlier presidents had seen classical learning as an entrance to training in republican ideas and virtues. As classical learning waned in the curriculum, so did it diminish as a guide to the good life.

All in all, the optimism that permeated the earlier presidents' rhetoric is much reduced, no doubt because of world events. The world is a more hostile place, and there is a sense of burden that accompanies the preparation of young Christians to be sent out into it. There are no guarantees that Christian civilization will win out.

---

20. This is not to say that Smith and the college were unfriendly to or unsupportive of aspiring young ministers. All through his tenure there were active pretheological clubs on campus, and he was always encouraging to those preparing for the ordained ministry (testimony of Robert Ayers, a pretheological student, 1944–47).

Charles Smith the Man

Since there are many persons still living who knew "Dr. Charlie," we have a better personal picture of him than we could have of the earlier presidents. Compared to the reserved formality of his immediate predecessor, John Morehead, Smith had a lighter personality and was given to humor and congeniality. "Dr. Charles Smith was always a very reassuring and charming person," says Robert Ayers. "He had a fairly deep voice and a resounding, affirmative chuckle. His words were fully rounded in pronunciation. I never heard anything negative come from his lips. His pulpit style, in full volume, fell only slightly below the flamboyant. He spoke and preached with breath that was pulsed from the chest and with a mild nasality. (Sort of a sacred snort.) His gaze was direct, and when he talked to or greeted you, you felt that you had his entire attention. Then he moved on to his next goal. He lived just across High Street [from the college] and was a visible presence, walking to and from home, with hearty greetings to all."[21]

Nevertheless, he always appeared in a suit and tie and had presidential dignity. The students respected him highly, and his personal warmth was effective with donors as well. He became friends with many of the movers and shakers of the Roanoke Valley, which helped to regain their affection and respect for the college, something that had been badly damaged by the controversies of the Morehead years. He was active in the Rotary and the Chamber of Commerce; was awarded an honorary Doctor of Laws degree by Gettysburg College in 1931; and was elected into membership of the William and Mary Chapter of Phi Beta Kappa.[22]

His oratorical skills made him a sought-after speaker in the region, especially on educational topics. He preached and prayed with extemporaneous eloquence; though he evidently composed his sermons for chapel extemporaneously, the product was polished. One can taste his locutionary facility by reading a section from his "Salute to Seniors" in the 1947 Roanoke College yearbook, *The Rawenoch*:

> At any rate, college days have been happy days in spite of these tragic years for humanity. I look forward to commencement when I shall be privileged to hand you the diploma which makes bachelors out of boys and girls alike. Both Roanoke College and its President will follow your careers

21. E-mail exchange with Ayers, class of 1947.
22. Eisenberg, *First Hundred Years*, 404.

with true interest and every helpful purpose, applauding you when we may and apologizing for you when we must. You and your College have traveled together this long and we travel together in affection even to the end. In this spirit I salute the Class of 1947. May your days be long, your labors great, and your happiness supreme.[23]

The Curriculum during Smith's Tenure

David Bittle, the founding president of Roanoke College, was probably the only president who was able to integrate his religious and intellectual vision fully into the life of Roanoke College. After Bittle, the faculty increased in size and power, and its members were able to shape the curriculum and ethos of the college more decisively than its presidents could—especially true because of the long tenure of highly respected faculty members. The presidents, though, were effective in passing the vision and ethos on to new faculty and to students by osmosis, as it were. Moreover, because all of Roanoke's presidents were necessarily involved in incessant fundraising and student recruitment, they simply did not have the time to involve themselves deeply in curricular matters.

The old-style liberal arts curriculum persisted with surprising continuity from its beginning in 1853 to the end of John Morehead's presidency in 1920, nearly seventy years. The curriculum featured versions of classical learning, history, math, and science, all of which were deemed compatible with a generic biblical religion. (Luther Fox dominated the offerings of the religion and philosophy department from 1882 until 1925.) Over those first seventy years, more practical subjects and more electives were gradually introduced into the curriculum, but its basic shape stayed the same.

However, the twenty-nine years of Charles Smith's tenure certainly did see some dramatic changes. In the following I will chart in general the curricular changes, with special attention to those that occurred in the philosophy and religion department. By 1925, the integrated old-style curriculum

---

23. *The 1947 Rawenoch,* 88. Given Smith's reputation as a public speaker, it is very odd that the Roanoke College archives have little of Smith's writing. Besides the edited accounts of his speeches at and reports to the college offered by Eisenberg, his periodic columns in the college's *Collegian,* and a copy of his 1949 commencement address, there are no copies of his other writings or speeches in the archives. For all his legendary facility with words, there seems to be little trace of his written use of them.

was pretty well gone, replaced by discrete departments featuring specialized approaches to knowledge. An attempt at integration was made when the faculty decided to require a philosophy course, placed in the senior year; otherwise, the curriculum began to look very much like a modern liberal arts curriculum. Two courses in Latin were still required in 1925, but by the mid-1930s they were gone. Roanoke did continue a strong classics department right to the end of Smith's tenure in 1949; but the Greek and Roman classics—grammar, literature, philosophy—diminished markedly as a major source of wisdom and republican values.

A liberal arts core was required: that meant plenty of courses in English, foreign languages, social and natural sciences. An amusing section in the college's catalogues from 1925 through 1945 was one that outlined "Penalties for Poor English," which seemed to be levied on poor English used anywhere in the academic life of the college. (The tradition of sharp attention to proper grammar and punctuation lived on until the beginning of the 1980s, when the English Department relaxed its discipline.) But the required liberal arts courses were far fewer than they had been earlier. Some of the newly available curricular space was inhabited by courses required by specific majors (initially called "concentrations"). Science concentrations dominated, but the business concentration took off as a real option. Fulfilling the requirements of a major occupied a significant portion of the curriculum, but ample space was left for electives.

All in all, there was less cohesiveness and coherence in the curriculum, just as the faculty became less involved in moral formation. Nevertheless, the college and its presidents remained formally committed to the Christian republican project. This was indicated in the college's attempts to articulate its mission. As the college moved forward through the years, its catalogue expanded as explanations were added for some of its curricular additions, resulting finally in 1945 with a full-blown purpose statement for the college.

In the mid-1930s, the college catalogue reiterated its long-held commitment to a "broad" Christian foundation while eschewing "narrow sectarianism." It spoke of "training the mind" and "developing character, personality, and appreciation of culture." In 1945, its purpose statement commended the boilerplate "training young men and women in the arts and sciences," but it added that the college cultivates "an atmosphere dominated by Christian ideals of service and conduct." Moreover, its education played a "vital part in the life and culture of a democratic state."

Philosophy and Religion

Luther Fox's long domination of the college's philosophy and religion of-ferings came to an end with his death in 1925. During the forty years of his teaching tenure he taught three required courses in philosophy that were laden with Christian moral concerns. He also taught the required three-course sequence in English Bible and one course in Christian apologetics (for which he wrote his own textbook, on evidences for life after death). With the gradual waning of the old-style liberal arts curriculum and the arrival of a new philosophy and religion professor, Frank Longaker, major changes occurred in the philosophy and religion course offerings. The de-partment's purpose became the impartation of a "just and consistent view of the universe" in which "faith and scientific knowledge are a unity." The one required course in philosophy in the new curriculum was offered in the senior year, and it was intended to "bring knowledge into a coordinated whole." So the old desire for a coherent curriculum did not completely ex-pire with the disappearance of the old-style curriculum.

For the first time, however, ethics was dropped from the required cur-riculum; it was now offered as an elective, along with a generous number of other philosophy electives. Longaker taught the philosophy courses and a number of psychology courses. He also taught two required courses in Bible, which incorporated elements of apologetics that argued that the his-torical study of the Bible and evolutionary thinking were not incompatible with biblical Christianity. He set a pattern that required all students to take two courses in Bible; this pattern lasted for decades. It is interesting that no electives were offered in religion; that, too, remained a pattern at Roanoke for many years.

Longaker, who earned a PhD in history at the University of Pittsburgh, developed his own text for the required Bible course in Old Testament, en-titled *The Meaning of the Old Testament*.[24] The text is well written and per-suasive. It incorporates historical criticism of the Bible without conceding essentials of the faith, though he interprets those essentials in moral rather than religious terms. It claims that the biblical narrative of creation does not conflict with scientific accounts because the former deals with the "what" and "who" while the latter deals with the "how." After his initial interpreta-tion of the creation story, he seems to accept further biblical miracles with-out a qualm, though he tries to find ways to make the miracles seem less

24. *The Meaning of the Old Testament* (Ann Arbor, MI: Edwards Brothers, 1936).

87

miraculous. One of his students reported that he suggested that the miracle of the feeding of the five thousand was actually a case of everyone "sharing their lunch." The book's organizing motif is the unfolding of the grand narrative of redemption. In the introduction, Longaker says that he relied theologically on Johann Heinrich Kurtz's *Manual of Sacred History*, which was a theological staple of the time. Kurtz was a well-known German systematic theologian of a strongly orthodox Lutheran bent, though in his *Manual* he assumes Luther's thinking rather than explicitly citing it. Longaker likewise makes no reference to Lutheran themes or ideas in his text. It represents a moderate, "enlightened" Protestantism.

Longaker retired in 1945, toward the end of Charles Smith's tenure at Roanoke. James Rikard replaced him as professor of philosophy and religion and also became the college chaplain. Rickard, a son of Southern Lutheranism but one who had earned a master's degree at Harvard (one of his professors was Alfred North Whitehead), brought changes after the twenty years of Longaker's reign over the realm of philosophy and religion. The last required course in philosophy departed from the curriculum during Rikard's tenure. However, the "Reading Course," a two-course sequence adapted from St. John's College's Great Books program and initiated by Roanoke's academic dean, Edward Myers, required a good deal of outside reading, especially in philosophy. "Jimmy" Rikard was famous for teaching it to several generations of Roanoke students. The two required courses in Bible remained, though with less theological overlay than the way Longaker taught them. Students of Rikard who are still living report that Rikard "made the Old and New Testament figures and stories come alive" with his "unorthodox" style of dramatizing Scripture.

There were many electives in philosophy but few in religion: this duplicated a long-standing pattern in which a number of courses of a religious nature were offered under the rubric of philosophy, while only two required Bible courses were offered as "religion" courses. During these many years the department of philosophy and religion was aptly named: it offered a philosophical emphasis without any real elaboration of religion courses, and no concerns of a Lutheran nature were addressed in its courses.

The academic dean from 1945 to 1952, Edward Myers, had a strong impact on Roanoke College, considering that he was academic dean for only seven years. A graduate of the college in 1927, he earned an MA and a PhD from Princeton. He was perhaps the first *bona fide* trained Christian intellectual at Roanoke. He carried on a highly disciplined intellectual life himself and taught courses at the college that brought students into genuine intellectual reflection on the great issues of the day from a Christian point of view. One of those students, James Crumley, who was to become the presiding bishop of the Lutheran Church in America, offered this: "Of all my teachers in college and seminary he did most to show me the way through some tough intellectual problems. He was my mentor."[25] Myers knew Arnold Toynbee personally and brought him to the Roanoke campus. He also wrote a bibliographical volume in Toynbee's massive *Study of History*. After his brief but significant stay at Roanoke, for which he was honored by the student yearbook of 1952, Myers taught at Washington and Lee University and then entered government service as a cultural attaché in several venues. He died in 1969, leaving an extensive library to the college.

Ethos

Unsurprisingly, the general trajectory over Smith's twenty-nine years as president was toward fewer and fewer rules. The catalogues during this time had a section entitled "Religious and Moral Culture," which is where the college made known its expectations. That section and the rules it included—prohibitions of the use of alcohol, automobiles, and firearms on campus—disappeared by 1949.[26] Required attendance at chapel services was reduced from five times a week in 1920 to one in 1949. The content of chapel programs also was modified from a worship emphasis to one featuring outside speakers, though President Smith frequently used the chapel period for his own sermons and talks.

It is noteworthy that the YMCA—and later the YWCA—still played an important part in religious formation and the enrichment of the student body during the whole time of Smith's tenure. The role of the "Y's" was remarkably consistent in Roanoke's religious life and extended back to Dreher's time (1878–1903). For almost seventy-five years it organized Bible stud-

---

25. E-mail conversation, Jan. 24, 2014.

26. The rule against firearms was unfortunately still in place when one of the living witnesses ran afoul of it. Robert Ayers, a student leader in many organizations, including Blue Key, shot out a quad streetlight "in a moment of tipsy foolishness." He adds, however, that he "hit a target the size of a football at a distance of probably one hundred yards, with plain sights." For this he was "properly but mildly excluded from attendance for six weeks and from residence forever. I am sure that Dr. Smith played some role in the leniency. Dean Myers, for whom I think I was a favorite student, reached into his Oxfordian lingo and informed me that I was to be 'sent down to rusticate'" (Robert Ayers, e-mail correspondence, Dec. 4, 2013).

ies, had weekly religious gatherings, offered recreational opportunities, and took up charitable causes in the community. Faculty wives offered teas for the YMCA members on Sunday afternoons.

Denominational groups proliferated at Roanoke to supplement and particularize religious life on campus. And the venerable Clericus, founded for preministerial students during Dreher's time, continued to flourish. Many talented and highly committed young Southern men prepared for seminary at Roanoke, and it was supported vigorously by "Dr. Charlie." All in all, Roanoke's claim that it was characterized by a genuinely "Christian atmosphere" during Smith's tenure was arguably true. No doubt there were many student rebellions against that culture, but it was obvious that those actions were violations of something clearly established.

Conclusion

Charles Smith saw Roanoke College through great growth over his nearly three decades of stewardship: the college had 163 students when he became president in 1920, and it enrolled 633 when he retired in 1949. The faculty grew markedly during that period, and many new buildings were built. He successfully raised an endowment adequate for accreditation. He raised money, recruited students, and led the college successfully through many financial challenges. He saw the college become a modern liberal arts college. Indeed, one commentator summed up his work: "Dr. Charlie was just perfect for Roanoke College at that stage of its existence, a modest legend in his own time. He had the right 'presence' for the hour."[27]

Smith pressed forward with the college's traditional commitment to Christian republicanism over that span with impressive consistency. He saw its mission as the intellectual and moral formation of young Christians for service to the church, nation, and world. Like his predecessors, he affirmed a broad base of Christian faith to sustain that project rather than a more specific theological rationale. The college depended on generic American Protestantism to provide the faculty and students for its mission. And, for the most part, the Baptists, Presbyterians, Episcopalians, Methodists, Lutherans—joined then by Northeastern Catholics—came through. The broad-based Christian culture held: at the end of Smith's tenure in 1949 one could still comfortably talk about Roanoke as a "Christian college."

27. Robert Ayers, e-mail correspondence, Dec. 4, 2013.

The means needed to sustain the Christian republican project, however, seemed to be weakening. The curriculum certainly did not pay attention to ethical instruction as it once did, nor was it as intellectually integrated. Religious instruction played a receding role. Faculty members became more interested in professionalized teaching than in moral formation. And the faculty did not articulate a clear theological rationale for the mission of the college; a broadly Christian base was assumed. Faculty selection was thus done less by conscious intention than by personal affinity.

Charles Smith was given the honorific title of "provost"—plus a $6,500 annual stipend—after he retired in 1949. For the next eighteen years he lived a quiet and unassuming life, continuing his involvement in the college, church, and community.[28] In 1967 he was honored on his eighty-fifth birthday at the college commons. Shockingly, he had a heart attack in the midst of the celebration and died later that day. Like David Bittle before him, Smith died right in the midst of the college life he loved. It was thus a fitting end. Like Dreher, he was buried next to Bittle in East Hill Cemetery.

28. Charles Schumann of Richmond, Virginia, a Lutheran layman and long acquaintance of Smith, reported in a conversation (Sept. 12, 2013) that he and Smith were the only two persons at a Virginia Synod gathering in the early 1960s who voted against a motion that supported continuing segregation of the races.

5

Builder of the Body and Caretaker of the Soul

By the time Sherman Oberly became president of Roanoke College in 1949, the postwar influx of returning veterans who enrolled in the college under the GI Bill was beginning to wane. Indeed, the college enrollment began to drop precipitously—from 633 in 1949 to 364 in 1951. It took Homer Bast, a young and energetic history professor, track coach, and admissions director, to turn the tide toward growth. For the first time, full-time administrators were hired to fill offices of admissions, public relations, alumni relations, business affairs, and student life. And by the early 1960s the college had a full-time director of development. It took some time to coordinate these new offices, and Oberly, with his experience at the University of Pennsylvania, had the qualifications and skills to bring order to Roanoke's somewhat chaotic organizational life.[1] Roanoke was taking modern shape.

A great deal of building went on during the fourteen years of Oberly's tenure—several dorms and a new library—partly because of the new fundraising capacities of the college. The completion of a new library in 1962 was particularly important because the college's accreditation was at risk. By 1963, there were over eight hundred students at the college; and the faculty

---

1. From an interview with Don Sutton, longtime dean of students (1956–76), who worked closely with Oberly on this project. Another important administrator, Clarence Caldwell (a 1941 graduate of the college), was put in charge of business affairs during Oberly's time. Caldwell, also influential in community and church circles, stewarded those affairs until 1982. Three administrators who began their work in the Oberly era—Bast, Sutton, and Caldwell—were memorialized by the college by dedicating buildings in their names.

was also growing—from thirty-six in 1950 to fifty-seven by 1963.[2] The management of the college was solid, allowing it to enjoy, from the mid-1950s onward, a long period of being "in the black." In short, the college grew gradually but soundly.

The culture of the 1950s was stable and coherent. Though the Cold War provided a sober background, the American Dream was alive. More and more young people were financially able to go to college and elevate their status in life. When they graduated, jobs were plentiful even for undergraduates. Families were growing and churches were full. The culture—the meaning and values system—shaped by the biblical and republican traditions was still intact: there was respect for authority and tradition; a strong work ethic; sexual restraint; patriotism; confidence in America and its role in the world; and strong adherence to religion. To be an American meant to be a Protestant, Catholic, or Jew—and vice versa.[3]

In such a stable and confident culture, one would correctly anticipate little change in the college's articulation of its identity and mission. The statement of purpose written by Charles Smith in the mid-1940s continued to set the vision of the college throughout Oberly's tenure, and the curriculum remained basically the same. Oberly was a caretaker of the vision and mission of the college; he was by no means an innovator. However, just at the end of his administration, in 1963, a new mission statement was written that was a harbinger of what was to come later in the sixties. It represents an interesting weakening of the Christian republican tradition that had held sway for one hundred and ten years. But a sharper departure from the tradition awaited the turbulence of the late 1960s and early 1970s.[4]

2. Mark Miller, *Dear Old Roanoke—A Sesquicentennial Portrait, 1842–1992* (Macon, GA: Mercer University Press, 1992), 213–32.

3. I am particularly interested in this phase of the life of Roanoke College because I would have been a student during Oberly's tenure as president had I gone to Roanoke. From 1955 to 1959, I went to a sister Lutheran college, Midland College (now University), which was similar in many ways to Roanoke, except for the presence of many more Lutheran faculty and students. The general culture of the fifties certainly held sway at both colleges, as it did in most places in America.

4. There is a good argument to be made that the sixties really were the years between 1965 and 1975. The early sixties shared much of the optimism and idealism of the fifties, whose traits were magnified in the Kennedy years. But from 1965 on a huge shift in America's culture, society, and politics took place. That upheaval calmed down after 1975 with the close of the war in Vietnam and the presidencies of Ford and Carter. However, many movements of the 1960s persisted to reshape American society in its many sectors. Above all, the sexual revolution was and is a cultural movement that has had enormous continuing effects.

The Formation and Vision of Sherman Oberly

Oberly was the first president of Roanoke who had no earlier connections with the college, in contrast to all the preceding presidents (except the founder, of course), all of whom graduated from the college and had many contacts with earlier presidents, graduates, and faculty. He was also the first president who was not "churchly," that is, deeply involved in the life of the Lutheran church and its organizations. Moreover, he was born in Illinois in 1898 and received all his schooling in the North. But he did have connections to the Lutheran tradition: his father, Frank Oberly, was a Lutheran minister who served briefly in Virginia before Sherman was born. His brother, Robert, became a Lutheran missionary to India and Africa. Sherman went to Muhlenberg College (Pennsylvania), where he earned his BA in 1920; he did graduate study in psychology at the University of Pennsylvania and earned a PhD in 1924 with a thesis on the subject of visual perception. He then taught in the psychology department at Penn until he was appointed dean of admissions in 1939. He was elected president of Roanoke in 1949 after a lengthy search period by a committee of the board. Besides being the first Roanoke president from the North, he was also its first president with an earned doctorate. He began his tenure as president at the age of fifty-one, older than any other Roanoke president was at the beginning of his presidency.

Oberly's personal style offered a sharp contrast to that of his direct predecessor, Charles ("Dr. Charlie") Smith. Smith, one of the most beloved of the school's presidents, was warm, positive, congenial, and eloquent. Oberly was cooler, a bit abrasive, something of an introvert, and lacking in oratorical skills. On the other hand, Oberly's administrative skills were superior to those of his predecessor. After he came to Roanoke College, he served on the board of the Southern Society of Psychology and Philosophy, which hosted a large academic conference at Roanoke in 1951. Long before he arrived at Roanoke, he had married Charlotte Peters, and they were the parents of a son and daughter. "Sherm" was an avid amateur photographer and moviemaker.[5]

Like earlier inaugurations of Roanoke College presidents, Oberly's was held during the spring commencement ceremonies at the end of his first academic year. But the inauguration ceremony of 1950 was quite different: it featured a major outside speaker, President Harold Stassen of the University of Pennsylvania, and a very brief speech by Oberly, unlike the extended

5. Online history of the Lindamood family.

inaugural addresses given by earlier presidents.[6] What it lacked in length, however, Oberly's speech made up for in clarity. It was clear about his commitment to continue the Roanoke College Christian republican tradition, set so many years ago by David Bittle. In fact, he began his speech with an explicit commitment to that tradition, and the cornerstone of the speech was the famous dictum of David Bittle: "The momentous duty of one generation to another is its education." He went on to recount the sentences that follow that Bittle quote, which emphasize that the college is to inculcate the kind of intellectual and moral virtues in its students that enable them "to be better men than we, better qualified to incur the responsibilities of life, to possess superior wisdom, and a more refined humanity."[7]

An amusing footnote is that Oberly twice erroneously claimed the sainted Bittle for the North. Early in his speech he said that "Dr. Bittle was brought from the Commonwealth of Pennsylvania in 1842 to found the educational institution which in 1853 was chartered as Roanoke College by the Old Dominion State." In truth, Bittle grew up in a slaveholding section of Maryland, went to seminary in Gettysburg, Pennsylvania, but began his ministry in Virginia, where he and Christopher Baughman decided—they were not "brought"—to begin a school in Bittle's parsonage in 1842.

A bit later in his address, Oberly noted that Roanoke College stayed open during the Civil War, attributing that to Bittle's coming "from the North." This probably referred to Bittle's friendly agreement with a Lutheran Union commander (Bittle knew the latter's pastor from his seminary days) to spare Salem and the college from a destructive attack late in the war. Though Bittle did make a helpful contact with that Northern Lutheran soldier, he was neither from the North nor was he a Union partisan. He was vigorously pro-Confederate; but when the hostilities ended, he immediately renewed his connections with the North without bitterness or enmity.

Historical errors about Bittle aside, Oberly went on to list the titles of the inaugural addresses of all his predecessors, again aligning himself with

6. There are scarcely any public writings by Oberly to be found in the college archives. This is in sharp contrast to the copious writings available of earlier presidents. This perhaps is due to the kind of education that Roanoke College presidents had. The early presidents were broadly educated and were highly practiced writers and speakers. Later presidents were hired as professional administrators for whom such activities were less important. Furthermore, from Oberly on, the presidents had diminished opportunity and power to effect the mission statements of the college; that responsibility resided increasingly with the faculty.

7. Sherman Oberly, in a hand-typed manuscript of his inaugural address; the following excerpts are also drawn from that manuscript, which evidently went unpublished.

the Christian republican tradition of the college. Locating himself in that revered stream, he chose a "comprehensive title to express [his] ideas for a blueprint for the future of Roanoke College: 'Education for Citizenship.'" A sentence later, he expanded the idea to "education for *world* citizenship" in honor of the guest speaker, Harold Stassen, who was very interested in world affairs during the intensification of the Cold War.

Oberly then moved on to insist that the colleges of America are in their own "cold war" in the field of education. One side in the battle claimed that the days of the liberal arts college were over. However, he took the other side: "In my opinion, the liberal arts college must survive if we are to have a democratic education for citizenship." Roanoke, as ever, aimed to supply virtuous citizens for the republic.

It is noteworthy that Oberly decried the temptations of liberal arts colleges to become dependent on the government. He cited the warning of the president of Yale, Charles Seymour, that the ever-present strings to government grants can compromise the school's freedom to educate in its own way. Here we had some reverberations of the persisting American notion that the religious freedom to shape church and educational life according to religion's own light was a great and rare blessing from God. Entanglement with the government would curtail a series of freedoms—religious, political, academic, economic—that were crucial for the flourishing of a free society.

He then quoted Thomas Jefferson: "I know of no safe depository of the ultimate powers of society but the people themselves; and if we think them not enlightened enough to exercise their control with a wholesome discretion, the remedy is not to take it from them, but to inform their discretion by education." It is difficult to state republican philosophy any better than that.

Instead of relying on government support and entanglement, Roanoke would move in another direction. The church, Oberly declared, would take an increased role in funding and supporting its church-related institutions. The United Lutheran Church in America designated 1950 as a "year of decision" to support its colleges and seminaries. This push would renew "the hope of our forebears, 'who amidst toil and great sacrifice' built our institutions." So there was still solid confidence that the republican tradition would continue to rest on Christian foundations at Roanoke. This hope for a *Christian* republicanism was reinforced as Oberly depicted the characteristics of a Roanoke education. Quoting the statement of purpose written by Charles Smith, he said that the college was "dedicated to the task of training young men and women in an atmosphere dominated by Christian ideals of service and conduct." Furthermore, he referred to the slogan for the Higher

Education Year of the United Lutheran Church in America: "For Christian leaders tomorrow."

> Our best investments today are those which preserve our freedom. Our greatest challenge today is to provide for a way of life for our citizens of tomorrow, who may live in an uncertain world. We aspire to prepare our students for world citizenship, ever mindful of the Christian ideals under which this institution came into being more than a century ago.

Oberly went on to say that he assumed his new role in a humble manner, asking for human and divine support for the task ahead. Only with such help would he be able to proceed in the manner of his predecessors. He closed his speech by quoting at length the remarks made by Julius Dreher, the only other layman in the pantheon of Roanoke presidents up to that point. Dreher had also had a guest speaker at his inauguration (in 1879), a scholar from the University of Pennsylvania, Prof. Charles Porterfield Krauth, the great Lutheran confessional theologian. Sensing the parallels between that day and his, Oberly ended by offering Dreher's welcome to Krauth as his own welcome to Stassen, concluding with Dreher's parting remarks to his Pennsylvania guest: "Heartily reciprocating the sentiment that the Republic of Letters is world-wide, and hence in America, knows no North or South, no East or West, but one common country to be blest with the best means of Christian culture, we beg you to bear back to your venerable university cordial congratulations and an earnest godspeed from your younger sister Roanoke."

Oberly's brief inaugural address offered a succinct articulation of the persisting mission of the college: the shaping of citizens for the republic and the world on the foundations of Christian ideals. There were a few more notable marks of the inaugural address besides its brevity and clarity. A respect for the college's tradition and past leaders permeated it. He humbly conformed his presidency to what had been already established by his predecessors. He offered no new thoughts or exciting horizons. He did expand citizenship to the world stage, but Dreher had done that more vigorously in his inaugural, as had Charles Smith when the community faced the aftermath of World War I. Furthermore, he refrained from any elaboration of either the republican or Christian components of the college's vision and mission, in contrast to earlier presidents, who were very interested in offering their own interpretations of both.

All this stasis, or, as I have called it, "caretaking the soul of the college," was probably the result of three factors, one personal and two social. On the personal side, Oberly was not trained in theology, philosophy, or the humanities in general; he was a scientist who was trained in a "hard" dimension of psychology, visual perception. He had neither the desire nor the ability to wax philosophical about educational matters. He had spent the last ten years before coming to Roanoke in admissions work—thus an administrator, not a philosopher. On the social side were two further reasons why he was more of a caretaker than innovator. First, by Oberly's time, the Roanoke faculty was more in charge than ever of articulating the mission of the college and shaping its curriculum. Humble man that he was, Oberly was not presumptuous enough to take on those tasks for himself. He wisely chose to stick with the inherited tradition. Second, the 1950s were a calm time, a time when the traditional verities and moralities held. Except for Sputnik and the distant Soviet threat, nothing terribly provocative was shaking the foundations of the college. Change was not necessary. However, it is instructive that at the very end of his tenure, the faculty decided to change the college's existing statement of purpose. It took a survey and then constructed a new statement, which I will discuss next. Such a change was precipitated by the arrival of many new professors, not only holding doctorates but also having a growing sense that faculties were in charge of the academic program of the college.

Roanoke College Statement of Purpose

Until the mid-1940s, Roanoke College had no purpose statement in its catalogue or admissions materials. It simply included a brief historical sketch of the college and an affirmation of its liberal arts approach to education. In 1943 a statement of purpose appears, no doubt written by its president at the time, Charles Smith. Its rhetoric—ornate, complex sometimes to the point of unintelligibility, and homiletical—reveals its source. It is a rather full-blooded statement of the college's Christian republican tradition. It pays attention to both poles: building the character of its students and the Christian moral tradition as its foundation. It emphasizes its liberal arts character and its decision to offer only two bachelor's degrees—in liberal arts and in science.

Liberal arts colleges were facing increased competition from public colleges and universities, with their more pragmatic emphases. The coming of World War II accentuated the need for small liberal arts colleges to define themselves. Therefore, it was necessary to write statements that not only praised and defended the liberal arts tradition but also connected that tradition with the republican purpose of the college along with its Christian undergirding. Further, the president was the proper leader to craft such a statement. Here is Smith's rendition, which was to endure for twenty years:

> More than a hundred years ago Roanoke College was dedicated to the task of training young men in arts and sciences in an atmosphere dominated by Christian ideals of service and conduct, with full realization of the vital part higher education must always play in the life and culture of a democratic state. Roanoke College from the beginning understood its educational task to include—the cultivation of the art by which an individual realizes himself as a member of a society whose tabernacle is here, but whose home is a house not built with hands; the development of processes by which he learns the best, enjoys the best, and produces the best in knowledge, conduct and the arts; the cultivation of the ability to express himself intellectually, physically, spiritually, and emotionally; and, finally, a complete and everlasting faith in a moral order and the continuing process of which it is itself, an integral and dynamic part.[8]

Contrast that with the new faculty-shaped statement of 1963:

> Roanoke College, founded in 1842 as a liberal arts college, is dedicated to training men and women in high standards of scholarship in the arts and sciences, and developing in every way possible the individual's intellectual ability. The College seeks to give the student a broad competency in a field of specialization and an understanding of the essential components of his own and other cultures. At the same time it is interested in having the individual become proficient in the disciplines necessary to his social, moral, and economic well-being.
>
> In a Christian atmosphere, it strives to foster in each student an emotional maturity and to endow him with high ideals so that with his superior education and his understanding and appreciation of the heritage of scholarship he may assume his responsibility in the contemporary world.[9]

According to a system of raw score-keeping, the first version had four religiously oriented themes, the second only one. Both statements men-

---

8. *Roanoke College Catalogue* (1943–44).
9. *Roanoke College Catalogue* (1962–63).

tioned moral concerns three times, but the earlier one pointed to explicitly republican themes three times, the later one only once. Further, there was a noticeable shift from pursuing substantive objective ends in the first to striving to acquire efficient means to realize subjective ends in the second. The first statement gives clear ends toward which the student is being educated: the student was to become educated in order to contribute to the life and culture of a democratic state; he was to learn, enjoy, and produce the best in knowledge, conduct, and the arts; he was to have faith in an objective moral order that he incorporated dynamically in his life.

The 1963 revision focused on competencies that can be used for individual ends. The college offered "high standards of scholarship," the opportunity to enhance the student's "intellectual ability," the chance to acquire "competency" in a field of specialization and "proficiency" in the disciplines necessary to his well-being. Even so, the 1963 statement ended with a claim that all this will be done in a "Christian atmosphere" in which high ideals would be encouraged, so that the student's education could enable him to "assume his responsibility in the contemporary world." The Christian republican themes were still present, but in a diminished and muted way.

Curriculum

There was little change in the curriculum during Oberly's time as president. A good dose of English (twelve hours, or four courses) continued to be required. Students were required to read and write well; indeed, the public penalty for poor English used in any spoken or written work persisted throughout these years. Repeat offenders had to report to the English Department for remedial work; and, after multiple admonitions, students could lose course credit.

Social studies continued to expand incrementally to eighteen required hours, and the natural sciences held their own at sixteen. Six required hours of physical education and hygiene were introduced; foreign languages, math, and religion all held at six hours each. Remarkably, the great books "Reading Course," an intensive reading requirement, persisted throughout the fourteen years of Oberly's presidency. Roughly 60 percent of the liberal arts curriculum was required, while 40 percent was devoted to a "concentration" or to electives.

Faculty selection continued "by affinity," though that strategy began to break down as the college sought more PhDs to strengthen its academic reputation. In the mid-1950s, two promising professors with degrees from prestigious Northern schools were hired by the college. Both could be characterized as "nonbelievers" with regard to Christian conviction and practice. They were joined by several more skeptics in the late 1950s and early 1960s. As fate would have it, those new hires became leaders of the faculty and, in turn, hired more faculty members with their profile. They were apathetic and perhaps even hostile to the Christian base of the college's republican tradition. This weakening of the college's sense of mission—and hiring faculty according to it—became an ingredient in the later marginalization of the college's Christian heritage. It is fairly certain that little effort was being made to hire Lutherans as members of the general faculty, though it appears to have been a concern on the religion side of the department of philosophy and religion. In general, new faculty members seemed to possess characteristics similar to those who hired them. For the most part, they were church-going mainstream Protestants who were assumed to support the general Christian republican aims of the college. They were asked by the dean where they went to church. A majority of the faculty continued tacitly to support the college tradition but with perhaps less unanimity and conviction. Oberly was a fitting leader for such a mode.

The philosophy and religion department continued to be primarily responsible for teaching the "Reading Course," which replaced a required philosophy course in the mid-1940s. James Rikard became lodged in the oral history of the college by his rigorous teaching of that course. On the religion side, the college continued to require a course in Old Testament and one in New Testament, which were listed under varying titles through the years. That precedent had been established by Frank Longaker after the death of Luther Fox in 1925, and continued to the early 1960s, when the two-course religion requirement was amended to require one course in "The Judeo-Christian Heritage" and one course in "Comparative Religion."

The general pattern of offering more courses in philosophy than religion continued through the Oberly years: "History of Philosophy," "Ethics," "Logic," "Problems in Philosophy," "Philosophy of Democracy" (which was later changed to "Political Philosophy"), "Contemporary Philosophy," and "Philosophy of Science" were offered. When Roy Bent arrived in 1958, he started up an "Introduction to Philosophy" course, plus one in "Aesthetics."[10]

10. Bent (1927–1999), educated at Hofstra and Episcopal Theological School, was a high-church Anglican steeped in the mystical tradition. He taught philosophy with a strong religious accent from 1958 to 1990. In the 1960s and 1970s, he was known for his lively engagement with students inside and outside of class. He often began classes with the query "What Feast Day is it today?" Then he invited students "to share in [his] confusion." He was

SHERMAN OBERLY (1949–1963)

The two required religion courses continued to be taught by James Rikard, supplemented by temporary faculty throughout the 1950s.[11] When Rev. Guy Ritter came onboard in 1956, religion courses were slowly expanded to include "Christian Ethics," "Prophets," and "Development of Christianity." Ritter, Rikard, and Bent shared the new responsibility of teaching the required courses of Judeo-Christian Heritage and Comparative Religion. While there was expansion in elective courses in both philosophy and religion, the required courses in Christian studies were cut to one course. One can find but small traces of Lutheran content in the titles of the courses, but it is probable that Ritter gave a Lutheran construal to the required course in the Judeo-Christian Heritage and in the electives he taught.

Ritter (1919–2013), a native Virginia Lutheran and 1948 graduate of Roanoke College, was a conservative confessional Lutheran educated at the Philadelphia Lutheran Seminary. He was perhaps the first professor in Roanoke's history to teach Christianity from a self-consciously Lutheran theological perspective, teaching there from 1958 to 1984. He was a man of many talents: he painted portraits of many prominent Roanoke College personages; he designed the college seal; he painted the flora and fauna of Virginia; he was a gunsmith, saddle-maker, and Bentley automobile mechanic; and he was an active outdoorsman. He supplied many Lutheran parishes in his long life as a pastor. The college named one of its dorms for this colorful character.

Ethos

Chapel continued to be required once a week. After the college acquired the old Methodist church in the early 1950s, chapel was held there.[12] The

---

firmly in the Roanoke tradition of offering much of its religious and moral teaching through its many philosophy courses.

11. One visiting professor, during 1950–51, was Alan Hauck (1925–2009), who had just received his ThD at Hartford Theological Seminary. Coincidently, Hauck later taught at Midland College in Nebraska (in the late 1950s), where I had him as my religion professor. He was instrumental in my getting deeply interested in Christian ethics. In the required senior course in Christian ethics, Hauck insisted that we read Reinhold Niebuhr's *An Interpretation of Christian Ethics*, which was incredibly stimulating to me. I then took independent courses with him in logic and Kierkegaard.

12. As part of the United Lutheran Church's commitment to Christian higher education, the Virginia Synod raised $100,000 for a new chapel at the college. However, the college decided instead to buy the Methodist church, as well as its parsonage and parish house, and it used the synod's grant for that purchase.

once-a-week pattern persisted during the Oberly years. In its 1958 catalogue the college reaffirmed that chapel was "required of all students, regardless of their own faith." But those who may have been nervous about that requirement were assured that many of the programs offered during the chapel hour were nonreligious. Furthermore, the college saw the chapel sessions as oriented mainly toward character development. Oberly was not the orator or preacher that "Dr. Charlie" was, so chapel-goers were not favored with the impromptu sermons of the old preacher-president.

Corresponding with the general character of chapel, the college continued, up until 1960, to tout its "broadly Christian" character—even though it was related to the Lutheran church. Indeed, it claimed that its "catholicity of spirit has given it wide appeal."[13] Roanoke expected "spiritual development" of its students, but it also insisted that its student body be "cosmopolitan rather than local." As always, the college needed to appeal to incoming students from a broad base of religious backgrounds as well as from a rather wide geographical area.

By the early 1960s, the college amended its language and dropped the "broadly Christian" language under prodding from the Virginia Synod, which then pledged $100,000 for the construction of a college chapel.[14] This apparent show of conviction on the part of the synod, however, had been precipitated by a weakening of Lutheran presence on the college's board: there were only two Lutheran clergymen on the board, a prestigious pastor from Richmond and the superintendent of the Virginia Synod. They were there by informal consensus, not because of any bylaw that stipulated a level of formal church representation. This practice continues to the present day. By the decade of the 1960s, the board was dominated by wealthy and powerful businessmen, including Stuart Saunders, of the Norfolk and Southern Railroad, and Henry Fowler, of Goldman and Sachs.

In the early 1950s two organizations that had been crucial in the religious life of the college—the YMCA and the YWCA—were merged into the Stu-

13. *Roanoke College Catalogue* (1950–51), 19. The following material about "ethos" was gathered from the catalogues of the time.

14. Miller, *Dear Old Roanoke*, 229. Perhaps this narrowing of the "broadly Christian" language indicates a further withdrawal by the college from any trace of earlier evangelical affinities in favor of those of the mainline Christian denominations; that is, tipping toward Lutheranism was accompanied by a further distancing from evangelicalism. The professors teaching religion were hardly sympathetic to evangelicalism, though they taught many evangelical students. It had been a long journey from Bittle's full-blooded evangelicalism to a generic mainline Protestantism, colored a bit by Lutheranism.

dent Christian Association (SCA), which aimed at the growth of personal religion, contributing to a wholesome campus life, providing Bible study and weekly services, offering recreational opportunities, and rendering service to various charitable groups, including the Lutheran orphanage and the Boy Scouts. However, the SCA disappeared by 1962, supplanted by a profusion of denominational groups, including the Newman Club for Catholic students. Clericus, an organization begun in the early 1920s for those preparing for church work, continued to provide support and discussion opportunities for its members.

At midcentury the college continued to call all its students to a high sense of duty and a wholesome way of life. It claimed to provide a "moral atmosphere," but the rhetoric about the faculty being crucial role models for the moral formation of the students was now absent.[15] At the beginning of the 1950s, a set of clear rules governed the student body: autos only by special permission; no firearms in the dorms; marriage only by permission of the dean; and no alcohol use on campus. By 1963, those rules were gone, replaced by a general requirement of "high standards of personal conduct," so that each Roanoke College student could contribute to a "wholesome moral atmosphere." Dress codes for men and women continued, along with rather strict rules governing life in the dorms (women's dorms were more rulebound than men's were). The college's honor system was maintained during this whole period, though with some interruptions and difficulties. And, as was typical of the 1950s, there was little open student rebellion against the moral consensus that still prevailed, though—as always in human history—no doubt there were many who transgressed it.

Conclusion

The era of Sherman Oberly was certainly characterized by growth in buildings, professional administrative staff, organizational complexity and sophistication, and in the number of faculty members and students. Administrators and faculty were generally chosen on the basis of affinity with the generic

15. Don Sutton, who became the college's first student life professional, and Homer Bast, history professor, registrar, and track coach extraordinaire, took on the role of mentor for many students in this era. Both had extensive military experience and seemed to combine moral sternness and compassion in a particularly effective way. Some of the men and women who were to become major supporters of and donors to the college in later years were nurtured and encouraged by these two men.

Protestant character of those who chose them. The expansion of the faculty in the late 1950s and early 1960s included many professors who would teach at Roanoke for the next twenty to thirty years—into the 1980s and 1990s.

On the educational side of things, the commitment to the liberal arts was steady, typified by the maintenance of the Reading Course. As always, Roanoke's ample programs in the natural sciences were well respected in academic circles. The philosophy and religion department was expanded to three members, and they shared the teaching load for one required course in philosophy (the Reading Course) and two in religion (one in the Judeo-Christian tradition and one in comparative religion). For the first time, Lutheran themes were introduced into the teaching of religion by Guy Ritter. The college continued to draw capable pretheological students, who went on to seminary and then entered the ordained ministry. But its rhetoric about raising men for the ministry and the mission field had disappeared. The college persisted in its *in loco parentis* role, but with increased parental "flexibility."

The student ethos was as steady as the surrounding culture: conservative, strongly patriotic, and generically Protestant.[16] A few Jews and Catholics had by then entered the student body—and even organized their own clubs—but all fit comfortably within the religious and political consensus of the day. Many graduates went on to excel in a society abounding in postwar opportunity.[17]

However, it must be noted that clarity about and zeal for the college's traditional commitment to Christian republicanism were beginning to wane. It was not that its age-old mission was under attack or explicitly rejected. Rather, it was complacently assumed that a coterie of southern Christian gentlemen would implicitly and quietly convey the Christian foundations of the college's republican mission to a homogeneous and agreeable student body. Those assumptions seemed to need little defense at the time: Ike was in the White House and all was right with the world. In such a settled world, citizens could pursue their own individual objectives, and the college could help them succeed in that. The college could even afford to have dissenters from its Christian foundations on its faculty.

16. Miller, in *Dear Old Roanoke*, reports that a student mock election in 1956 resulted in Eisenhower swamping Stevenson by a vote of 262–82.

17. Students from this era who went on to successful careers are currently some of the main benefactors and servants of the college: Robert Wortmann ('60), John Turbyfill ('53), Paul Capp ('52), Donald Kerr ('60), and Morris Cregger ('64).

6

PERRY KENDIG (1963–1975)

Contending with the 1960s

Looking back at that turbulent time in America's history, Donald Sutton remembered challenges at the college:

> The strict and polite life at the College changed radically in the late 1960s and early 1970s, and some of the changes were needed. But what saddened me was the new attitude of many undergraduates. Roanoke has long been a home to wonderful, affable young people. But gradually the students in the seventies became less friendly, less cooperative, and more surly and wild.[1]

It seems to be something of a mystery how a college under the administrative leadership of morally upright, sober, churchgoing, strong-willed ex-military men—Kendig, Sutton, Bast, Caldwell, Lautenschlager, as well as many military veterans among the faculty—could be dramatically transformed by that surge of "wild" students in a surprisingly short period of time. Truth be told, however, the changes could not have happened without the acquiescence of a good portion of a faculty that was increasingly distant from the Christian republican tradition of the college.

In preceding chapters I have discerned a sense of mission that originated in David Bittle's founding vision and persisted throughout the college's his-

---

1. Donald Sutton, Dean of Students from 1956 to 1976, as quoted in George Keller, *Prologue to Prominence—A Half Century of Roanoke College, 1951–2003* (Minneapolis: Lutheran University Press, 2005), 30.

tory. I have termed that sense of mission "Christian republicanism," after a movement originating in the Second Great Awakening (1800–1850), which used colleges as one of the main instruments for "Christianizing the nation." During that period many colleges were founded on explicitly Christian convictions in order to supply citizens of virtue from all classes and walks of life for the new American Republic. Roanoke was definitely in that tradition, its presidents constantly emphasizing that its students would be formed in crucial republican virtues by immersion in a Christian ethos and Christian learning. The college was committed to supplying such students to the church and world by grounding them in the solid foundation of Christian faith and life. New faculty members were selected by "affinity" with the older Southern Christian gentlemen who carried the tradition, which was clearly articulated in the purpose statements up until 1963, when a weaker one was written by the faculty. More seriously, new faculty in the 1950s and 1960s were selected more on the basis of their professional credentials rather than their commitment to the traditional set of purposes.

"Transformed" is not too strong a word to depict the changes occurring in the college, which go far beyond changes in the student body. During Perry Kendig's time as president, the two required courses in religion were dropped in favor of choices in the elective curriculum. The Reading Course—a "great books" course—was excised from the curriculum. A new curriculum (1969) and purpose statement (1971) were forged, both of which featured a diminished commitment to Roanoke's traditional mission.

The politics of the 1960s made their appearance on campus in a fairly moderate form. In the spring of 1970, a moratorium on the Vietnam War was observed, and students could choose whether or not they wished to finish the semester. Earth Day was celebrated. Countercultural celebrities performed on campus. Marginal students were given a second chance to keep them from being drafted.[2] More than a few radical notes were sounded.

Required weekly chapel attendance ended in 1967. As early as 1964, students protested the college's alcohol policies; by the end of that decade, beer was served in the student lounge. Alcohol consumption was allowed in dorm rooms, and public keg parties were held on campus. Drug use became commonplace on campus by the early 1970s, and the honor system came to an end as well. Dress codes went the way of all flesh in 1969. Dressing up for a served dinner in the student dining hall was replaced by casual dress for

---

2. These many happenings are chronicled in Miller, *Dear Old Roanoke*, 246–75, and in Keller, *Prologue*, 30–31.

informal eating in a cafeteria setting. Visitation hours were cast aside—along with single-sex dorms—by 1974. The initiation process (run by students), which required freshmen to learn the history of the college, was terminated by that year, and other long-standing traditions vanished. The college annually hosted one of *Playboy* magazine's "playmates of the month."

It is often credibly argued that one's political stance can be predicted by one's assessment of the 1960s, an era that I have argued is actually the decade from 1965 to 1975. The period from 1960 to 1965 was characterized by "liberal idealism," which involved a positive, "can-do" attitude toward solving the nation's great challenges: racism, urban decay, and poverty. After 1965 that up-beat posture changed toward a more polarizing revolutionary attitude. The antiwar movement, the urban riots, the shift from civil rights to Black Power, the emergence of a revolutionary student movement, sexual liberation, and the beginnings of the feminist, gay liberation, multiculturalism, and environmentalist movements made the decade bracing indeed. The traditional cultural lid that governed American society was blown off by liberationist movements fueled by a burgeoning baby boomer population. In that upheaval, both positive and negative impulses were dramatically and powerfully expressed. What one ultimately makes of them is crucial to determining one's current political and cultural stances.

Certainly some important positive things happened. The double standard between men's and women's behavioral requirements was sharply diminished. The college accepted, without any disturbance, its first black student in 1964. Students became more aware of the outside world by way of the lively politics on campus. Students became more involved in the governance of the college. Freshman hazing came to an end. "Through the first six years of Kendig's presidency the college would build more buildings, purchase more property, and raise more money than at any other time in its history."[3] That meant three new dormitories, four fraternity houses, a new chapel, and two massive new science buildings. Student enrollment increased from 813, when Kendig first took office in 1963, to 1,138, when he retired in 1975. The curriculum was liberalized to allow more student choice among more electives.

George Keller perhaps catches the jagged character of the 1960s decade (1965–75) for the college with the following summary paragraph:

The countercultural outbursts of the late 1960s and the early 1970s are often seen as a semi-nihilistic and hedonistic period of increased sex, po-

3. Milller, *Dear Old Roanoke*, 247.

litical frenzy, booze, and rock-and-roll. There is no denying that it had destructive elements. But at Roanoke College the period helped introduce long-needed reforms, and in some ways brought the separate entities, such as students and trustees, closer together. The period was both a wrecking ball and a stimulus to renovate the college for an emerging new world.[4]

Perry Kendig: The Man and His Formation

Perry Kendig was the first Roanoke College president who did not have a Lutheran upbringing. His Pennsylvania forebears were Mennonites who later became members of the German Reformed Church. Born in Lancaster, Pennsylvania, in 1910, Kendig had his early schooling in Lancaster and then naturally went on to Franklin and Marshall College, a German Reformed college located in his hometown, where his acumen as a student was rewarded with membership in Phi Beta Kappa. After college he briefly taught high school, but then went on to graduate studies at the University of Pennsylvania, earning his MA in 1936 and his PhD in English in 1947.[5] He spent five years in the US Navy (1942 to 1946), ending his tour of duty as a lieutenant commander. He taught English at the University of Pennsylvania briefly, but then moved to Muhlenberg College as an English professor. He became chairman of that department before going to Roanoke College as dean of the college in 1952. He spent twelve years as dean of the college under President Oberly, during which time he sought out and hired a number of new faculty members with doctorates from prestigious universities.[6] As president, he

4. Keller, *Prologue*, 32.

5. Kendig continued the historic Roanoke connection with the University of Pennsylvania, dating back to David Bittle's mentor, Samuel Simon Schmucker, who studied with the Lutheran theologian Hellmuth at Pennsylvania. John Morehead, president from 1903 to 1920, studied philosophy at Penn while he was at the Lutheran seminary in Philadelphia. Sherman Oberly, president from 1949 to 1963, received his PhD in psychology from Pennsylvania and then served as admissions officer there, from whence he was called to be president of Roanoke. Oberly invited the president of the University of Pennsylvania, Harold Stassen, to speak at his inauguration in 1950.

6. My first and only encounter with Perry Kendig was in the parking lot of St. John Lutheran Church in southwestern Roanoke County, where we were both attending church in the fall of 1982, long after he had retired. I noticed the Phi Beta Kappa pin that he proudly wore on a watch chain. He greeted me by noting my PhD from the University of

tried to hire faculty with completed PhDs (not easy during that era) and encouraged those who had not finished the doctorate to do so, thus raising the percentage of faculty with the PhD degree from only 20 percent in 1964 to 60 percent by the time of his retirement in 1975.

Kendig was a scholarly kind of man: always dressed in a suit and tie, he was formal and dignified but not cold; he was also urbane, witty, and un-flappable. He was often seen "walking the campus." Though affable, he did not like fundraising. One of his deans complained that he had "too high a boiling point"; yet his calmness evidently served him well during the many times he came under duress in the 1960s. He was a bird watcher and loved to tell stories. He wrote a history of his home church in Pennsylvania, as well as translated and wrote an introduction to *The Poems of St. Columba* in 1949. He worked hard to establish more scholarships for Roanoke students. He sat on many private and public boards in the Roanoke Valley and was recognized as an influential citizen. Though no "cradle Lutheran," he was a very faithful member of College Lutheran Church and participated actively in regional and national expressions of the church. He and his wife, Virginia, whom he married in 1947, had a daughter and two sons. He died in 1987 and is buried in his home county in Pennsylvania.

As one who had spent many years teaching in the classroom, Kendig was comfortable in public speaking roles, and he often gave the commencement address to graduating Roanoke seniors. As an English professor, he was also comfortable writing his many speeches, so we have a good deal of his writing in the college archives. It is to his written vision that we now turn, especially to his inaugural address, which he gave on a cold day in April 1964, in front of a thousand listeners, including faculty and dignitaries representing 235 colleges and universities.[7]

Kendig's Inaugural Vision for Roanoke College

Kendig opened his address with the requisite set of thanks to those who pre-pared for the day and for those assembled. Though he noted the presence at the ceremonies of his two living predecessors, Charles Smith and Sherman

---

Chicago. "We have some very good degrees at Roanoke College, too," he said, obviously promoting the reputation of the college.

7. Miller, *Dear Old Roanoke*, 252. The portrait of Kendig offered above is a compilation of remembrances by a number of people who knew him.

Oberly, unlike his predecessors he did not enumerate the accomplishments of the seven presidents who had preceded him. He merely mentioned that they were "a most distinguished line."[8] Instead, he called special attention to his friend and mentor Theodore Distler, former president of Franklin and Marshall College, Kendig's alma mater. Distler gave the main address at Kendig's inauguration, and in it he strongly developed the theme of "education for service," a common focus in the lingering republican vision of the role and mission of a liberal arts college.

Kendig began with a quote from Thomas Jefferson in order to have the audience "understand what I deem the essential principles of this government." The first essential was the freedom of a liberal arts college to "free [the student] from the bonds of ignorance, superstition, and fear."[9] This meant to pursue truth wherever it might lead; and it meant an affirmation of academic freedom.

This one-paragraph description of the purpose of the liberal arts college was in sharp contrast to the amount of time devoted to it by most of his predecessors, who felt compelled to lay out the contours and purposes of liberal arts education at each inauguration. But that justification became briefer with each president, which seems a bit odd considering the rise of the large public universities, which were now enrolling more American students than ever before and which were articulating the same sort of justification— service to the country. Furthermore, the trend seemed to be toward shorter inaugural speeches in general by each incoming president.

Continuing, Kendig addressed a number of practical issues. He affirmed the necessity of an excellent faculty, which to him included continuing scholarly activity and even research. As a former dean, he recognized the need for well-supported faculty, and he no doubt gained strong support from the faculty by putting its agenda front and center. He spoke of the need for "innovation," which to him meant the use of planning techniques. (However, a real strategic plan had to wait until the arrival of Kendig's successor, Norman Fintel.)

Kendig then talked of the need for cooperative efforts among the schools of Virginia, especially those in the Roanoke Valley. He pointed approvingly to a plan that Roanoke College had already made cooperatively

8. Unpublished manuscript of Kendig's "Inaugural Address," housed in the Roanoke College archives, 1.

9. Kendig, "Inaugural Address," 2. The following page references are all drawn from that manuscript.

with Lutheran Theological Southern Seminary to offer graduate training in theology for ministers of all denominations in the Roanoke Valley. It is worth noting that, at that point in his speech, his rhetoric became more vivid. He called for more interdependence between the college and the Virginia Synod of the Lutheran Church in America. The relationship between the two, he said, should be symbiotic rather than merely tolerating each other—"like an unhappily married couple skittering on the edge of divorce." The church should support its institutions to the utmost of its ability, and the church colleges must do their part "to conduct their affairs within the framework of the Christian philosophy and ethic."[10]

> If there is really no discernible difference between a church-related college and a secular college, then we ought to get a divorce. I want to be crystal clear at this point. Piety is no substitute for scholarship. To justify their existence church-related colleges must be excellent institutions. Young people want to know the truth. They have a right to know the truth, for it is truth alone that can set them free. We must not compromise on this point.[11]

The "difference" that Kendig was calling for was consistent with the classic Christian republicanism of the college: moral formation, which was to happen in the "ethos" of the college rather than in the classroom. Attention had to be paid to the development of character, integrity, decency, and "Christian principles" in general.

> Mankind will need all the moral fortitude it can muster to face the seeming chaos that surrounds us in a rapidly changing civilization. The only inexhaustible source of this fortitude comes from the realization that this is God's world, created by Him and redeemed by Him. Pointing out this all important truth is one of the ineluctable responsibilities of the church-related college.[12]

10. Kendig, "Inaugural Address," 6. Kendig's emphasis here implies that an estrangement of the college and the church had emerged during Oberly's administration. His call for more cooperation between the college and the Lutheran Church in America resulted in a new covenant between the church and college in 1970.

11. Kendig, "Inaugural Address," 7.

12. Kendig, "Inaugural Address," 7. It is interesting that Kendig uses the language of the Lutheran Church in America to describe the college: "church-related college" rather than "college of the church," which was the language of the American Lutheran Church. The

Kendig's conclusion exhibited the most rhetorical power of the address. He issued a vigorous call to the constituencies of Roanoke College to continue and even increase their support for the ambitious plans he had in mind for the college. "If the American people want freedom, they must invest for it; for the independent college is one of Freedom's last bastions." Moreover, if the church wanted educated leaders, it had to support its colleges; the most important "products" of the college were its men and women. To some extent they are what the college makes them. "The fate of the world will be in their hands. They will need the best of which we are capable."[13] He closed with a plea for divine guidance and help.

This vigorous call to the college and its constituency to produce citizens of virtue was remarkably consistent with the traditional definition of the college's mission. The republic needed citizens of virtue for ordered liberty to survive, especially in a world challenged by totalitarianism and in a country about to experience genuine turbulence. The Christian ethic could form those citizens for the republic, even as it could shape leaders for the church. The Christian resources rested in the "atmosphere" of the college, not in its curriculum. Kendig's approach was a noteworthy departure from the older Christian republican heritage of the college. Moral formation of students in the older era (1853–1920) was certainly contingent on a faculty and a student body that shaped the moral atmosphere of the college. But that moral formation was also supported by strong doses of moral philosophy in the core curriculum of the college. Moreover, Christian formation was not only moral but also intellectual. There had been a formidable array of required courses that shaped the students' worldview, including Bible, theology, philosophy, and Christian apologetics. Little of this was now required.

The new president of Roanoke College seemed rhetorically to endorse the Christian republican mission of the college without a couple of important ingredients: a faculty who perceived one of their main roles to be moral

---

LCA's language reflected a theological commitment to the proposition that church-related higher education was guided by human reason, imagination, and experience in the classroom. Therefore, the intellectual happenings in the classroom of such a Lutheran college would exhibit no great difference from that of a secular school. The search for truth was unfettered by any sort of Christian convictions. The wisdom and insight from Christian revelation played no real role in either the curriculum or the classroom, except for those of the religion department. This arrangement offered little encouragement for "faith and reason" interaction.

13. Kendig, "Inaugural Address," 8.

exemplars for the students and a curriculum that included required courses in Christian philosophy or ethics.[14]

Other Themes in Kendig's Writings

Kendig spoke at other Roanoke College commencements and on many other occasions. A number of themes run through these speeches. One of his favorite themes was "developing a philosophy of life." He inveighed on this topic in many addresses in which he exhorted students to develop such a "philosophy of life," by which he meant the "beliefs, attitudes, and understanding that you hold concerning the world in which you live and your relationship to it." Further, it is a "code you believe in and live by."[15]

He advised students to develop a philosophy that involved a constructive view of their relationships to themselves—their minds and bodies—and to their society—its politics, economics, education, culture, and religion. They should ponder their relationship to God, he said, though "religion is one of the most difficult things in the world to *think* about because it's all wrapped up with our emotions; but we ought to think about it sometimes."[16] Kendig was no relativist in these matters. He believed that it was good to develop a strong faith in God and to belong to a church; it was good to have a more intelligent and mature philosophy of life, which would include service to others "as the highest form of human activity": "It is important to have the moral principles which will help you consistently decide for the right side, the good side, the decent side."[17]

Another of his favorite themes was *moderation*, which was understandable considering the rather unstable social and political situation that characterized a good deal of Kendig's presidency. He lamented the "generation

14. This certainly does not mean that the college lacked faculty members who served as fine moral exemplars. There were many of them. But it seemed clear the faculty no longer saw itself primarily in that role. Furthermore, required courses in religion and philosophy were soon to disappear in the curricular revisions of the late 1960s.

15. Kendig, "Some Thoughts on the Perils of Polarization," commencement address at Roanoke College, May 31, 1970, unpublished manuscript, 3.

16. Kendig, "Developing a Sound Philosophy of Life," commencement address at Radford College, March 17, 1967, unpublished manuscript, 9. This emotive view of religion seems to devalue its intellectual content, which, in turn, would devalue the role of theology in the curriculum of the college. Students should think about religion, but not necessarily be instructed by its intellectual manifestation, theology.

17. Kendig "Developing a Sound Philosophy of Life," 10.

gap," which was such an issue of contention in the 1960s. He argued that the current gap between the student generation and his own was not only deplorable but also dangerous, because it contributed to the polarization of the country. He feared that such polarization could undermine democracy, which to him was of highest value because it occupied the middle ground between two extreme political options. The extreme left moved toward anarchy, while the extreme right moved toward repression. The students of the left in America represented the former, and the political right was inclined to repress the left. Kendig appealed to the students to avoid both extremes and hew to the middle ground—American representative democracy. He reinforced his point by pointing out that many of his generation fought in World War II to protect the democratic project. He went on to admit that our system is not perfect. But, he said, it is the "best system under which to live as free men and women. . . . We dare not polarize ourselves into two enemy camps, into revolution."[18]

His appeal for moderation and calm was poignantly illustrated in his brief address to the Roanoke College faculty and student body after a group of student activists tried to close down the college for the duration of the semester after the violence at Kent State University in May 1970. In explaining why he would neither dismiss classes nor close the college, he said, "It is better to talk than to fight." Such civil interaction was the democratic way, and he strongly believed in it. As to making a public statement about the Kent State situation on behalf of the whole college, he demurred: "I can speak on Roanoke College policy, but cannot do that on national policy. There is no consensus among us."[19] He went on to say that normal operations of the college would continue, which would include alumni day, exams, and commencement. He concluded with a heartfelt prayer for those who lost sons and daughters in the violence.

Kendig's writings, as he steered the college through troubling times, indicate a firm commitment to democracy and its republican virtues—civility, moderation, restraint, loyalty to country, and service to others—and he was aided in part by the college's distance from the flash points of 1960s turbulence, as well as by the conservatism of Virginia, which many Roanoke College students and faculty called home. He also commended a humane philosophy of life in a winsomely avuncular way to a student generation that

18. Kendig, "Some Thoughts," 9. He gave this unpublished address shortly after the Kent State violence in the spring of 1970.

19. Kendig, "Remarks to Faculty and Students," May 8, 1970, unpublished manuscript, 2.

was less and less trusting of its elders. He inserted Christian themes into his talks on the need for democracy and a philosophy of life, but they resembled grace notes rather than independent themes themselves.

However, like the presidents before him, Kendig affirmed the college's relationship to the Lutheran church; he even desired to strengthen that relationship. Under his leadership the college established the Office of Church Relations in 1975. Yet, in all his writings and speeches there was scarcely a trace of any Lutheran themes or ideas. This is not at all surprising, considering that the college always insisted on being "broadly Christian" and that even those presidents who were trained in Lutheran theology rarely if ever expressed Lutheran notions in their speeches or writings. Furthermore, unlike his clergy predecessors, Kendig had not been formally educated in Lutheran theology.

Statement of Purpose

The statement of purpose written by the faculty under Sherman Oberly in 1963 lasted less than a decade. Another version was adopted by the faculty and the college in 1971, a version that lasted nearly thirty years. The changes featured in the new one were reflected in many ways in the presidential rhetoric.[20]

Here is the statement from 1963:

Roanoke College, founded in 1842 as a liberal arts college, is dedicated to training men and women in high standards of scholarship in the arts and sciences, and developing in every way possible the individual's intellectual ability. The College seeks to give the student a broad competency in a field of specialization and an understanding of the essential components of his own and other cultures. At the same time it is interested in having the individual become proficient in the disciplines necessary to his social, moral, and economic well-being.

In a Christian atmosphere, it strives to foster in each student an emotional maturity and to endow him with high ideals so that with his

20. As I have observed in previous chapters, the newly elected presidents of the college seem to size up the current sense of mission of the college and adapt to it. Of course, they project idealistic rhetoric and can at times sketch out a new direction, but for the most part they adapt to the sense of mission that is already extant.

superior education and his understanding and appreciation of the heritage of scholarship he may assume his responsibility in the contemporary world.[21]

This is the statement from 1971:

Roanoke College is dedicated to educating men and women in high standards of scholarship and in creativity in the arts and sciences. It seeks to give students a broad understanding of their own and other cultures and competency in a field of specialization. It also recognizes a responsibility to serve its community.

The College believes it can serve a free society by developing in students a capacity for responsible leadership. It seeks to achieve this purpose through the intellectual, emotional, spiritual, and practical aspects of a liberal arts education. It strives to provide its students with the knowledge, skills, and adaptability needed for the successful pursuit of their careers.

Roanoke is a small college with a concerned and dedicated faculty, nurturing sensitivity, maturity, and a life-long love of learning. It honors its Christian heritage and its founding by Lutherans in 1842, while welcoming and reflecting a variety of religious traditions.

The latter statement was supplemented in the catalogues with a section on "How It All Began and Why It Continues," which featured a brief history and description of the college. It claimed its affiliation with the Lutheran Church in America but assured the reader that, "never sectarian in its outlook, the college admits students of any race, color, religion, national and ethnic origin, or sex to all the rights, privileges, programs, and activities generally accorded or made available to students at the college." That was followed by its nondiscrimination policies, which included nondiscrimination on the grounds of religion. This latter policy was fateful, because it was later interpreted by the board to nullify the requirement that anyone—including the president of the college—be a Lutheran or Christian for any position.

Throughout Kendig's time as president, the statement underwent various small changes. For several years the purpose statement did not appear in the college catalogue at all; in other years the statement was paraphrased. In Kendig's final year, 1974–75, the college statement assured the reader that

21. *Roanoke College Catalogue* (1962–63).

"Christian experience is available."[22] But "Christian atmosphere" was no longer claimed. Yet there was much continuity in the statements, including the college's commitment to "high standards of scholarship" in the arts and sciences; to understanding the student's own and other cultures; to educating the whole person; and to providing the specialization of a major.

The traditional republican concerns of the college were evident in its pledge to train students for responsible leadership to serve a free society. The college continued to aim at moral formation: high ideals, maturity, sensitivity, responsibility. The basic gist of this statement of purpose lasted nearly thirty years, before it was changed (in 2000) under pressure from the college's accrediting agency.

Clearly, a distinct weakening of the college's Christian claims had occurred in the 1971 version.[23] It no longer claimed to provide a "Christian atmosphere" that morally shaped the student. Rather, it "honors its Christian heritage and founding by Lutherans," which can mean almost anything, from that historical statement alone to something far more ambitious. We shall see presently which intention prevailed.

Curriculum and Faculty

If the foregoing indicated what the president and the college thought they were doing as a college, how did its curriculum bear that out? While it would be tedious to indicate all the curricular changes in each of Kendig's eleven years as president, it is important to note the major changes over those years. The changes were dramatic, and they reflected the great changes in the college and the country.

22. *Roanoke College Catalogue* (1974–75), 3.

23. One can see this weakening when comparing the 1971 statement with the ancillary statements the college made in the 1963 version right after the purpose statement. There the college declared that it "believes that ideal education consists of intellectual development in a Christian atmosphere" (*Roanoke College Catalogue* [1963–64], 7). Likewise, in most of the catalogues during Kendig's presidency, he had a "Personal Word" that introduced the catalogue. In the early years (1963–69) Kendig made a direct claim: "This is a Christian college with an honor code. Here the student is expected to grapple with ideas about God and religion and personal honor and integrity." In the 1974–75 *Roanoke College Catalogue*, Kendig's final "Personal Word" makes no reference to religious themes or issues. There was no longer any claim that Roanoke was a "Christian college." Furthermore, the rhetoric about an ideal education was gone and was replaced by the assurance that the college was "proud of its distinguished heritage as America's second-oldest Lutheran college" (8).

There was a veritable "curricular revolution" during 1968–69, which then issued in a new curriculum described in the 1969–70 catalogue. In brief, it was a sharp shift from a prescribed core curriculum to one of choice within various areas—a "distribution" approach. The former approach had required 69–76 hours (out of 124) in various subject matters, including the Reading Course in philosophy and the comparative religion and Judeo-Christian heritage courses in religion. The curriculum was heavy on math, the natural sciences (two full-year lab courses), and English (four courses), with a fair number of choices in the social sciences (six total courses).

After the revolution, the 1969–70 catalogue listed only two required courses: a composition and a literature course in English. Beyond those two courses, two courses were required out of an array of courses in each of a number of areas: science and math, social studies, humanities, and one from the new interdisciplinary courses. Students could choose which courses they wished to take. (In 1969–70, the reading course was listed among those interdisciplinary options; by the next year that course was gone, but a number of new ones were available.)

The big losers were the natural sciences, which were reduced from two year-long lab courses in two different sciences to two one-semester lab courses in two different sciences; English, reduced from four to two courses; the Reading Course; and religion, which lost two required courses. Religion and philosophy courses became optional: they were now choices within the humanities area. This was an important departure from the Roanoke pattern of requiring two courses in religion, a pattern that began in 1926 and persisted for nearly fifty years. Before that there were far more required religion courses, as well as a generous number of required ethics courses. After the demise of the Reading Course, which included many readings in philosophy, there were no required courses in philosophy or ethics either. Another loser along the way was the classics major, as well as the battery of courses that made it possible. This was another significant departure from the college's republican tradition. Throughout most of its history, courses in the Greek and Latin language and literature were held to exhibit the kind of virtuous life the college wanted to inculcate. The college had moved far from the time in which David Bittle exclaimed in his inaugural with regard to the presence of so many courses in the classics: "Classical literature is the same as American literature. It commends a virtuous life."[24]

The winners were the social sciences, which could benefit from more

24. See chap. 1 for further information about the role of classics in the early Roanoke.

student choices in their area. From 1969 onward, the college offered a bachelor's degree in business administration, with a hefty number of required courses in its major, along with its bachelor of arts and bachelor of science degrees. In 1973 the faculty also began to offer a short-lived bachelor of liberal arts degree.

By the end of Kendig's administration, the faculty was in charge of defining the mission of the school and involved in shaping its curriculum. However, Dean Edward Lautenschlager, Kendig's academic dean for most of his presidency, was the mover and shaker behind the curricular revolution. His authoritarian leadership, though, cost him dearly with faculty members. Fewer members of the faculty had received their undergraduate degrees from Roanoke, diminishing from about 25 percent to 10 percent in that same time frame. Likewise, the number of Lutheran faculty members dropped, though no formal count was kept of that statistic.[25] The administration, however, did continue to be dominated by Lutherans: the president, the academic dean, and the business manager were members of the Lutheran Church in America. The president was still required by the college's bylaws to be a Lutheran. However, as I have suggested above, there was little in the president's rhetoric or approach that signaled Lutheran convictions. And the Christian themes articulated tended to be generically Christian.

The new faculty members who had PhDs were also more specialized and less likely to have come from small church-related, liberal arts colleges. Therefore, they were less likely to be able to agree on a common core of required learnings and more likely to develop a curriculum featuring student choices from among several fields—a so-called distribution system. They were also less likely to even know about the inherited Christian republican tradition of the college, let alone support it. The biblical and republican strands that had shaped the college were no longer passed on by "affinity" from one faculty generation to the next.

Reports on what "Christian" requirements were exercised in selecting faculty and staff are varied. President Kendig asked one key staff member in his job interview: "Do you believe in God?" The president was content when he received a positive response. Others reported that the dean or president asked what church they attended. In the early 1970s, a woman applicant for

---

25. The fact that no count of Lutheran faculty was kept is quite revealing. It meant that the Lutheran vision and ethos—which could be borne best by observant Lutherans—was not publicly relevant to the educational life of the college. The college continued to hire mostly Christians in general, but in an undisciplined and informal manner.

a position in the psychology department was reported to have retorted to that query: "I don't go to church." She was hired anyway. A faculty member who *was* Lutheran recalled that he was never asked about his church membership or his beliefs. A significant portion of the faculty was indifferent, if not negative, toward the faith's role in the college and toward the college's connection with the Lutheran church. The old assumption that the college and faculty were Christian was breaking down.

In addition, by the mid-1970s a number of faculty members had been much affected by having pursued their graduate degrees in the 1960s, a time when the academy was much politicized. The rather conservative political and cultural consensus of the older faculty and administration—deeply conditioned by the Depression and World War II—was now mixed with those who were far more skeptical about America's virtue and its benevolent role in the world. The "hermeneutic of suspicion" that arose in the 1960s and sharply questioned all inherited tradition became something of a serious challenge to Roanoke's Christian republicanism. At the very least, it broke up any consensus on that tradition.

The Philosophy and Religion Department

The philosophy and religion department entered the Kendig years with three members: James Rikard was chairman and taught the Reading Course as well as courses in religion and philosophy; Guy Ritter taught mostly in religion; and Roy Bent taught mostly in philosophy.[26] None of them had doctorates and thus were handicapped for leadership roles. They were assisted by the new chaplain, John Keister, who arrived in 1963. Courses in philosophy were many and varied, which continued a Roanoke tradition: many courses and a major in philosophy; few courses and no major in religion (though two courses in religion had long been required of all students). The courses in philosophy were often permeated by religious concerns, so that for many years students grappled with serious religious issues in philosophy courses. The two-course religion requirement had changed in 1963–64, from a course in Old Testament and one in New Testament to a course in the Judeo-Christian heritage and one in comparative religion.

The department not only lost its two required courses in the new cur-

---

26. For more detailed sketches of these members of the department, see notes in the preceding chapter.

riculum of 1969–70; it also lost the Reading Course, for which it had taken major responsibility. In 1972, James Rikard retired from full-time teaching, and V. Truman Jordahl came to Roanoke as the new chair of the department of philosophy and religion with the rank of associate professor. Jordahl was a Midwestern Lutheran who had a bachelor's degree from Luther College, a strongly ethnic Lutheran college, a bachelor of divinity degree from Luther Seminary in St. Paul, and a PhD from Durham University in England. Up to that point he was the best-credentialed religion professor the department had ever had. He soon increased the number and variety of religion courses to match those of the philosophy side of the department, and initiated a major in religion. Courses with a Lutheran flair were introduced: "The Reformation," "Life and Teachings of Jesus," "Life and Teachings of Paul," "Contemporary Religious Thought," and "Issues in Christian Behavior." Jordahl was also instrumental in getting the bachelor-of-liberal arts track adopted by the faculty. Brian Hinshaw, a graduate of Lenoir Rhyne College and Southern Lutheran Seminary, helped to teach the new courses during the years between 1969 and 1974. For the first time in Roanoke College history, religion courses straightforwardly incorporated Lutheran history, themes, and ideas. This remarkable change was no doubt facilitated by Jordahl, who was the product of a more heavily Lutheran education and environment. The loss of required courses was partly compensated for by the introduction of many more religion courses and a religion major.

Two members of the philosophy and religion department (Bent and Hinshaw) joined the politically active students in protesting the Vietnam War and were identified with the student protest movement in general. But the other two members (Ritter and Jordahl) were strong conservatives who deplored the protests.

College Governance

The Roanoke College board of trustees during the Kendig years was dominated by wealthy and influential officers of major corporations, a pattern that was begun during the Oberly administration (1949–63). They were generous in their giving to the college, on the one hand, but they exercised fiscal restraint, on the other, ensuring that Roanoke would continue to run a balanced budget. They did not feel comfortable deliberating about the religious mission of the college. Though they refrained from micromanaging college affairs, they exercised formidable power over its major business decisions.

Another pattern established in the Oberly administration persisted throughout Kendig's: by tradition, the board of trustees included three Lutheran pastors. One was the president of the Virginia Synod, and the two others were distinguished pastors of large Virginia Synod churches. But, by all accounts, the clergy were rather quiet in the presence of powerful, executive-type businessmen. There were few wealthy Lutheran, and therefore influential, laymen on the board.

The college signed a new covenant with the Virginia Synod in 1970: "Both the college and the church pledged their mutual support and respect and hoped to work more closely together in the future."[27] A church-relations office was established by the college in 1975 as a product of the covenant. It focused on increasing college hospitality to synod functions and on sending college faculty and administrators to appear in local parishes.

The 125th Anniversary of the College's Founding

During the 1967–68 academic year the college celebrated its 125th birthday. In contrast to other such milestones, which featured days of celebration with speeches by dignitaries, music by bands, orations by students and faculty, worship services, and festivities with the townspeople of Salem and Roanoke, the college this time elected to have a year-long series of lectures by well-known scholars, an impressive array that featured the poet Richard Wilbur, the political philosopher Hans Morgenthau, the historian Daniel Boorstin, and theologians Harvey Cox, Thomas Altizer, and Jerald Brauer. The selection of theologians indicated something of a fascination with the "new" that had emerged in many fields during the 1960s. Harvey Cox had recently published *The Secular City*, something of a smash hit of that era, which argued that God's work is primarily this-worldly and of a distinctly political stamp. Religion that was church-centered and concerned with individual salvation was obsolete. Thomas Altizer was a notorious leader in the "God is dead" movement, which radically reduced religion to ethics. Both represented a departure from traditional Christian claims about Jesus and his mission in the world, titillating the minority of progressives and disturbing the traditionalists in the town-and-gown audience. Jerald Brauer, dean of the Divinity School of the University of Chicago and a noted Lutheran

27. Miller, *Dear Old Roanoke*, 262.

historian of American religion, no doubt offered a more detached analysis of the current role of religion in a turbulent America.

Ethos

It was the college's way of life—its ethos—that underwent the most noticeable changes during the Kendig years. I have listed many of the changes in the introduction to this chapter, but let us take another look. The sharpest change was precipitated by the college dropping nearly all of its *in loco parentis* rules and regulations. Students arriving at the college in the mid-1960s pressed hard for the elimination of the whole battery of those binding rules. In a brief period of time the college set student life free from the constraints that had long followed from its Christian republican tradition. It engaged in one grand experiment to determine what unregulated student life might look like. The effects of that experiment were to be felt for more than a decade.

The honors code, the dorm rules, and the dress codes disappeared. (The college even had a plague of "streakers" in 1974—naked males running in public places.) But perhaps the most damaging to student life was the surge in alcohol and drug use. Nancy Mulheren, a student of that era—and subsequently a great benefactor and board leader of the college—said this about her time there (1968–72): "When I entered Roanoke as a freshman in 1968, there was considerable drinking, but mostly beer and mostly on weekends. There was still a good family atmosphere. By my senior year, however, more drugs and heavier drinking became prevalent."[28] Another student of the time remembered that by 1970 the younger lower classmen were more deeply into drug and alcohol usage than were the upperclassmen.[29]

The change in atmosphere from an absolute prohibition of the use of alcohol on campus in 1963 to selling beer in the student center, not only for off-campus consumption but also for on-campus use in 1968–69, was quite a transformation. The text of the 1973–74 catalogue states that "the college does not encourage alcohol use," but then acknowledges that beer was for sale in the Cavern (the student canteen) and that it could be consumed in the dorms and at public parties.[30] The college did prohibit the use of any drugs,

28. Nancy Mulheren, quoted in Keller, *Prologue*, 31.
29. Conversation with Macmillan Johnson ('70), who later became Roanoke College's vice president for student affairs (Aug. 1, 2014).
30. *Roanoke College Catalogue* (1973–74), 24.

but that prohibition was widely ignored. The same catalogue calls for "high standards of ethical conduct and a wholesome moral atmosphere"—but offers no specific rules to reinforce those qualities.

Another serious loss was the student orientation system for incoming freshmen. Though somewhat puerile, it had been completely run by upperclassmen, who demanded a certain level of manners from the younger students, and also required them to memorize a passage on the college's history from the student handbook. It had provided a socialization into the life of the school by the students themselves. That element of student self-government disappeared, never to be regained.

The deterioration of student life was reflected in the number and quality of students that the college was able to recruit during President Kendig's years. After gradual increases from 1963 (813 full-time equivalents) to 1972 (1,216 full-time equivalents), the enrollment of the college gradually declined for six years until 1978, when it again registered over 1,200 students and stayed in that range until 1984. With respect to quality, the student SAT scores began to fall from the 1100s in the early 1970s to the 1000s between 1973 and 1987. In terms of the average high-school rank of entering freshmen, the average fell from a typical student being in roughly the top 35 percent of his or her class in the early 1970s to being in roughly the top 45 percent in the ensuing years (1975–87).[31] The upheavals of the mid-1970s had effects on student quality that lingered into the mid-1980s.

Not surprisingly, religious life on campus contracted during that time.[32] The loss of required once-a-week chapel in 1967 was replaced by a Sunday morning service led by the chaplain. The chaplain also introduced a number of other worship services and religious retreats and conferences. The number and quality of pretheological students declined. Though the chaplain tried hard to expand and deepen the religious life of the student body, it was peripheral to the college's social life (and was "practiced lightly"); it was a concern of the "God squad," a small portion of the stu-

31. It is significant that three of the persons—Sutton, Johnson, and Nancy Mulheren—who were at Roanoke College between 1968 and 1972 all estimated a change for the worse in student behavior from 1972 on. The statistics for the period come from the Office of Institutional Research of Roanoke College. However, the interpretation is my own.

32. About one-third of the incoming students in 1975 failed to respond or indicated no preference to the question concerning their denominational affiliation. The high percentage who answered that way in the mid-1970s was never reached again in subsequent years, even now in the era of the "nones."

dent body.[33] The catalogue of 1973–74 calls for "spiritual development" on the part of students and notes that courses in religion are available.

A new chapel, Antrim Memorial, was dedicated in 1971. A lovely and striking building, its size indicated what role religion was projected to play in the present and future life of the college. Its seating capacity was at most 350, roughly a quarter of the student body, which indicated that the planners had no expectation that the majority of the student body and faculty would ever worship together or that the chapel could be the location for a baccalaureate ceremony.

Of course, the *political* turbulence of the 1960s affected Roanoke College, but lately and mildly. Though a number of polarizing political personages appeared on campus—Spiro Agnew and George Wallace on the right, and "political theologians" Harvey Cox and Thomas Altizer on the left—and there was an attempt to bring the school to a halt in the moratorium of May 1970, the college did not experience severe disruption. President Kendig worried about polarization (see his speech on that topic above), but the student body was fairly balanced. There was a fringe of (politically and culturally) radical students on the left but also a faction of "hard-hat patriots" on the right. But most students were in the "fun-loving, apolitical middle."[34]

A gradual but important change in this era was the withdrawal of faculty members from involvement in student life. As the faculty professionalized, members did not see their role as participants in and monitors of student social life. They, like the college, abjured their *in loco parentis* role. Moreover, as the students got more rambunctious, a natural response of more mature faculty was to distance themselves from such frivolities. This vacuum was filled by student-life personnel, whose professional role was to try to manage the life of the students.

Conclusion

One of the most potent signals of change in the Christian republican mission of the college is conveyed by the change in President Kendig's religious rhetoric from the 1968–69 college catalogue to the catalogue of 1973–74, his last year as president. In the 1968–69 catalogue, Kendig still refers to the college as "a Christian college where students are expected to wrestle with

33. Interview of Macmillan Johnson, Aug. 1, 2014.
34. Interviews of Donald Sutton and Macmillan Johnson.

the idea of God and religion." However, by the 1973–74 catalogue, all religious rhetoric is absent from his "Personal Word." This significant shift was probably less an indication of change in Kendig's own convictions than in his assessment of where the faculty and the college were on the matter.[35] He sensed that the Christian base of the republican mission of the college was no longer affirmed by a consensus of the faculty or the trustees. Therefore, it would be discomforting—and dishonest—to speak any longer of Roanoke College being a Christian college.

Why this loss of consensus on the Christian base of the republican project? It had to do essentially with the fact that the college *assumed* that it would have a sufficient number of solid Christians in the faculty to supply the Christian base for the republican mission.[36] It did not take pains to define its mission as a Christian college carefully enough and then to hire for mission in a disciplined fashion. It needed to hire at least a critical mass of strongly committed Christian faculty to provide the Christian base for its traditional mission. But it failed to do that. Instead, faculty members were hired for their professional credentials rather than for their loyalty to the traditional mission of the college.

After some time, the number of "nay-sayers" in the faculty ranks grew. There were those who were hostile toward religion in general; there were those who were simply apathetic and wanted to be left alone with regard to religious matters; there were those who, even if they were religious, did not see any relevance of religion to the college's educational task; there were those who were appalled by the laxity of student behavior and didn't think the college could honestly call itself "Christian"; and there were those who were friendly toward the traditional role that Christianity played in the life and mission of the college. But there was enough pluralism to prevent any further claim that the college was "Christian."

A similar fate met the "republican" part of the college's traditional mission, but not in the same way. The idea that a main purpose of the college was to supply virtuous students for a civilizational role in the American republic was shattered more by the surrounding ethos of the 1960s than by a failure of

35. I have noted in earlier chapters that Roanoke College presidents after the founder, David Bittle, tended to assess and then follow the sense of the faculty with regard to the mission of the college rather than to try to change it.

36. It has been stunning to me how many Roanoke College people—administrators, faculty, former students—said that the college "simply assumed" its Christian nature; it did not define it carefully nor publicly speak of or advocate it. It was a background assumption until it wasn't. "Assuming" slowly had become "forgetting."

the college to state its mission and then hire for it. The college still insisted that it was producing students "to better assume their responsibilities in the contemporary world"; but its main focus, instead, was on helping students realize themselves. Thus did the emerging individualism of the 1960s take hold among its faculty and student body.

Furthermore, the earlier assumption of America's innocent and benevolent role in the world was shaken by the turbulence of the 1960s. The liberation movements of that period—social, economic, political, cultural—were fueled by a good deal of suspicion of all traditional authorities, including those of the nation. It would have been almost as difficult for President Kendig to speak of Roanoke as an American college as to refer to it as a Christian college. While only a small segment of the student body was self-consciously radical, the majority was shaken in its confidence in the nation and its role in the world. More significantly, a good portion of the faculty imbibed a more sophisticated skepticism. Though a number of conservative faculty were still there, no real consensus was possible on the worthiness of the American project. As Kendig said in his message to the college during the 1970 moratorium: "I cannot speak on national policy. I can't do this among our own faculty and students, where beliefs vary widely—and no man can speak for everyone."[37]

The college's diminished commitment to its traditional mission issued in a loss of confidence in performing its *in loco parentis* role. Under great duress, it simply set student life free, and the results were not positive. This was typical of many colleges and universities of that time. The tsunami of the student "revolution" was extraordinarily powerful and accounts for how and why a college led by upstanding, military-shaped, morally strict Christian men could preside over such a transition.

Certainly the college did not collapse: there were many fine faculty members and students. Achievement went on. But the college was wounded in both its quality and its soul.

37. Kendig, unpublished remarks of May 8, 1970, Roanoke College archives.

7

NORMAN FINTEL (1975–1989)

Launching a Recovery

When Perry Kendig, the seventh president of Roanoke College, announced his intention to retire in the fall of 1973, the college searched for a year and a half for Norman Fintel. And what they found was someone quite different from any president up to that point: a Midwestern Lutheran from an ethnic German Nebraska culture who was used to dealing with robust Lutheran educational institutions. Fintel was the first Lutheran president who was not from the South or East, and he made quite a difference. This chapter charts that difference. Its subtitle indicates a "launch," a set of new initiatives that at the same time "recovered," at least to some extent, something older: the classic purposes of the college, albeit clad in new attire. The launch initiatives also added a new ingredient to the old, the desire to become officially recognized as a regional—then national—liberal arts college of excellence. That purpose was begun in the Fintel years, but it was realized in administrations that came after him. In fact, the new ingredient—national recognition as an excellent liberal arts college—became an important new ambition of the college, though its commitment to its Christian republican mission was continued in a new way.

By the time of Fintel's arrival in 1975, the college was experiencing its own version of the malaise of the 1970s. It had a worrisome drop in enrollment and a decline in student quality, due in part to the unruly student life that was set off by releasing students from almost all constraints. To counter the drop in enrollment, the college indulged in very high acceptance rates. It was led by a generation of leaders who were near retirement and were exhausted by the challenges of the 1960s. Its faculty was by now diverse, no longer unified in a commitment to its historic purposes of Christian re-publicanism, which meant a commitment to form students from all walks of life into virtuous citizens for the republic. The college believed that such formation was based most effectively on a Christian religious and moral foundation. The Christian foundation was always broad, encompassing many Christian traditions, though under the leadership of ecumenically minded Lutherans. Such formation in virtue also provided leaders for the church. The assumption that a critical mass of observant Christians made up the faculty no longer held; by this time, many faculty members would bridle at the college's being called "Christian." Moreover, the 1960s had brought forth professors who were skeptical about the character and role of the American republic itself. The college's commitment to providing citizens for that re-public seemed time-worn, if not retrograde.

Furthermore, the 1970s were a time of political and economic uncer-tainty. In many ways, the story of the college tracked that of the nation as a whole. Politically, the Vietnam War wound down, and the election of Rich-ard Nixon had returned the country to conservative governance. But the sta-bility that seemed to bring was quickly dashed by the Watergate scandals and Nixon's resignation in 1973. Jimmy Carter's election in 1976 promised a new beginning but was soon shattered by the resurgence of the Soviet Union and the emergence of Communist agitation in other places of the world. America seemed to be weak, and it was difficult to drum up patriotic commitment to its purposes. To add to that malaise, Carter presided over the deadly combi-nation of inflation and economic stagnation. "Retrenchment" was a key word of the time, both politically and economically. These new conditions served to dampen the political and economic impulses of the 1960s.

What did not abate was the cultural revolution touched off by the 1960s.[1] The 1970s mainstreamed what had been initiated by a revolutionary mi-nority in the 1960s. Above all, the feminist movement gained strength and penetrated all institutions, opening them up to the participation of women, as well as to feminist perspectives. After the cooling of the more extreme agitations of Black Power, the country settled down to include blacks into its institutions through affirmative action. The movement for "diversity" gained momentum. The huge change in sexual morality initiated in the 1960s con-

---

1. As I have argued earlier, the 1960s were really the decade of 1965–75. The sixties before 1965 were characterized by "liberal idealism." After the escalation of the Vietnam War in 1965, the liberal confidence in reform turned into a more revolutionary posture that had powerful political, economic, and cultural effects. The upheaval lasted until the mid-1970s.

tinued and expanded into the 1970s. Gay liberation made gains. Popular culture became suffused with sexual excitation. Music, dress, and generational interactions were altered. The "counterculture" of the 1960s, shorn of its excesses, was absorbed into the larger culture.

If the travail of the college matched that of American society of the 1970s, the college also seemed to awaken with the renewed vigor of the 1980s. That is the main story of the Fintel administration; it was pivotal.

Ronald Reagan was elected for his first term in 1980 and proceeded to inject strength and optimism into American political life. After some economic difficulties in the early 1980s, the Reagan administration was able to free the economic engine of America for a remarkable and lengthy expansion. The mid-to-late 1980s featured widespread economic growth. Even the cultural revolution was quieted a bit, though certainly not extinguished. Social and cultural conservatism made something of a comeback with a conservative President in the White House and a number of popular initiatives, such as the Moral Majority, emerging in society.

The Fintel years can be divided into two roughly seven-year phases that mirror those of the larger society. The first seven years were occupied by coping with the aftershocks of the 1960s and the malaise of the 1970s, which lasted into the early years of the 1980s decade. The last seven years were characterized by a vigorous renewal of the college and its mission—as well as its new ambition to become a nationally ranked college—that persisted long after Fintel's departure in 1989.

The Formation of Norman Fintel

Norman Fintel was born in 1925 in California during his family's brief sojourn there. His father and mother had left Nebraska to find a better life in the West; but, after a short time driving a taxi in Monrovia, California, and finding only disappointment in work possibilities there, the elder Fintel returned the family to Nebraska, where he ran a pool hall in the town of Byron, near the Kansas border. Shortly thereafter, in 1928, Grandfather Fintel asked Norman's father to farm several of the eight farms that he had acquired over the years. The grandfather had immigrated in 1888 at the tender age of fourteen to the southern Nebraska farmland near the town of Deshler. He had obviously found the land to be "sweet and good."

Young Norman was brought up in a staunch German Lutheran tradition that emphasized hard work and a quiet piety. Regular Sunday school and church attendance were a must. He went to a one-room country school for four years, and then to a Lutheran parochial school for another four. Confirmation followed strict instruction in Luther's Catechism. Participation in Luther League not only offered some leadership training but also awakened a sense that he should lead a life of service, perhaps even in the ordained ministry. Off he went to Deshler High, where he excelled as a student and continued to work hard for his father. As a member of the Great Generation, he graduated from high school in 1943, right in the middle of World War II. After a brief deferment to help his father and grandfather with the harvests in the fall of 1943, he volunteered for the Army Air Corps early in 1944. He trained to be a navigator on a bomber, but the war ended before he got into advanced training.

Mustered out of the service when the war ended, he attended the University of Nebraska in 1946, but he had little sense of direction. As a lark, he entered a contest to win an airplane and, to his great surprise, he won it. He worked in 1947 as an aircraft engine mechanic while he flew around the region in his plane. In one of his trips he stopped to see his old high school football coach, who was by then teaching at Wartburg College in Waverly, Iowa. In a lively conversation between the two, the coach recommended strongly that Norman come to study at Wartburg. He followed the coach's advice and spent the next four years at Wartburg, graduating in 1951. He continued to plan to enter the ordained ministry for a "life of service," but that call was intercepted by a request from the college to become its director of admissions and public relations, and he spent nine successful years in that role.

Between the eighth and ninth years as admissions director, he spent a year earning a master's degree in educational administration from the University of Wisconsin at Madison. After returning to Wartburg for a year, he was called in 1960 to be an assistant to the American Lutheran Church's executive director of the Division of College and University Work. When the director, Sidney Rand, became president of St. Olaf College in 1964, Fintel became executive director. He spent the next ten years overseeing, coordinating, and instructing the seventeen schools—colleges, junior colleges, and high schools—that made up the American Lutheran Church's educational system. The many challenges that those schools experienced led him to organize and conduct management audits in all the schools, as well as in other church-related institutions. He had a hand in keeping those institutions solvent and faithful to their Christian mission. Along the way he received a PhD from the University of Minnesota in education administration, and during those years he found that his "life of service" would be focused on higher education. After fifteen years in that administrative position in the American Lutheran Church's national office, he was called to Roanoke College.

There are three important elements in Norman Fintel's formation that were crucial for his work at Roanoke. First, he had a strong formation in a "thicker" and more defined Lutheranism than that of his immediate two predecessors, Oberly and Kendig. Midwestern ethnic Lutheranism of a German, Swedish, or Norwegian stripe preserved its confessional identity and sensibilities more than did the Eastern Lutheran traditions, partly because ethnic insulation slowed down their accommodation to American culture and religion. Their people had immigrated to the Midwest in the late nineteenth and early twentieth centuries. Midwestern Lutheran churches of those traditions not only kept Lutheran doctrine intact, but they permeated their many institutions with their ethnic ethos and familial networks. This was in contrast to Southeastern Lutheranism, whose forebears had been in America since the eighteenth century. And, as we have seen in earlier chapters, that Lutheranism had accommodated to American religion, first to the evangelicalism of the Second Great Awakening of the nineteenth century and then to the generic Protestantism of the twentieth century. Fintel came to Roanoke deeply embedded in the Midwestern ethnic Lutheranism.[2]

A second important element that prepared Fintel for his Roanoke presidency was his deep immersion in Christian higher education; no other Ro-

---

2. Midwestern Lutheranism itself featured both the ethnic and "Eastern" varieties. The United Lutheran Church of America (1918–62) represented the latter. Based in Philadelphia, it was strongly affected by generic American Protestantism. The ULCA, the largest of the Lutheran bodies, claimed many members from the East—especially Pennsylvania—who had migrated to the West. It also gathered and churched many immigrants who wanted to become fully American faster than was offered by the ethnically based churches. Their churches were often called "English Lutheran," to distinguish themselves from the ethnic varieties. (Those laymen who wanted to become Masons were even more attracted to the ULCA, which allowed its members to join fraternal lodges.) The ULCA churches were also affected more by the religion of the frontier, especially Methodism, with its emphasis on temperance, moral probity, and enthusiasm for gospel hymns and songs. I grew up in a ULCA church in Nebraska, which featured the characteristics just mentioned. That contrasted with the ethnically based Missouri Synod (German) and Augustana Synod (Swedish) churches of our region, and with the American Lutheran Church (German) in which Fintel grew up. Like the "Eastern" Lutherans of Virginia, we in the ULCA never worshiped in or spoke German, and we had Communion with grape juice because of our affinity with the temperance emphases of the religion of the frontier. But both strands of Lutheranism had their periods of vigorous growth up to 1965, which was the high point of membership in mainstream Protestantism in the United States.

anoke president had had such a depth and breadth of exposure to Lutheran higher education as had Fintel. Some Roanoke presidents had served as deans or faculty members at Roanoke or other Lutheran colleges before- hand, but Fintel not only had long exposure to a robust Lutheran college, Wartburg, but also extended dealings with the seventeen different educa- tional institutions of the American Lutheran Church.[3] He knew what the strong version of Lutheran higher education was all about. This gave him the ability to assess where Roanoke was on the continuum between the poles of full-orbed Christian colleges and those en route to secularization. His background also gave him clues as to what was needed to strengthen the Lutheran character of the college.

A third important element in Fintel's preparation for his work at Ro- anoke was his experience in the "management audits" in which he shared as executive director of the Division of College and University Work. Like Roanoke College in the early 1970s, some of the ALC colleges he worked with met serious economic challenges during that period, which not only threatened their continuing existence but also their mission as colleges of the church. Fintel assembled a team that visited all the ALC schools, scrutinized their management and planning practices, and guided them in strengthening those capacities. This ambitious project had absorbed a good deal of his time and energy, but it brought significant beneficial effects to the colleges of the ALC as it strengthened his own managerial capacities.

This extensive involvement in the "management audits" also inspired Norman Fintel and his wife, "Jo," to resolve that, when he accepted the presidency of Roanoke College, it would be a team effort. They had had enough of Norman being away; now was the time for the two of them to act in concert. Norman and Jeanette ("Jo") Kosbau had wed in 1953 and had three children who were nearly "out of the nest" when they embarked on

3. The colleges of the old American Lutheran Church (1930–60, then the "new ALC," 1960–87) were called "colleges of the church" rather than "church-related colleges," as the Lutheran Church in America named them. This subtle difference in nomenclature actu- ally represented a significant difference: the ALC schools were more closely related to the church and its mission. They were also more ethnic in makeup. Thus, they had a more robust Lutheran identity than their LCA counterparts. By "robust," I mean a higher percentage of Lutheran faculty and students, more courses in Lutheran studies, more required chapel, and a more overt appreciation of their ethnic Lutheran heritage. The colleges associated with the LCA (1960–87), whose major predecessor was the United Lutheran Church in America (see note 2), were more generically Protestant and less robust in the sense described above. They tended to secularize earlier than the ALC schools.

the leadership of Roanoke. Fintel insisted that their presidency would be a 49/51 percent effort, with the small edge going to Jo. The two of them were deeply involved in hospitality to the students, the extension of meaningful connections to Roanoke and Salem leaders, and service to the community. Jo was also strongly influential in personnel decisions: candidates had to pass muster with her.

The Fintel Vision for Roanoke College

Given his dealings with many robust Lutheran colleges of the Midwest, one might expect Fintel to offer an explicitly Lutheran vision for Roanoke College; but that was not to be. Indeed, presidents who could have done such—Morehead and Smith, for example—refrained from that kind of approach, mainly because they perceived that they were coming to a college with an established identity that was not distinctively Lutheran. Fintel was no different. But he did articulate a vision that resonated with the historic Christian republicanism of the college, albeit in somewhat muted form.

Inaugural Address

Fintel gave his inaugural address at the commencement ceremonies on April 23, 1976, at the end of his first year, which had become a Roanoke tradition. The address was entitled, oddly, "The Valley Waits," which was a pretext for elaborating on his main theme—leadership. The title came from a book by T. F. Gullixson, a writer who marveled at the great valleys of the Midwestern rivers—Ohio, Missouri, Mississippi—and anticipated how they would develop under the stewardship of good leaders. Fintel saw an analogy in the Roanoke Valley, which needed good leadership as well.

He asked rhetorically: What could he and Roanoke College do to supply quality leadership to the valley and beyond? After all, "in some mysterious and awesome way we have been created by a power we cannot fully understand, yet we are held accountable for what we are and how we use our resources in the valleys of our lives."[4] Drawing on his experience in observing and helping to manage colleges, he argued that effective colleges have a clear

4. "The Valley Waits," unpublished inaugural address by Norman Fintel (Apr. 23, 1976), in the Roanoke College archives, 2. All the following quotes are from this inaugural address.

NORMAN FINTEL (1975–1989)

sense of mission. Those colleges are then able to organize their programs and hiring policies in alignment with that mission. They also engage in effective planning because they know what their goals are. But they must have an attitude "in which planning is a natural part of doing."[5]

A second thing he drew from his experience of dealing with other colleges: they all intend to provide leaders for society. He then quoted words from the founding of Harvard: "The college will train the schoolmasters, the divines, the rulers, the cultured ornaments of society—the men who will spell the difference between civilization and barbarism."

He then emphasized that leadership is for the sake of service to others, not for personal gain or even institutional status. He lamented that all "have sinned and fallen from our purposes and missions," but we need not wallow in our shortcomings. He said that we have to regain moral fiber so that we live and work for others.

What drew him to Roanoke was the opportunity to share his commitment to transmitting the value of service to a new generation, as well as the managerial capacities he had recently developed in his last position. The community had already talked about mission and planning, and he was confident that they were in the process of rediscovering the college's mission.

This section of his address was certainly an indirect way to talk about some important Christian—and, more specifically, Lutheran—teachings: that we are stewards of the creation in all its facets; we have vocations that provide ways to serve our neighbors; we tend toward sinful self-serving, but we can bend that selfish impulse outward to the neighbor by the proper kind of leadership. Stewardship, servanthood, vocation, and sin are concepts that lie below the surface of Fintel's text. But he refrained from any explicit articulation of the Lutheran/Christian basis for those teachings, though he later affirmed his own anchoring in the Christian faith as the source of his values. He assumed that the audience could better accept these values in a nonreligious guise. Again, like his predecessors, he did not appeal to Lutheranism as the specific Christian heritage of the college. This, too, was congruent

---

5. Interestingly enough, Fintel did not mention Roanoke's sense of mission or its capacity to plan in his address. In an interview on September 4, 2014, he was asked why he did not talk about those subjects. He responded that he did not mention them because he thought there was little clarity about the mission of the college by the board and the faculty, and therefore little ability to plan effectively. When asked whether the purpose statement outlined a clear definition of mission, he retorted that few paid attention to the purpose statement. Therefore, he had to take up some of its themes—leadership and service on a Christian basis—and give them a new lease on life.

with the "broadly Christian" self-definition of the college; but it certainly indicated a shift from the specific to the general by a person who had been deeply involved in a Christian higher education that proudly trumpeted its Lutheran specificity. This was another example of presidents accommodating to the already extant sense of identity of the college.[6]

Fintel then moved into an explication of "paths to leadership," which included four dimensions—the intellectual, emotional, spiritual, and practical.[7] The content he gave to each category is interesting. By "intellectual," he meant competence in the liberal arts as a whole and in a particular field of knowledge. He also included "problem solving" as a part of competence. Roanoke College would try to nurture intellectual competence in its students so that they might become leaders. By "emotional," he meant growth toward maturity—that is, sensitivity and balance. Though he admitted that hardly any college or university really did this well, he nevertheless thought that emotional maturity was a path to leadership.

The "spiritual" dimension is of particular interest in this inquiry. The Christian college was to stimulate spiritual growth in its students; leadership without this dimension was deficient, but church-related colleges could actually focus on it. Spiritual growth was not fostered by indoctrination but by "confrontation with the full range of ideas and explanations of the realities of life and death" (5). Though contemporary society seemed to focus on science and technology, there was still room for the important questions of "why and how." Fintel said, "There is room for God." These questions were not out of bounds for a college like Roanoke, which had been founded, tended, and attended by many church people as well as members of other faiths. "We must continue to ask the ultimate questions, confident that God is the ultimate reality and that, for those of us who are Christian, he is best represented in the life and witness of Jesus the Christ" (5).[8]

6. This diffidence about speaking in a Lutheran vein was sharply different from Fintel's talks to Lutheran groups, including presidents of Lutheran colleges. There he showed his familiarity with Lutheran themes and their relevance to Christian higher education. So it seemed a self-conscious strategy to talk in more general terms in the Roanoke context.

7. These four dimensions are the same that are listed in the Roanoke College Statement of Purpose, which asserts that imparting these four qualities is an essential part of the college's main purpose: "to serve a free society by developing in students a capacity for responsible leadership" (*Roanoke College Academic Catalogue* [1975–76], 3). This is a clear statement of the historic republican purpose of the college.

8. In his section on the "spiritual dimension" of nurturing leadership, Fintel signaled several interesting things: (1) that he was unabashedly Christian, but that faith was one of a number of options that the college welcomed; (2) that Roanoke stood for inquiry rather

The fourth path to leadership was to equip students with practical skills so they might enter the marketplace: "Without sacrificing the liberal arts, we must find ways to relate what we learn to what we earn" (5). Hence, the college had to marry the liberal to the practical. He then called on the faculty to become models and "catalysts" of these four dimensions. He put a heavy challenge on them: to help themselves "and the student reach the deepest interiority of being and thereby learn about meaning, about life, and about death." Responding to this challenge would be an ongoing and unfinished process for both faculty members and students. They would always be on the way. "Such a person will be a fruitful gardener of all the valleys in his or her life" (5).

Fintel then argued that developing these paths to leadership was not alien to the historic life and mission of Roanoke College. However, that sense of mission had to be sharpened, and commitments to it had to be strengthened. He bowed to the work of his predecessors in general, and particularly to President Emeritus Perry Kendig, but he did not perform obeisance to the great figures of the past—Bittle, Dreher, Morehead, Smith—that his predecessors usually felt obligated to do.[9]

He finished his address by listing his personal commitments: to liberal arts, to competence and quality, to working hard for what he believed, to an education in values (and "in my case to the Christian faith as the fundamental source of values"), to be a servant leader, to flexible management, and to "be himself and honor all others who try to be the same, so that together we may be fruitful and multiply and have dominion over the valleys of our lives that lie waiting for us" (6).

Themes in Other Fintel Writings

Like all Roanoke presidents, Fintel had many occasions to speak publicly. In the next few years of his presidency, he spoke at commencement exercises

---

than indoctrination; (3) that the spiritual dimension of life and leadership was important; (4) that the spiritual dimension had an intellectual aspect—questions of ultimacy about the why and how of all things were important; and (5) that Jesus revealed the way we ought to live for those who are Christian.

9. Perhaps Fintel did not yet feel part of that grand tradition of presidents. He was new to the college and especially to the region—its history and ethos. It would take a while for a Midwestern German-American Lutheran to identify with the Southern tradition of the college. Besides that, a certain humility might have inhibited such an identification.

and at faculty workshops. In his talks he distilled his inaugural address to two themes: competence and conscience. He praised the college's achievement in competence, but he summoned it to more work on conscience. He said, "We cannot teach morality or intelligence or wisdom per se, but we can raise value questions—Is it right? Is it true? Is it just and is it fair for my neighbor?"[10]

The graduates of 1977, he believed, would be graduating into a new kind of context, one in which there were limits to external growth. But this simply meant that growth could become inward, a "new frontier where the mind and soul of humankind can grow to a new flowering unknown and almost unthinkable to our present generation."[11] Over and over in his later addresses, Fintel called for servant leadership, stronger formation in moral values, and developing strong leaders for a society beset by many challenges.

At the end of his tenure in 1989, he had the opportunity to reflect on the previous fourteen years in his last commencement address. He reiterated the commitments he made in 1976 in somewhat revised form: that a liberal arts education was the best way to educate for life; that competence had to be wedded to conscience; that conscience was formed by strong values, which to him were grounded in the Christian faith; that servant leadership was an important ideal, service to a cause beyond the self; that management had to be flexible; and that students should honor others' efforts in all they did. His last admonition to the students was to "give generously to those not as fortunate as you are."[12]

Statement of Purpose

Until the mid-1940s, Roanoke College, like many other colleges, had no formal mission statement.[13] Then Charles Smith wrote a robust one that

10. Fintel, "Competence and Conscience," unpublished commencement address, May 22, 1977, 2.

11. Fintel, "Competence and Conscience," 3.

12. Fintel, "Farewell Address," unpublished commencement address, April 29, 1989, 4. It is noteworthy that in all these public speeches to the college's various constituencies, Fintel does not mention the college's relationship to the Lutheran Church. Yet one of his first moves as president was to invite the Virginia Synod to relocate its offices on the Roanoke campus. He also acted decisively to strengthen what was then the philosophy and religion department. These actions conformed to one of Fintel's adages: "Don't talk about it; do it."

13. An irony might be pointed out: when the college had no formal statement of purpose, it had perhaps its sharpest sense of purpose and mission, located in the collective mind of the president and the faculty. By the time a formal statement of purpose was drawn up,

was clearly the product of his own hand. In 1963, the statement of purpose crafted by the faculty—upon prodding by an accrediting agency—replaced Smith's statement. This statement, with one significant change, existed for nearly forty years, until an accrediting agency again demanded a revisit. The change had to do with the college's Christian heritage. In 1963 the purpose statement declared that the college's education would take place in a "Christian atmosphere." In a bit of tinkering in the mid-1970s, the college mentions that learning will take place in a "setting in which Christian experience *is available*." But in a further statement, which was affirmed by the board of trustees, the Roanoke College faculty, and the Virginia Synod in 1977, a third formulation was accepted and lasted until 2000: "It honors its Christian heritage and founding by Lutherans in 1842, while welcoming and reflecting a variety of religious traditions."

These changes reflected a gradual weakening of the college's formal commitment to its Christian heritage—from "atmosphere" to "availability" to an "honoring its heritage and founding," which could be, minimally, a reference to its founding in the college's ancient history rather than a continuing part of its present mission. Yet the statement itself perhaps affirms something more substantial:

Roanoke College is dedicated to educating men and women in high standards of scholarship and in creativity in the arts and sciences. It seeks to give students a broad understanding of their own and other cultures and competency in a field of specialization. It also recognizes a responsibility to serve its community.

The College believes that it can serve a free society by developing in students a capacity for responsible leadership. It seeks to achieve this purpose through the intellectual, emotional, spiritual, and practical aspects of a liberal arts education. It strives to provide its students with the knowledge, skills, and adaptability needed for the successful pursuit of their careers.

Roanoke is a small college with a concerned and dedicated faculty, nurturing sensitivity, maturity, and a life-long love of learning. It honors its Christian heritage and its founding by Lutherans in 1842, while welcoming and reflecting a variety of religious traditions.

---

there was less clarity about identity and mission, and perhaps the writing of such a statement indicated an effort to sharpen an already weakened sense of purpose.

From 1963 until the turn of the twenty-first century, the college's statement of purpose continued its commitment to leadership, responsibility in community and society, and the development of students in a holistic way, including in a spiritual way. These aims were to be nurtured by means of a liberal arts education. The college also intended to impart specialized knowledge and skills for successful careers.

However, when Fintel gave his inaugural address in the spring of 1976, he pointedly omitted any praise for the college's sharp sense of purpose, even after he had observed that the strong colleges he knew had that quality. He refused to sing the praises because, in his judgment—along with that of Dean Gerald Gibson, who arrived eight years later (1984–85)—there was little sense of purpose on the part of the faculty and board.[14] The statement of purpose had fallen into benign neglect. Gibson noted that the scattershot distribution-type curriculum that had been in place since the 1960s was a sure sign that the college lacked coherent purpose.[15] Though the college revisited the statement of purpose in 1977, it made only one noteworthy change in that statement—the one concerning the college's relationship to its religious heritage.

Dealing with the Hangover of the 1960s

The period from 1975 to roughly 1983, the first half of the Fintel administration, was occupied in clearing the deck of the wreckage resulting from the 1960s and preparing the college for major steps forward. The first thing to do was to bring on new personnel to replace those who had grappled with the 1960s and had been exhausted by it, had proven to be incompetent, or just didn't fit into plans for the future. The dean of students, weary after serving twenty years in that office, was moved to the office of alumni relations. A brash but inventive new dean of students was brought on to cope with the chaotic student life; a recent graduate of the college became his assistant. The struggling director of the Roanoke College Choir was replaced by a young and dynamic director. A new admissions director was hired in an

14. Interview with Fintel on Sept. 4, 2014; interview with Gibson on Sept. 24, 2014.

15. After the curricular revolution of the late 1960s, which I have described in the preceding chapter, the general curriculum remained basically unchanged until 1989–90, the first year of the Gring administration. However, the movement toward a renewed general education curriculum began with the planning of the new honors program immediately upon the arrival of Gibson in 1984–85.

effort to increase student numbers and quality. A young and imaginative new chaplain was brought in to succeed the older chaplain, a conventional pastor. The chair of the philosophy and religion department had seen his fortunes sag rather quickly. He was eased out, and a new beginning for the department was concocted (about which, more later).[16]

Fintel moved Roanoke College's athletic teams from Division II of the NCAA to Division III, ensuring that the college would not get involved in the ambiguous practice of offering athletic scholarships. That entailed a new coach as well as a new approach. A highly skilled director of development replaced an equally skilled director, who, in turn, left to direct development efforts at Harvard Law School. Henry Fowler, a distinguished graduate of the college who was treasury secretary in the Lyndon Johnson administration, became an influential member of the board of trustees in 1977.

Edward Lautenschager, academic dean under President Kendig, tendered his resignation. C. Freeman Sleeper, a PhD in New Testament but recently a dean in the New York Community College system, was selected as the new academic dean. Upon his arrival in 1976, he had to trim the college's budget to keep its record of "being in the black" intact. He made a significant effort to freshen the faculty with new professors committed not only to teaching but to scholarly pursuits. That meant more PhDs from distinguished research universities. (In his eight-year tenure, from 1976 to 1984, Sleeper replaced one-third of the faculty.) He also garnered a number of outside grants to help increase the skills and scholarship of the faculty.[17]

It is noteworthy that the first half of Fintel's tenure also featured a number of major building projects. Olin Hall, a fine new theater and fine arts center, was completed in 1977. That enabled the college to introduce into the curriculum majors in theater, music, and art. It also provided a handsome place for the college to host the Roanoke College Children's Choir, the Roanoke junior symphony, and the Kandinsky Trio. Fintel also recruited donors

---

16. The 1970s decade was a time of retrenchment at the college. The board refused to grant new tenure-track positions to the faculty, keeping the tenure-track faculty at about two-thirds of the whole faculty. Thus, faculty members who were hired during that period were given three-year contracts. Because of this, the administration had more flexibility in the dismissal and acquiring of faculty.

17. George Keller, *Prologue to Prominence—A Half Century of Roanoke College, 1951–2003* (Minneapolis: Lutheran University Press, 2005), 35–38. Keller traces the history of the college from the time it applied for a Phi Beta Kappa chapter in 1951 to the year in which it finally acquired one, 2003. He, too, saw the decade from 1975 to 1985 as a prologue to major positive changes during the rest of the 1980s.

to purchase and install several modernist sculptures on campus. The Homer Bast Physical Education and Recreation Center was dedicated in 1982. The college acquired what had been the old Roanoke County courthouse for additional classroom space, as well as the former Elizabeth College Campus, which had been occupied for many years by the Lutheran Children's Home of the South. The student center was refurbished and enlarged, and Sections, a revered old dormitory, was renovated. Furthermore, the college announced a $25 million Sesquicentennial Campaign for its 150th anniversary in 1992.

Four other initiatives were necessary for the takeoff of the later 1980s. The first was the innovative and energetic efforts of the college to raise money, led by Jack Hills, the director of development from 1976 to 1986. Hills taught the college that it had to "spend money to make money," and in that he was extraordinarily successful. The college was able dramatically to increase its endowment as well as its annual fund.

A second major initiative was provided by William Miller, whom Fintel moved from student affairs to admissions in 1984. Miller concocted a brilliant strategy to increase applicants exponentially, which then allowed the college to expand its student body and to become more selective in a short time.

The third important initiative was the establishment of the Fowler Program in 1983, which enabled the college to invite national leaders to address questions of public policy. In time, the program funded a professorship, scholarships, contests, and study in Washington, DC, and abroad. Its emphasis on public policy and public service was a major effort to recapture the republican strand in the college's classic sense of mission. Its gala launch in the spring of 1983 featured former Secretary of State Henry Kissinger addressing an audience of five thousand in the Salem Civic Center.

A fourth initiative was the college's discovery of its ability to do strategic planning. As I have noted earlier, Fintel came to Roanoke after having just completed planning audits of many church-related colleges in his role in the American Lutheran Church. He believed that Roanoke College had not engaged in serious planning and that it needed to. He insisted that each vice president draw up plans for his or her own division. At a famous planning retreat during the fall of 1984, Fintel became exasperated that the various plans were not fitting into a coherent whole. He told the vice presidents that he would take a nap, and when he returned, he said, he expected a more coherent plan. Voila! When he returned, the vice presidents presented him with the outline of Roanoke College's first comprehensive plan, which eventually became the "1992 Plan."[18] Since then, the college has done several more effective comprehensive plans. These plans have tended to sharpen the trajectory of the college, especially its effort to reach regional and national recognition.

The Major Launches

Following this seven or eight years of prologue, the period from 1983 to the conclusion of Fintel's administration saw several launches that not only lifted the college to another level of excellence—and gained regional and national rankings for it—but also recovered in new ways the classic emphases of the college: service to the nation on the basis of Christian foundations.

In the following pages I will depict four significant changes—in the college's ethos, its curriculum, its faculty, and its relationship to its Lutheran/Christian heritage. I will employ a "before-and-after" approach in each section that will heighten the difference between the earlier and latter parts of the Fintel tenure at Roanoke College.

Ethos

In the preceding chapter I observed that student life remained relatively settled and civilized in the early 1970s, even as, one by one, the rules and regulations of the *in loco parentis* approach fell by the wayside, mostly under student pressure that had been fueled by the spirit of the 1960s. But after 1975, the year of Fintel's arrival, the full bloom of student "liberation" could be observed.[19]

18. Keller, *Prologue*, 47. Gerald Gibson notes that, before that famous retreat, Fintel insisted on planning by the vice presidents but not a comprehensive plan for the college. The retreat produced a real "break-through."

19. Oddly enough, when asked whether he was aware of the turbulence in student life at the college, Fintel noted that it was "more open" than the Midwestern Lutheran colleges with which he was familiar, but he could not remember being alarmed by its excesses. Such equanimity is perhaps the result of being the president and living in a home somewhat removed from campus. (Later, the Fintels were to move from the president's stately home to a smaller home, newly purchased by the college, that was right on campus.) It is also possible that the lieutenants around him shielded him from reality by not reporting those excesses to him.

Macmillan Johnson, at the time a recent (1970) graduate of the college, and one of the student leaders who had earlier pressed for more liberalization of student life, was hired on the spot in the spring of 1976 by William Miller, the vice president and dean of student affairs, to become assistant dean of students. Johnson had been, in fact, merely applying for an internship when, to his great surprise, he was offered the assistant dean position. Upon accepting the job, Johnson was returning home along the west side of the campus, where, he said, he witnessed quite a spectacle. Several kegs of beer were being consumed by a large group of students who were dancing to very loud rock music in front of three fraternity houses. The students blocked Market Street, and some were sitting on faculty members' cars in the parking lot. Many who were drunk and/or high on drugs were also present. The new ethic seemed to be, "If it feels good, do it." With something of a sinking feeling, Johnson realized that he had his work cut out for him. Very soon after that incident, he observed that almost all the student organizations he had known as a student were gone. There was little evidence of upperclassmen socializing the younger students. Furthermore, since Roanoke had enrollment and retention problems, the college had also become a "second chance" college for students who had flunked out or had been dismissed from other colleges—or even those who had failed at Roanoke.[20]

George Keller records a similar story:

Roanoke staff members and graduates in those years (1976–1985) admit that it was often a "wild" time in student life. While a minority of students prepared earnestly for graduate and professional schools, many were inclined to boisterous fun-seeking, and lax about rigorous study. During the early 1980s, Roanoke became known as "party school" among school counselors and prospective students. For some undergraduates, heavy drinking led to academic failures and, tragically, to student deaths in three cases.

"Wednesday Night Live" in the Cavern often featured beery gaiety and exuberance, and on each Halloween, a colorful costume party. And when two graduates, James McEnerny and Robert Rotanz, opened their food-and-drink bistro called Mac 'n' Bob's on Main Street in 1980, the pub quickly packed in standing voluptuaries from Thursday to Saturday nights. It was like Yale in the 1920s. The Kappa Alpha fraternity became so unruly

20. Interview with Johnson, August 1, 2014.

that college officials revoked its charter and suspended it for five years, and all other fraternities—except Sigma Chi—were also disciplined.[21]

I arrived at Roanoke College in the fall of 1982, having no inkling about the nature of student life at the college. I was appalled at what went on in the dorms after the chaplain took me on a tour of the dorms on a Friday night. He told me of the many alcohol and drug overdoses he had to get to the hospital, as well as the abortions he had to arrange for young women who accidentally became pregnant. Widespread damage to furniture was obvious. Keg parties on Wednesdays in the fraternity houses meant that fewer students came to class on Thursday mornings. Moreover, a highly negative effect of such debased life was that it drove away good students. They could not get rest or find suitable intellectual partners. I had many advisees leave the college in my first several years. With the shocking death of three students, however, the college began to wake up and get more control of student life. President Fintel appointed a panel to report on student life and make recommendations for saner life on campus. The faculty, having similar experiences to mine, put great pressure on the administration to get things under control. Slowly but surely, student life began to change after those unfortunate episodes. Luckily for the college, liability laws were not as stringent as they are today, or the college may have found itself in deep legal trouble.

The student alcohol-related deaths became an occasion for reform of student life. President Fintel appointed a blue-ribbon committee that issued a number of strong recommendations to curb drinking. Keg parties were soon forbidden. By 1984–85, the Cavern no longer sold beer, which meant that "Wednesday Night Live" lost much of its allure. However, federal and state laws governing the drinking age were perhaps the most crucial aid in bringing alcohol consumption under control at the college. In 1985, those who were born after July 1, 1966—most college students—could not purchase beer until they were twenty-one. By the next year, almost all college students were underage. This change in law gave Macmillan Johnson, who succeeded William Miller as dean of student affairs in 1981, the means by which to sharply limit drinking on campus. Johnson soon brought in a former military man to oversee the disciplining of students. Even the faculty

---

21. Keller, *Prologue*, 39. In later years, when student life was under more control by the college, officials of the college asked the owners of Mac 'n' Bob's to move toward a sit-down restaurant that catered more to adults and families. They responded by building the pub into what has become a large, well-known restaurant in Salem.

Christmas party, which had become rather boozy and bawdy, was toned down. It was moved to Bast Gym, where it became a grand but sober annual event.

After serving several years as assistant to the president, Miller moved to admissions in 1984. He soon devised a brilliant strategy to increase the applications to the college dramatically. More student applications meant that the college could be more selective. Soon thereafter, the quality of students began to rise, as measured by a sharp increase in their SAT scores and a noticeable elevation of their rank in their high-school class. More selectivity meant that fewer "second-chance" students needed to be accepted, something that pleased the faculty but upset some alumni who prized the wide-open life of the late 1970s. Moreover, better students and a better environment meant a higher retention rate; good students did not leave as readily.

The academic quality of the student body rose with the introduction of an imaginative and challenging honors program in 1986–87, which recruited twenty-five high-achieving students each year. This was made possible by the arrival of Academic Dean Gerald Gibson in 1984–85, who made sure that the faculty desire to shape a new honors program was realized. With that program in place and growing, the college was creating new subcultures that were not only not attracted to partying but also intolerant of rambunctious behavior in the dorms. Other subcultures emerged with the introduction of new varsity sports or the strengthening of those already established. Coaches recruited and cultivated athletes who were also good students. The athletic subcultures helped students resist the allure of the party culture. The athletes also benefited from winning teams in basketball, lacrosse, and soccer. Their successes also drew hundreds of student supporters to games, thus elevating student spirit.

Though partying no doubt continued, it was forced off campus. Thanks to the various strategies concocted by the student life office, campus life took on a new civility that was conducive to study and serious discussion. That was aided by the proliferation of public events sponsored by the three endowments on campus: the Fowler Program, the Center for Church and Society, and the Jordan Endowment for the Humanities. In addition, a weekly convocation was added to the college event calendar, which also featured outside speakers, often sponsored by the three endowments.

A more positive ethos was also engendered by a stronger choral music program, led by a commanding professor/conductor who insisted on a disciplined college choir. A strong drama program continued to produce plays attended by large numbers of the student body and community. The chaplaincy program slowly weakened during the first five years of the Fintel administration. Under the guidance of a solid but conventional pastor, it emphasized different kinds of worship events, along with a Sunday morning Lutheran service in Antrim Chapel. The chaplain offered good preaching of a "progressive sort."

The chaplaincy offered counseling as well as participation in a number of small denominational clubs, along with an interdenominational club, the Campus Christian Community. There was no longer a club for pre-theology students. The assessment of religious life on campus was that it was a minority phenomenon, attractive only to a small "God-squad." "It was assumed but practiced lightly." It was not vigorous enough to take up the tough challenge of appealing to a rather large cohort of students who responded to the college's request to list their religious preference on their student record by choosing "no response" or "no preference." In 1976, 32 percent of the students responded to the query that way, and in 1977 nearly 34 percent.[22] Never before had that large a percentage of the student body at Roanoke College been so religiously indifferent.

Similar to his decisive action regarding leadership of the philosophy and religion department (which I will discuss later), Fintel decided religious life on campus needed a strong stimulant. On the advice of his assistant, William Miller, he brought Pastor Tim Swanson to campus in 1980 as chaplain and director of church relations.[23] A most unlikely pair ever to grace the life of Roanoke College, Miller and Swanson were remarkable. Both graduated from Bethany College in Kansas, a school with a pietist Swedish background that could scarcely hold this bold, inventive, brilliant, dashing, eccentric, and risk-taking pair. Miller came from Brooklyn, New York, and Swanson's father taught at Bethany after serving for many years as a missionary in Tanzania. They took Roanoke College by storm. Miller innovated many programs in

22. Roanoke College Office of Institutional Research.
23. Miller tended to dream up brilliant schemes and leave them soon, bored with the details of actually running them. His flamboyant style caught up with him about the time Fintel retired. He moved on to found his own consulting firm. Swanson, I should mention in the interest of full disclosure, was instrumental in getting me to Roanoke College. I had him as a student at the Lutheran School of Theology at Chicago in the early 1970s, when there was great turbulence surrounding the Vietnam War. Swanson negotiated his way through the seminary while he worked full-time running a bar. He evidently spoke well of my work at the seminary and suggested to Fintel and Sleeper that I would be a good candidate for restarting the philosophy and religion department. They acted on his suggestion. Swanson's time at Roanoke College was dynamic and brief; he left after only six years.

various roles but was especially important in developing the college's first modern admissions strategy.

For the following five years, campus religious life was indeed renewed. Swanson was energetic, youthful, imaginative, and innovative. As a product of the 1960s, he was close in age and style to the students and could identify with them. He engaged them vigorously in many ways. He started up the Religious Life Center in Trout Hall, which had been the old chapel. He taught New Testament courses in the philosophy and religion department. He installed many programs and collected several vigorous chaplains of other denominations to minister to their students at Roanoke. He spent freely to bring speakers to campus and take students on trips abroad. He visited many churches and hosted numerous events as the director of church relations. He became heavily involved in student crisis-intervention. He became so busy that the college decided it needed a second chaplain to perform the more traditional duties of a chaplain. It called Pastor Paul Henrickson in the spring of 1984, and he then embarked on a long tenure of a faithful, solid, but more conventional ministry. Programs begun by Swanson to engage the students were extended and deepened by Henrickson in his "ministry of presence."[24] Later, Henrickson began major initiatives that coupled the Christian heritage of the college with its republican tradition—building houses for the poor (Habitat for Humanity) and establishing a Center for Community Service under his supervision. He also organized a Center for Counseling Services as part of the chaplaincy program.

Curriculum

Major changes in the curriculum of the college were part of the great pivot of the mid- to late-1980s. From 1975 until the initiation of a new honors program in 1986 and, a bit later, the inception of a new general-education curriculum in 1989, the old distribution approach from the late 1960s held

24. When I interviewed Chaplain Henrickson on January 28, 2015, he characterized his "ministry of presence" as an attempt to show genuine care for students, staff, and faculty. He was the "go to" person in both tragic and happy events. His presence in rites of passage—including death—gave him the chance not only to offer human support but to openly proclaim the gospel. These occasions were also times to invite persons who were cared for to consider an encounter with Christ, though that invitation was always noninvasive and noncoercive. Many times it was refused. Nevertheless, the "ministry of presence" always included that invitation.

sway. Besides two required courses in English (composition and literature), students were allowed a wide variety of choices within prescribed areas. This scattershot approach was accompanied by a January interterm that had less than a minimum of academic integrity. Students could take some courses abroad whose content had no relationship to where the students were located. They could, for example, study math in Luxembourg for three days a week and then be set free for the rest of the week for fun and travel. (This was before liability laws tightened up considerably.)

In the early 1980s the faculty exhibited a strong desire to change things, starting with an imaginative new honors program. Before his arrival in 1984, Dean Gerald Gibson surveyed Roanoke's department chairs to discern their priorities; a new honors program came out on top. He chose a task force to work on the project, and it took up the task enthusiastically. The efforts resulted in an innovative curriculum that emphasized interdisciplinary approaches to related subject matters.[25] The proposal for the new program passed the faculty without great difficulty, partly because the new curriculum would affect only a minority of the faculty. Those who disagreed with it or were uninterested could avoid it. C. William Hill, professor of political science and director of the Fowler Program, became its first director.

The honors program began with two semesters of "Literary Reflections and Responses" and one of "Formative Visions," which surveyed the major philosophical and theological visions that deeply influenced the West. It continued with "Turning Points," a history course that focused on hinge moments in history. "Artistic Imagination" aimed at the history of art as interpreted from visual, audio, and dramatic artistic viewpoints. "Individual and Society" called on psychology and sociology to help understand the human condition. "Wealth and Power" enlisted economists and political scientists. "Scientific Milestones and Millstones" examined great scientific discoveries according to their effects on the human project. A capstone course entitled "Contemporary Challenges" examined major societal issues by using the various perspectives students had learned in their earlier courses. The cur-

25. The interdisciplinary model was modeled on the University of Chicago approach ("Ideas and Methods") that assumed that every discipline has a "way of thinking" underlying it. Different ways of thinking were paired in each course, e.g., economics and political science, with the expectation that excellent students would not only understand that underlying method in each discipline but also discover how they related negatively and positively to each other. Sometimes it was difficult to recruit faculty who themselves understood the underlying paradigm, but mostly the faculty engaged this approach with eagerness. It was a learning experience for all involved.

riculum also required an independent study in the student's major as well as "Plenary Enrichment Colloquia," which required the student to attend a certain number of intellectual enrichment events each term. In addition, two math courses, two laboratory sciences, and proficiency in a foreign language to the intermediate level were required.

Of the many students who applied to enter the honors program, only twenty to twenty-five were accepted each year. They were given handsome scholarships and were closely advised by the honors program director. As the program grew year by year, the number of high-achieving students coming into the student body elevated it. Dean Gibson supported it strongly with funds and personnel. The deficient January interterm was terminated in 1987 and was later replaced by a May term that involved courses whose content was closely related to their location abroad or at home. President Fintel instituted a weekly convocation that was held late in the morning on Thursdays, and it became a prime venue for speakers invited by departments—and funded by the three endowments—to speak to the faculty and student body. Students were often required to attend by professors who thought the speaker would have something relevant to say to their classes.[26]

The new honors program was meant to be a "primer" for the construction of a new general-education curriculum to replace the old distribution system. By the fall of 1989, the general-education curriculum was ready to go, though its adoption was more hotly contested than was the honors program. It required most faculty members to be involved, and it occupied 15.5 units out of the 36.5 units needed for graduation. Further, all departments were summoned to participate in some fashion. Also, it called for the return of a required course in religion and philosophy after a twenty-year absence, an initiative resisted by the secularist wing of the faculty. Nevertheless, the curriculum passed and held sway for over twenty years.

The new curriculum included a full year of the "Writing Course," a three-course sequence in Western Civilization called "The Civilization Requirement," a junior-year religion and philosophy course called "Values and

26. At one such convocation the students in all the religion and philosophy courses were required to come to hear Eleanore Stump, a Catholic philosopher who was one of the world's authorities on Thomas Aquinas, speak on a rather rarified topic in Aquinas's thought. She was used to small audiences for such topics. When she came into the old ballroom, which was filled with several hundred students, she was stunned: "What an academically alert student body you have here," she offered. The illusory nature of required attendance, however, was exposed when the vast majority of students exited once the formal talk was over and the question-and-answer period had begun.

the Responsible Life," and a senior capstone course entitled the "Reading Course," which was the reintroduction into the curriculum of that famous course of earlier times after a long absence. In addition, students were required to take courses in—or test out of—a foreign language, complete two courses in math, two one-unit laboratory courses in different scientific disciplines, two courses in the social sciences, and two physical education courses. Beyond that, they were free to engage in majors and minors in specific departments.

The curricular changes carried out in the latter half of the 1980s represented a return to a more coherent liberal arts education. It also meant a reintroduction of required courses that emphasized the Christian basis of responsibility in society, an important dimension of the historic Christian republican mission of the college. These advances were major accomplishments, given the increasing fragmentation of the academic world and the individualism of the faculty. They owed a good deal to a dean who was willing to push forward the ideas and programs of a portion of the faculty who favored a return to a more robust education in the liberal arts.

Faculty

In accordance with Roanoke's new ambition to become a regionally and then nationally known liberal arts college, its faculty increased in both number and in the quality of its credentials. In 1980 the faculty numbered seventy-two; by 1990 it stood at ninety. The percentage of faculty with terminal degrees improved from 70 percent to 85 percent.[27] The incoming faculty tended to be more interested in ongoing scholarly activity, and Dean Gibson supported them by introducing "scholarly activity" into the criteria used for tenure and promotion. Furthermore, since the college was expanding its student body by the mid-1980s, the additional tuition enabled major salary raises for the faculty.[28]

With the credentialing of the faculty, however, came more professionalization and specialization. The great research universities were turning out

27. Miller, *Dear Old Roanoke*, 306.

28. Gibson was so popular with the faculty that when Fintel retired in 1989, and before David Gring arrived as president, a faculty petition to keep Gibson on as dean in the new administration was supported almost unanimously. This affirmation diminished sharply a short time later, when the "scholarly activity" requirement began to be applied to those embedded in the traditional "teacher only" ethos of the older Roanoke faculty.

PhDs whose educations were increasingly narrow and whose work was becoming more specialized all the time. Furthermore, faculty members tended to be more concerned about their standing in their academic guilds than in a full-blooded commitment to the college. While the faculty became more qualified in a technical sense, it became less interested in joining the common enterprise of the college. Yet, in spite of that new faculty direction, the college was able to enact the curricular changes described above.

While the effort to recruit a more credentialed and scholarly faculty was successful, the same could not be said for the effort to select faculty committed to the classic Christian republican mission of the college. President Fintel and the "purpose statement" of the college could rhetorically claim that mission, but little effort was made to select faculty who supported it directly.[29] Faculty hiring was delegated more and more to the departments, and they tended to hire faculty according to specialized departmental needs. Finalists were interviewed by the dean, whose major interest was whether the prospective faculty member would fit the liberal arts agenda of the college. As to the college's historic Christian identity and mission, the most he asked concerned their level of comfort about teaching at a church-related college. The general response was: "That doesn't bother me." The implicit assumption was that the college's relationship to the Christian tradition was fine as long it meant no obligations on the part of the candidate.[30] President Fintel did not interview finalists, but did strongly intervene in some faculty hiring when he thought it was essential.[31]

Naturally, given the location and history of the college, candidates who

---

29. Gibson introduced a fourth criterion—besides teaching, service, and scholarship—for tenure and promotion. That was "institutional fit." That criterion was used to select faculty who supported liberal arts education—often in spite of their narrow graduate study—but it was not used to select Christians or eager republicans to the faculty. Such use would have been widely and strongly resisted by those who thought that such criteria were publicly irrelevant to the educational mission of the college. However, a small number of department chairs actively looked for Christians—even Lutherans!—as well as those who believed strongly in the American project. But that was not official college policy. No doubt those considerations should have been discussed as criteria for institutional fit but were not, perhaps because of a premonition that they would be rejected.

30. Interview with Gibson on September 24, 2014. He wasn't pleased with such an answer, which sometimes led to his suggesting another candidate to the department chair.

31. Fintel's recruitment and hiring of me in 1982 was for the most part the work of him and Dean Sleeper. His hiring of a strong choral director a couple of years later was similar. He thought these positions were so crucial that he was willing to go outside the general guidelines and practice of faculty hiring.

were seriously religious and patriotic did find their way into the faculty; but for the most part that was fortuitous, perhaps even providential. Enough of them came to Roanoke to support the partial recovery of its Christian mission (a subject I will turn to next). But the temper of the Roanoke faculty was highly individualistic, suspicious of any common identity or mission. That was the effect of years of not "hiring for mission," but rather of hiring for departmental needs and for focusing on the effort to elevate the reputation of the college.

The Lutheran/Christian Heritage of the College

Though it looked as though the quality and reputation of the philosophy and religion department would be elevated by the arrival of its new chairman in the early 1970s, such was not the case. The chairman, a Midwestern Lutheran well-educated at Luther College, Luther Seminary, and Durham University in England, at first impressed the faculty with his intellectual firepower and educational vision. (He won an early version of the "outstanding professor" award and successfully proposed a degree in the liberal arts achieved by passing "Tripos" exams, a very English style of education.) But the romance with him soon soured. Fintel and Sleeper decided to ease him out. Using the fact that he did not have a tenure-track position, they were able to move him out of his academic role and briefly into an administrative role. He was gone from the college by 1980–81, but damage had already been done. The older members of the department were dispirited, and they receded in effectiveness and engagement.[32] All in all, the reputation of the department diminished markedly. By 1982 there was only one student majoring in philosophy and religion.

This situation was grist for the mill of the secularist wing of the faculty, those who would just as soon have decoupled the college from the Lutheran Church and changed the department into a religious-studies department in which Christianity was in no sense privileged. Indeed, an aggressive antireligious sentiment was openly expressed by that wing, which, though a minority, was vocal and intimidating.

32. Both Guy Ritter and Roy Bent had enjoyed some effective years at the college. Ritter taught religion from a vigorous Lutheran perspective, and he had many talents. Bent was a gadfly who spent much time conversing with students in the Cavern. Many alumni mention the two with affection. A dorm was named in honor of Ritter in the early 2000s.

When I arrived in 1982, I was shocked at that hostility because I had assumed that the Roanoke of the 1980s would be similar to its sister Lutheran college, Midland College, when I was a student there in the late 1950s. That was a naïve assumption, of which I was soon disabused.

Several instances of the denial of or the hostility toward the Christian heritage of the college come to mind. Sometime during my first weeks on campus in 1982, I attended a lecture by a historian in which he argued that the main reason for the establishment of small liberal arts colleges was that protective families wanted to keep their sons and daughters free of urban dangers. There was not one mention of the fervent religious motives of David Bittle, the first president of the college, nor of the religious motivations behind the founding of almost all the liberal arts colleges in the nineteenth century.

Another instance: When President Fintel appointed a blue-ribbon committee to report on alcohol abuse on campus after the deaths of three students, I was asked by fellow members of the committee to write a statement counseling moderation. I used Christian arguments as well as philosophical arguments for the virtue of temperance. One outspoken member of the committee objected to the mere presence of a Christian argument. "After all," she said, "everyone here is not a Christian," which made the false assumption that there had to be unanimity of conviction before any kind of argument could be made.

Another instance: In the late 1980s, in response to President Fintel's all-college convocations, and fearing that this was an effort to reestablish required chapel, a contingent of the faculty insisted that no religious content could ever be expressed at those convocations. Religion was to remain sequestered in the philosophy and religion department and in the private lives of faculty and students. It should have no wider public relevance to the college. This attitude was later exhibited in the resistance to the reintroduction of a required religion/philosophy course ("Values and the Responsible Life") in the proposed new general education curriculum. During the faculty debates about the curriculum in 1988, faculty members strongly objected to requiring anything that might smack of religious coercion. After the course came on line in the general-education curriculum, the director of general education monitored the course like no other course at Roanoke had ever been monitored. She reiterated the suspicion of part of the faculty that the course was a "Sunday school" course featuring outright "proselytization." Though the course, in fact, surveyed Western moral philosophy and theology—as well as a section on other world religions' moral teachings—in a sophisticated and noncoercive manner, the suspicion toward a required religion course was fairly widespread.

A majority of the faculty was not openly hostile to the Lutheran/Christian heritage of the college, but had little interest in defending, promoting, or strengthening it. They would have been alarmed at any effort to strengthen the connection. But there was a small minority who would have liked to have a more pronounced connection.[33]

Fintel, relatively fresh from his role in Christian higher education in the American Lutheran Church, recognized that the department had to be rebuilt if there were to be any credible Lutheran/Christian voice in the college. Furthermore, he knew that a stronger department would be an important way to arrest the secularizing trajectory of the college. He worked with both Dean Sleeper and Chaplain Swanson to find a Lutheran scholar—preferably one in Christian ethics—who was in mid-career and who could bring fresh energy, competence, and vision to a badly damaged department. In order to make their recruitment efforts more attractive to such a candidate, they raised money among Lutheran donors to endow a professorship and to establish some sort of center. (This strategy of raising money from wealthy Lutheran donors for professorships and chaplaincies was to become a very important instrument for building Lutheran/Christian presence and voice at the college. The groundwork laid by Fintel was brought to fruition during the tenures of later presidents.) They succeeded in getting the Jordan family of Richmond and the Trexler family of Florida to donate significant money to those endeavors. Thus, they were able to offer the Jordan-Trexler Professor of Religion position to a promising candidate, as well as an endowment that would support a center, the shape of which would be up to the successful candidate.

President Fintel approached me in 1981 about accepting that newly minted position. I was in mid-career and had published several books and was active on the lecture circuit.[34] I had also been tenured for a dozen years

---

33. In the early 1980s a small group of Lutheran faculty began meeting among themselves and with President Fintel. Members were concerned that the number of Lutherans on the faculty was getting ever smaller. Though there was no change in the college's hiring policy (no "affirmative action" for Lutherans), there were ad hoc efforts to hire more Lutherans by several department chairs and the president.

34. In early 1981, Fortress Press published my book *The Ethic of Democratic Capitalism: A Moral Reassessment*, which gained considerable attention, partly because it made a measured defense of the combination of constitutional democracy and market economic arrangements. The preponderance of Christian intellectuals was dismissive of capitalism and much preferred socialism, so my argument was somewhat unusual.

at the Lutheran School of Theology at Chicago. Soon after my arrival, President Fintel took me to lunch and laid out a set of expectations. He said he wanted me to work on four things: build an excellent religion department; develop the center; do my part to elevate the academic quality of the faculty; and explore ways to draw the college closer to its Lutheran/Christian heritage. Further, he said, since there would be some resistance from the faculty to several of these imperatives, "just do them and don't talk about them." He said he would quietly support my efforts but had to avoid the appearance that I would get special favors from him.

Strengthening the Department

The first task, strengthening the department, involved encouraging the remaining older members of the department. Both had low salaries that we were able to raise. Their teaching role was affirmed. When Guy Ritter decided to retire in 1984, Dean Sleeper moved from the deanship to the philosophy and religion department. He became the main professor in biblical studies. When I received a sabbatical in 1985–86, the new dean, Gibson, allowed us to hire a young professor, Ned Wisnefske, from his position in systematic theology at Luther Seminary in St. Paul, Minnesota. The next year he allowed that position to become a tenure-track position. Wisnefske soon proved himself to be a superb teacher. By that time we had three professors with PhDs from distinguished divinity schools in the religion faculty, plus several adjunct professors. We now covered the fields of Bible, theology, and ethics. As the department gained stature and accumulated majors (up from one to now twenty), Dean Gibson allowed us another tenure-track position, this one in church history (with a special focus on American church history) and world religions. In 1988–89 we selected Gerald McDermott from the University of Iowa, and he arrived just as Fintel retired. Now we covered the main fields of a full-blown theology department: Bible, theology, ethics, church history, and world religions.

By 1984 all members on the religion side of the department were teaching well and were engaged in scholarly research—all had PhDs—and the religion offerings of the department expanded rapidly. A combined religion/philosophy major, along with minors in religion/philosophy, religion, and philosophy were developed. Since the preponderance of courses and professors rested now on the religion side of the department, its name was changed from "philosophy and religion" to "religion and philosophy": the name represented a historic change from the Roanoke pattern of offering many more courses in philosophy than in religion. Along with this came the self-conscious molding of the department into a theology department—one that spoke *for* the Christian tradition, not only *about* it as one religion among many, as would be the case in a religious studies department. Though it did not seem wise to try to change "religion" to "theology," the movement toward a theology department (in spite of its name) seemed to fit the mission of a church-related college more fully than the route of religious studies did.

The religion and philosophy department supplied faculty for the honors program's "Formative Visions" and the general education curriculum's "Values and the Responsible Life"; it also graduated roughly eight majors and a like number of minors per year. Its electives drew well. Its teaching and publishing capabilities led Keller to call it "one of the finest at the institution."[35] The Christian intellectual base of the college took on considerable strength.

Defining and Developing the Center

Months before I arrived at Roanoke College in the summer of 1982, I began the pleasant task of defining and developing a center that had already been funded by an endowment raised by President Fintel. Since I was trained in the field of Christian Ethics and Society at the University of Chicago Divinity School, my inclination was to define and develop a center that would engage in a lively dialogue between Christian intellectual and moral perspectives and the pressing issues of church and society. That seemed to be what President Fintel and Dean Sleeper were looking for, so approval of my general thrust came quickly. Here is the definition of the mission of the Roanoke College Center for Church and Society, which has persisted for over thirty years:

> The Roanoke College Center for Church and Society aims at bringing to bear Christian religious and moral perspectives—particularly in their Lutheran interpretation—on contemporary challenges to the church and world. Its purpose is to cross boundaries between church and world, sacred and secular, religion and society; to operate at the dynamic interface between religious commitment and the multi-faceted life of the world.[36]

35. Keller, *Prologue*, 39.
36. Unpublished original proposal for the Center for Church and Society (August 1982).

At its inception the center had four purposes:

1. To feature speakers of note (especially Lutherans) in public lectures that would reflect on significant issues facing both church and society. The very first event happened in the spring of 1983, entitled "Religion and Evolution: Constructive Possibilities," featuring theologian Philip Hefner and biologist Jeffrey Wicken. "The Legacy of Luther" and "Religious Perspectives on National Defense" followed soon thereafter.
2. To propose and fund interdisciplinary and other needed courses to enrich the college and departmental curricula. "Religion and Contemporary Literature" was an example of the former, and a course in Judaism taught by an observant Orthodox Jew was illustrative of the latter. A pioneering course on the Holocaust was also sponsored by the center. After the "pump was primed" by the center, the college then took over the funding for these courses when they proved to be successful.
3. To enhance cross-cultural education by proposing and funding travel courses to Africa, Latin America, and Germany.
4. To develop continuing education events for clergy and laity. A perennial one was "Power in the Spirit," a successful summer event at the college that was jointly sponsored by the Virginia Synod, the Center for Church and Society, and the Roanoke College Office of Church Relations. Courses in lay theological education were held at the college and in Lutheran churches. Special lectures for clergy on Reformation Day were also some of the center's other offerings.

A fruitful partnership between the center and the Fowler Program (under the direction of C. William Hill) emerged, in which both the Christian and republican traditions of the college were renewed in programs that featured both religious and political perspectives on public issues. This partnership offered fine occasions for faculty, students, and the community to hear high-level discussions of pressing issues.

Perhaps the most significant and glamorous event in its early years was held in the spring of 1985. The topic of the event was "Germany and the United States: Signals of Danger and Hope," and it was analyzed and probed before a crowd of nearly three thousand in Bast Gym. It featured Helmut Schmidt, the former chancellor of West Germany, Walter Stoessel, the US ambassador to West Germany, Michael Naumann, the senior foreign editor of *Der Spiegel*, and Wolfhart Pannenberg, a leading German Lutheran theologian.[37] A sumptuous reception, which was attended by hundreds, was held in the newly opened Marriott Hotel near the Roanoke airport, and it featured food prepared by a German chef brought in from Washington, DC. In addition to this grand event, many other collaborations took place. For example, "A Celebration of Liberty—The Constitution, Culture and Change," featuring Martin Marty, James Kilpatrick, and Edward Albee, took place in 1987. Another noteworthy joint program that expressed both the Christian and republican interests of the college took place in 1988, entitled "The Meaning of Citizenship—Rights and Obligations in the 1990s," with social philosopher Robert Bellah, political scientist Lawrence Mead, and syndicated columnist William Raspberry as the speakers.

Elevating the Academic Quality of the Faculty

From his arrival onward, Dean Gerald Gibson was intent on encouraging the ongoing scholarly activities of faculty members. In order to honor those who were involved in scholarly writing and lecturing, he instituted a publication that listed those activities by the faculty. At the beginning, its issues were rather slim; but they soon began to expand, partly because of his insistence that faculty continue scholarly lives, but also because the new faculty coming out of the graduate schools in the mid- to late-1980s were intent on carrying on a scholarly life. In compensation for this new emphasis on publishing and lecturing, Gibson was able to reduce the teaching load for many professors from eight courses per year to seven by implementing a system of release time for scholarly pursuits.

As chair of the newly named religion and philosophy department, I instituted seminar sessions (called "Front Burner") in which members from other departments were invited to talk about their intellectual projects. It was important to get cross-disciplinary discussions going across campus. New faculty members were hired as the student body expanded dramatically after 1985; and increased faculty compensation and reduced course loads made Roanoke an attractive place to work. The quality of the faculty was elevated in accordance with the new ambition to become a regionally, and then nationally, recognized liberal arts college.

37. The lectures were later published in book form in an American-German Studies Series sponsored by the University of Virginia. Lore Amlinger, ed., *Germany and the United States: Changing Perceptions/Danger and Hope* (Stuttgart: Academic Publishing House, 1987).

Drawing the College Closer to Its Lutheran/Christian Heritage

Fintel made important moves to connect the college with its sponsoring tradition, the Lutheran Church: in the case of Roanoke, it was the Virginia Synod of the Lutheran Church in America, which became the Virginia Synod of the Evangelical Lutheran Church in America in 1988. One of his first moves was to forge a new "Statement of Partnership between Roanoke College and the Virginia Synod" in 1979. In it the college pledged to offer a value-laden education for the formation of whole persons, so that they might become responsible citizens; that it would cultivate a campus environment influenced by the Judeo-Christian ethos; that it would encourage students to enter the ordained ministry; that it would provide a chaplain and competent courses in religion; and that it would share its competencies with the synod. It committed itself to attracting to its work "the most qualified faculty, staff, and Board of Trustees . . . who will possess a sympathetic understanding of the purposes and goals of the college and its character as an institution related to the Lutheran Church in America."[38] The statement declared that the college would seek to enroll a significant number of qualified Lutheran students.[39] As a concrete symbol of this renewed relationship, the Virginia Synod was invited to move its headquarters to the college campus in a lovely old building—Bittle Hall—which had been the college library. This move put synod personnel into an active relationship with the college's faculty and staff, and vice versa. The synod and its leadership were no longer distant and undefined.

The synod, for its part, pledged to support the college in the above functions, mainly by helping to supply students, scholarships, and some modest financial backing. In an appendix, the document listed the many ways that the college and the synod currently cooperated, most of them having to do with the use of facilities and the mutual enrichment that each could provide.

Regarding governance, the college continued to retain, as was its custom, the synod president (or bishop) and two distinguished pastors from the synod on its board of trustees. But Fintel saw the need—in addition to the ecclesiastical presence—for the presence of wealthy Lutheran laypeople

38. These references are all from the "Statement of Partnership between Roanoke College and the Virginia Synod," accepted by both bodies in 1979.

39. It is noteworthy that no such aim—recruiting a significant number of qualified Lutherans—was actualized with regard to faculty hiring. At that point in the college's history, only the president was required by bylaw to be a Lutheran. Neither was there any stated aim to maintain a "critical mass" of Christians on the faculty, staff, or board of trustees.

on the board. These laypeople, usually business executives, could more per-
suasively support the religious purposes of the college by offering financial
backing for them. For example, one such Lutheran layman, Timothy Pickle,
endowed the chaplaincy. In his search for wealthy leaders like Pickle, Fintel also came across wealthy Lutherans whom he would later encourage
to endow professorships. The rest of the members of the board, while certainly not hostile toward the Christian heritage and mission of the college,
were not naturally attuned to discussing them either. Indeed, they generally
avoided giving much studied attention to those topics. But the Lutherans on
the board, and the representative whom the national church sent to board
meetings, could now and then remind the whole board of such concerns.

Another important move Fintel made was to appoint a successor to
Chaplain Swanson as director of church relations in 1987. He recruited a
Lutheran laywoman, Kathryn Buchanan, who came from a banking background, to take that position, but he placed her in resource development.[40]
She had excellent fundraising abilities that became extremely important in
the next decade for building a strategy of targeting Lutheran money to the
specifically religious functions of the college—professorships, scholarships,
and programs.

Though these institutional connections were important, it was far
more important to restore to the college a strong *intellectual* connection
to its Lutheran/Christian heritage. After all, the college was an educational
institution where intellectual matters were foremost. So it was utterly important not only to gather an impressive group of Christian intellectuals in
the religion and philosophy department to teach that tradition, but also to
demonstrate the public relevance of the Christian moral and intellectual
tradition in two other ways: the public programs of the Center for Religion
and Society, and faith/learning engagement in the formal academic life of
the college beyond the religion and philosophy department.

Regarding its teaching mission, the department was teaching a full array

---

40. I was initially appalled by his placing her in resource development because I
thought that would signal to the churches that the college was only interested in their money.
As it turned out, I could not have been more wrong. She was brilliant in finding donors who
saw their benevolence to the college as a Christian calling. She was instrumental in cultivating Lutheran donors who funded at least three endowed chairs in Lutheran studies. She
was also crucial in organizing and funding many programs of the center and the synod. The
effect of her work was magnified by her deep involvement in the Virginia Synod, in which
she held office and was much admired and respected. She also cultivated wealthy Lutherans
beyond the Virginia Synod, much to the benefit of the college.

of courses for its majors and minors by 1985, as well as attractive electives that were open to all students. By the end of the decade, it was teaching a required course—"Formative Visions"—in the honors program and preparing to teach a required course—"Values and the Responsible Life"—in the general-education program.

The center also supported courses that demonstrated faith/learning engagement, for example, "Capitalism and Justice" and "Religious Perspectives on Contemporary Literature." "Faith/learning engagement" meant a dialogue between the claims and perspectives of the Christian faith and those of "secular" fields. For example, the course "Religious Perspectives on Contemporary Literature" featured a close analysis of the religious underpinnings of the literary works of John Updike and Flannery O'Connor, while "Capitalism and Justice" involved a moral assessment of market economics and practices. Since Christianity makes comprehensive claims, it was important to put those claims in conversation with the claims of secular subjects. There was no assumption that one set of claims automatically trumped those of the other, or that they could be harmonized easily. A Christian college was called to engage in that sort of lively faith/learning conversation.[41]

Fortunately, faculty outside the religion and philosophy department also offered courses that engaged faith and learning. The college was providen-

---

41. Oddly, the theology of the Lutheran Church in America undercut faith/learning engagement by depriving the faith of publicly relevant intellectual content. It claimed that colleges were "First Article" institutions that prized knowledge ascertained by reason, experience, and science. It eschewed the terms "Christian college" or "Christian higher education." In this interpretation, the wisdom that comes from reflection on the revelation of God in the long history of Christian theology and ethics had no role in the search for truth that a college strove for. While rightly distancing itself from theology that would place a college in the realm of redemption (colleges cannot be baptized, repent, or receive forgiveness of sin), the LCA's theology—taken up later by the ELCA—made Christian truth claims irrelevant to the search for truth in the broader educational life of a church-related college. It was a formula for secularizing college education by making the Christian intellectual inheritance unimportant to the major task of the college. It sequestered Christianity in the religion department and then was tempted to make Christian studies into "religious studies" in which the faculty taught *about* the Christian tradition, not *for* it. To be fair, the document that outlined the LCA theology did list one question among several dozen that hinted at faith/learning engagement: "Do the other academic disciplines have a concern for theological issues and is there provision for their interaction with the theology of the church?" ("A Statement of the Lutheran Church in America: The Basis for Partnership between Church and College," Division for Mission in North America of the Lutheran Church in America [1976], 13). However, given the overall theology of the document, there was little reason to insist on such an interaction.

tially blessed with a sprinkling of Christian faculty who saw such engagement as part of their calling as professors in a variety of disciplines. Faith/learning engagement was emerging in the college in a vigorous, though fragmentary, way. More was to develop in later years.

Conclusion

The later Fintel years (1983–89) were pivotal. Though it was certainly true that the pivot was enabled by new physical improvements and increasingly effective approaches in resource development, admissions, and planning, the crucial changes came in launches that recovered a healthier ethos for the college and that renewed the Christian republican themes in the mission of the college. It recovered some of its soul. In addition, it set forth a new ambition: to become a widely recognized liberal arts college in the region and nation.

Those years featured the strengthening of the Christian voice at the college, and perhaps gave that voice its clearest Lutheran construal ever in the history of the college. The Lutheran/Christian voice was projected not only in the curricula of the college through a rejuvenated department of religion and philosophy, but also publicly through the programs of the Center for Church and Society. Though it could not be said that the Christian vision was the privileged organizing paradigm of the college, as it once was, it was true that it was now articulated by a strong voice among other voices at the college. It had a place in the required courses of the curricula, and it was increasingly expressed in the intellectual life of the college. It was transmitted through many more courses than it had been earlier. Likewise, the republican tradition of the college was strengthened by the institution of the Fowler Program, with its professorship and many public programs. And, fittingly, those who carried responsibility for the Christian and republican emphases of the college often cooperated in articulating them to the college and the community.

The curricula of the college—its honors program and general-education offerings—represented a recovery of a more coherent liberal arts education. Courses fit together in curricula that aimed at serious intellectual and moral formation of the students. The quality of the students went up with the coherence of the college's educational mission. Likewise, the ethos of the college was reshaped to be more hospitable to those students of an intellectual and religious bent. Though one could not claim that the whole student body shared those characteristics, room was made for subcultures that cared about them.

Partly because of its new emphases on scholarly achievement by the faculty, the college began to be recognized by rating agencies, especially the *US News and World Report*. The desire to be recognized became a major item—perhaps the uppermost item—on its agenda. Indeed, the desire for recognition became the rallying point upon which the faculty could agree. The college and its faculty moved forward on a number of fronts to further that goal. Improvement was palpable. But it was difficult, if not impossible, for the faculty to agree on a comprehensive vision of Christian republicanism. The college had not had a firm enough grasp of that historic mission to articulate it sharply and to hire faculty who supported it. The faculty became more fragmented on substantive meanings and values. While the college renewed its Christian republican voice, it was a partial renewal shared by only a portion of the faculty and the student body. Still, it was an important recovery, and it had a semblance of soul. Norman Fintel certainly led that recovery.[42]

42. Retired president Norman Fintel died in the morning of April 7, 2017, hours before he and his wife, Jo, were to receive the Roanoke College Medal in honor of their service to the college. Nevertheless, the award ceremony went on and his funeral was held in the college's Antrim Chapel on Sunday, April 9, 2017, with hundreds attending. His and his wife's ashes will be buried in a garden in front of the Fintel library.

8

DAVID GRING (1989–2004)

Incrementalist Par Excellence

As we have seen in earlier chapters, Roanoke College presidents have been surprising. One might have thought that David Bittle, the founder and life-long Lutheran, would have planted Lutheran themes and practices deep into the life of the college; instead, he embedded American evangelical themes in it. Or one might have guessed that Julius Dreher, who had a very constricted formation in the South, would have been a narrow zealot for his home region; instead, he became one of the most cosmopolitan of Roanoke presidents. One could have thought that John Morehead, a well-trained systematic theologian who taught in a seminary prior to his arrival at Roanoke, would have altered the theological substance of the college in general and the department of philosophy and religion in particular; instead, he succeeded in making the college "more efficient" and in constructing a significant number of buildings.

Likewise, when the search committee that was appointed in the spring of 1984 to find a successor to Norman Fintel selected David Gring, academic dean of the robustly Lutheran Concordia College in Moorhead, Minnesota, many expected—and some feared—that he would bring new and vigorous efforts to deepen the Lutheran character of Roanoke College. Indeed, several of the members of that committee worried a bit that he might be too assertive in doing so.[1] Was Gring to carry forward Fintel's efforts to renew the "Lutheran soul" of the college?

---

1. The recruitment of Gring was probably the first time Roanoke used "professional" methods for finding a president. A firm of "head-hunters" was hired, and the search commit-

Fintel had gotten the ball rolling in strengthening the Lutheran voice at the college by recruiting a Lutheran ethicist in mid-career to rejuvenate the religion and philosophy department. By the end of the 1980s the department was strengthened by the arrival of two more strong Christian intellectuals. A Center for Church and Society was under way. The Virginia Synod was now headquartered on campus. Fintel was raising money specifically for the religious functions of the college. A friendly dean, who had himself become a Lutheran, was supporting these efforts. Would the "Lutheran momentum" be continued? What about the other two elements in Roanoke's sense of mission: service to the community (which I have called "republicanism" throughout this book) and national recognition as a liberal arts college? This chapter will be devoted to answering those questions.

The Close of an Old and Beginning of a New Century

Upon his arrival in the fall of 1989, David Gring was met with two challenges that were to be definitive for his tenure at Roanoke College. The first happened soon after he moved into his office in an informal meeting with one of the most powerful men on the board of trustees, who said: "We want to have a chapter of Phi Beta Kappa, and we want you to bring it off."[2] Gring set about to meet that challenge, and it can be fairly said that his work was crucial in reaching that goal in 2003. The second challenge was external, but became closely related to the first. Soon after Gring arrived, the United States experienced a recession. The board, which included a

---

tee, which included several Lutheran members of the Roanoke faculty, met eight candidates in a neutral location. According to William Hill (whom I interviewed on January 6, 2015), the committee chose Gring with the expectation that he would foster the Lutheran heritage of Roanoke College more strongly than the others might. The heightened concern for that Lutheran heritage was probably a compensatory response to the board's move in 1989 to strike down the clause in the college bylaws that required the president to be a Lutheran. That move was instigated by a secular-minded member of the board, whose lawyer reported to the board that that bylaw would jeopardize federal programs at the college, a judgment that was dubious, to say the least. But the board did replace one requirement with another: "The President of the College should understand and support the long-standing relationship between the College and the Lutheran Church and be able to articulate effectively its beneficial influence on the College and society" (*By-Laws of the Trustees of Roanoke College*). It is interesting that the three presidents since that new provision was enacted have been Lutherans, even though they are no longer required to be so.

2. Interview with David Gring (March 12, 2015).

number of prominent businessmen, had to cope with that difficult situation in their own enterprises and expected the college to do likewise. The president was challenged by his board to maintain a stringent fiscal discipline.[3] Thus the 1990s became known among the college faculty and staff as the decade of "revenue neutrality." Every new expenditure had to be covered by new income; it could not come from the general budget. The result was that the college produced an excess of saving over spending throughout the 1990s, and that excess was ploughed back into the college. At the same time, Gring worked hard to raise money for many college causes—with great success.

This combination of fiscal discipline and increasing funds put the college in the strongest financial condition it had ever been in by the turn of the twenty-first century. That increased financial strength, distributed incrementally in crucial places, was instrumental in the college's acquiring of the Phi Beta Kappa chapter. And that achievement fit the college's newfound ambition to become a nationally ranked liberal arts college.[4]

If Gring experienced that fitting reward for the fruit of his labor toward the end of his tenure, two other events were not so positive. One was external: 9/11/01. That cataclysmic event led him to reflect more deeply about the "soul" of the college.[5] What really is its mission? How could the sense of mission become stronger and more coherent? A ready-made answer seemed to be presented by the Lilly Foundation's offer to the college to compete in a national contest for a $2 million grant to strengthen the teaching of Christian vocation at each college that won that grant. Roanoke College, after winning a preliminary grant to support the application, did indeed develop an ambitious proposal; but it was sharply challenged by the faculty, and the grant was lost. (I will have more to say later about the loss of this major chance to strengthen the religious dimension of the mission of the college.) But now a bit more about the 1990s and the turn of the century, the era during which David Gring was president of the college.

3. This tightening of the college budget pressed by the board's businessmen led one of the college vice presidents to opine: "That's when the board began insisting that the college be run like a railroad."

4. In 1993, *US News and World Report* ranked Roanoke as one of the finest liberal arts colleges in the South. This was but a prelude to higher rankings later in Gring's presidency.

5. George Keller, *Prologue to Prominence—A Half Century of Roanoke College, 1951-2003* (Minneapolis: Lutheran University Press, 2005), 75. Keller reports that Gring conveyed some remorse that he had not been able to address the issue of "institutional identity" as fully as he had wished.

After the initial recession in 1990, the rest of the decade was one of economic expansion, which even included a balanced federal budget by mid-decade. Politically, the end of the Cold War was paramount. It allowed the country to relax on the military front as the Soviet Union collapsed. But that calm didn't last long: the First Gulf War occurred in 1991, and ethnic wars in Africa and the Balkans exploded a bit later. Bill Clinton, elected for two presidential terms, presided over good economic times, though his administration was marred by his own sexual misconduct. He was a political moderate who knew how to find consensus on economic and political matters, so the country experienced a good deal of political comity.

As I mentioned above, the good times of Gring's administration came to a screeching halt in the second year of the new century when, on September 11, 2001, a major terrorist attack was made on the United States by radical, suicidal Islamic operatives.[6] Soon thereafter, the country again girded itself for war, this time against the radicals in Afghanistan and then in Iraq. The "national security state" emerged as a new and inescapable backdrop for all American institutions.

Culturally, the transformative energies of the 1960s continued to work their way into society. Identity politics increased their role in American life. What was once a common culture was broken into many subcultures. This fragmentation was accelerated and strengthened by the new technologies that were rapidly being adopted: computers, the internet, videos, cable and satellite TV, and mobile phones—to name just some of the innovations. These enabled individuals to pick and choose from an ever-increasing array of "lifestyle choices." Individualism of an expressive and utilitarian kind increased. "Diversity" and "inclusivity" became mantras that would last well into the new century; multiculturalism and social liberalism were both the causes and the effects of these slogans. These accumulated technological and cultural changes affected colleges and universities profoundly. I will trace some of those effects in the rest of the chapter, but now let's take a closer look at the president during this time.

---

6. Coincidentally, the first Palestinian students to come to the college arrived about a month before the September attacks. To its great credit, Gring's administration made sure the students were safe and secure in the turbulent days after the attack.

The Formation of David Gring

David M. Gring was born in Reading, Pennsylvania, in May 1945, of solid Pennsylvania Dutch (i.e., German) stock: his mother was Lutheran and his father Reformed. Though David's father was not a regular church attender during David's growing-up years, the family adopted the elder Gring's religious heritage. (Later, his father became quite active in a nearby Reformed congregation.) Through all this time David and his mother attended Reformed and Union churches faithfully. He went to local grade schools and graduated from high school in nearby Shillington, where his mother served as a school secretary—and from which the novelist John Updike also graduated.

The senior Gring was an engineer who had graduated from Penn State University in 1931, and who worked in high-level sales of specialized products to trucking companies. He also owned a fifty-four-acre family farm that featured an old stone house, ten acres of Christmas trees, and a huge garden.[7] Young David, along with his sister, was assigned daily duties in both agricultural enterprises. The whole family, modeling after the father, worked hard and had little time for frivolities. The work ethic was revered, along with a rather ascetic style of life. As it was for many parents who grew up during the Depression, having too much fun was considered something close to sin, and emotional expression was restrained.

In high school David began dating Susan Dietrich, a member of the Brethren in Christ Church. That relationship developed later into a lifelong marriage, enriched by two children. After high school, David went off to Franklin and Marshall College, an academically excellent school that was historically—but, by David's time, very loosely—connected to the German Reformed tradition. While in college he attended a large Lutheran church in Lancaster. At Franklin and Marshall he majored in biology and earned membership in Phi Beta Kappa, and his academic accomplishments enabled

---

7. Since his father believed that the labor of the two young Gring siblings was their unpaid contribution to the family farming enterprises, young David, desiring a bit of spending money for himself, asked a neighboring farmer if he could work in his large garden for a modest stipend. The farmer accepted his offer. Delighted, David announced to his father that he would be working in another garden for pay, expecting that his father would either begin paying him or free him from working in the family garden. "That's fine, David," his father said; "you can just get up at five a.m., when I do, and work both gardens" (David Gring interview [March 13, 2015]).

him to enter a highly regarded graduate program in genetics at Indiana University, where he was awarded a PhD in 1971.

He then spent five years teaching biology at Lebanon Valley College in Annville, Pennsylvania. But a teaching career was not the calling that Gring sought. He was not attracted to the "publish or perish" ethos of faculty life. Rather, he was interested in the broader enterprise of higher education, especially one devoted to the liberal arts. That meant moving into administration.

Following a year (1975–76) as an American Council on Education fellow, he applied for an assistant deanship at Concordia College in Moorhead, Minnesota, a solidly Lutheran and academically respected school. At that time Gring was not a Lutheran, and the president of the college, Paul Dovre, was intentionally maintaining a critical mass (70 percent) of Lutherans among the faculty and staff. Surprisingly, Gring was tapped for the job and quickly moved up the ranks to vice president of academic affairs, a position in which he served from 1979 to 1989.

During that time he became a Lutheran and acquired a passion for Lutheran higher education. He developed a sophisticated understanding of the role of a Lutheran college in its intellectual pursuits:

> The scholar at a Christian college ought to promote a world view that influences the selection, interpretation, and application of data from any discipline; and that Lutheran contribution to the theology of grace, the doctrine of vocation, and understanding the relationship between the secular and sacred (to name a few) are important to the manner in which scholarship and inquiry are conceived.[8]

Further, he pledged himself as dean to recruit such scholars in order to strengthen Concordia's commitment to faith and learning engagement. He and President Dovre interviewed and assessed all finalists for academic positions at Concordia to make sure they fit the liberal arts and faith-oriented mission of the college.

After ten years of successful academic leadership at Concordia, Gring was recruited to become a candidate for president of Roanoke College, a position that would give him opportunity to shape the "broader enterprise of

8. David Gring, "Christian Faith and the Liberal Arts: The Centrality of Faculty Recruitment and Retention," an unpublished address to the Concordia faculty at the opening worship, August 24–25, 1988, 7.

higher education" at another Lutheran-related college, albeit a very different type of that species. His candidacy was successful, and he arrived as the new president of Roanoke in the fall of 1989.

The Gring Vision for Roanoke College

His predecessors generally waited until the spring commencement to give their inaugural address, but Gring decided to give his in October 1989. The brief interval between his arrival and his address meant a rather quick "size-up" of what kind of institution he was addressing.

The Inaugural Address: "Marks of Significant Distinction"

Offering generous praise to the presidents who preceded him, he maintained that the "progress of this college has been extraordinary. During this period when many colleges lost focus, strayed from their mission and traded a vision of quality and excellence for something less, this college has grown in stature and reputation and has in these days emerged as a college of considerable strength."[9] Still, he argued, the "task is not yet completed." As the college moved toward its sesquicentennial in 1992, it should no longer be "content to be a college of considerable strength, but instead move vigorously to become a college of significant distinction." The latter phrase became a well-known Gring slogan.

After identifying the center of his vision for the college, Gring went on to define the marks of significant distinction. The first mark of distinction was having a clear sense of mission. Roanoke, he believed, had a good start in that task. Its purpose statement claimed that it aimed to "serve a free society by developing in students a capacity for responsible leader-

---

9. David Gring, "Marks of Significant Distinction," unpublished inaugural address given at a Roanoke College assembly, October 27, 1989. The quotes that follow are all taken from that address. While the sentence that congratulated the college on its progress was straightforwardly true, the praise for clear missional focus may have been a bit of inauguration boilerplate. Privately, Gring—like Fintel before him—believed that the college lacked a sharp sense of mission. When I interviewed him on March 12, 2015, Gring said that the college had "little institutional cohesion." Both presidents probably were comparing the deficit in clarity of mission at Roanoke with the sharper visions of Midwestern Lutheran colleges such as Concordia and Wartburg.

ship."[10] It would do so by promoting the "intellectual, emotional, spiritual and practical aspects of liberal arts education; engender an appreciation for and an understanding of our own and other cultures; encourage service to community; and emphasize the ethical dimensions of our Lutheran heritage and the more broadly defined Judeo-Christian tradition."

Noting that it was easier to claim these lofty goals than to do them, he congratulated Roanoke in actually pursuing them practically. He pointed to the new general education curriculum, the honors program, strengthened majors, and the emphasis on written and oral communication. He then argued that the thrust of the academic program was not merely intellectual; it aimed at shaping character, the most valuable possession an individual can have. This concern for character "captured the spirit of the founder and the power of our Judeo-Christian tradition rich in a theology that requires standards for individual action, service to the community in which we live, and the responsibility to humankind less fortunate than ourselves." These academic and moral tasks could only be carried out by a faculty that modeled these noble virtues and shaped young lives according to them. And it meant a faculty that should be 100 percent devoted to teaching and mentoring.

A second mark of a college of significant distinction was that it made its education available to a wide range of classes of students. It had to offer generous assistance to those who qualified for the college but could not pay the full price. A third mark was facilities appropriate to the quality of the academic program. He looked forward to the completion of the Fintel Library project, the renovation of the courthouse, the beautification of the campus, and increased support for state-of-the-art technology, especially in the area of computer services.

The fourth mark of a college of significant distinction was a commitment to community. Gring argued that all the great tasks of liberal arts education were best viewed as a communal project, one that was shored up by mutual commitment and support. The community included the college, the surrounding Roanoke Valley, the nation, and the world. The college, he said, was interdependent with each of those realities, and it needed to see its task in consort with them.

In concluding, Gring quoted the Bittle dictum that had become something of a mantra for the college: "The most momentous duty of one generation to another is its education." And the education that was communicated

10. This phrase in the college's statement of purpose so impressed Gring that he had it calligraphed and framed for his office.

was pointless unless it resulted in better men and women. In carrying out this duty, college leaders stood on the shoulders of their predecessors and drew on the commitment of the current generation of board, faculty, staff, and students. He named individuals from each category to individualize his point.

"Though we stand by the grace of God," he said, "we do not stand without responsibility, without obligation." Gring closed by again quoting Bittle on the purposes of higher education: "To enable our successors to be better persons than we are, better qualified to incur the responsibilities of life, to possess superior wisdom and a more refined humanity." He reiterated the four marks of a college of significant distinction and pledged his best efforts to work together with every Roanoke College constituency to realize those marks.

Commentary

David Gring clearly articulated the thrust of his presidency: to continue to move the college from a "college of considerable strength" to one of "significant distinction." Pursuing that goal was a continuation and enhancement of the efforts begun in the Fintel administration: it aimed at ever-higher recognition by key ranking agencies. This was at the time a relatively new goal of the college. It was one around which all constituencies could rally because it did not assume that all—or even a majority—agreed on the content of the college mission, which continued to have the theme of Christian service forthrightly stated.

Strengthening these more substantive historic goals of the college, though, would aid in the quest for wider recognition. Increasing intellectual excellence, plus a commitment to "responsible leadership" for all classes of students, had been goals the college had long sought. Generating those virtues from the base of the Judeo-Christian tradition had also been a staple. Enhancing intellectual excellence and responsible leadership would bring a higher ranking—and significant distinction.

Gring then offered clues about what priorities he would pursue: a faculty committed to teaching; the college commited to the community; better facilities; better pay for the faculty; and, fittingly, raising the money to support the sort of initiatives that might lead to acquiring Phi Beta Kappa status. What got rather short shrift in the address was what earlier presidents called "the religious element." The Lutheran heritage and the Judeo-Christian tradition got one mention—as sources for the ethical development of students. As other presidents had done, Gring viewed the broad Christian tradition as an instrument of moral formation. But whereas others had spent a good deal of time emphasizing this theme, Gring mentioned it only once, and that was a quote from the college's statement of purpose.

What was especially interesting was the contrast of his inaugural address at Roanoke with one of his addresses to the faculty at Concordia.[11] The former, as I have noted, barely addressed the religious dimension of the college mission, while the latter was a fulsome exposition of the religious mission of a Lutheran college, replete with references to faith and learning engagement. The former mentioned the recruiting of faculty who would be committed to teaching the liberal arts, while the latter promised to recruit faculty who would help advance the Christian mission of the college.

In the short time that Gring had to assess the nature of the college before he crafted his inaugural address, he obviously came to the conclusion that Roanoke was quite different from Concordia, especially with respect to the "religious element" in its identity and mission. This was no different from preceding presidents, who discerned where the college was in terms of its identity and mission, and then accommodated their address and their ensuing efforts to what they thought the college was all about. But what was happening over time was that the "religious element" of the college was being addressed less and less as presidents were discerning that neither the faculty nor the board of trustees had that element as a central concern. Indeed, the secularist wing of the faculty would have liked to see it diminish—or disappear completely. As long as it was merely a grace note to the main proceedings, they tolerated it.

On the many occasions after his inaugural that gave Gring an opportunity to articulate his vision, he was consistent in his emphases. "Significant distinction," of course, was the leading theme. "To serve a free society by developing in students the capacity for responsible leadership" came up repeatedly, as did "leading a responsible life of ethical decision-making." "Serving those who are less fortunate than you" was another theme. On more religious occasions, such as the annual Christmas dinner, he offered "thanks to One greater than we by whose grace we live and work in this vineyard." On the occasion of his last Christmas dinner, he affirmed that "Roanoke College is a sacred trust founded on the bedrock of Judeo-Christian values and venerable

11. Gring, "Christian Faith and the Liberal Arts," 3–8.

Lutheran tradition. With sacred trusts come sacred responsibilities to special people. You are those special people."[12]

Though his religious rhetoric was consistently mild, careful, and "inclusive," that does not offer a full view of how Gring actually promoted that religious element. What he does is better than what he says, as we shall soon see. Suffice it to say, however, the worries of several Lutheran faculty on the search committee that Gring would be too aggressive in pressing the Lutheran/Christian character of the college never came to pass.

The Sesquicentennial

Several major initiatives were in progress when Gring arrived at the college in the summer of 1989. Besides the beginning of a major library renovation project and the culmination of the 1992 campaign, the 150th anniversary of Roanoke's founding was being prepared. He participated in the preparations and celebration itself with gusto. In the sesquicentennial year itself, 1992–93, the newly renovated library was named Fintel Library in honor of the recently retired Fintels, Norman and Jo. Further celebrations of the anniversary included: the production of the play *Fashion*, which was popular in Roanoke's founding year; Founder's Day; a Sesquicentennial Ball; the publication of a new college history, *Dear Old Roanoke*, by Mark Miller of the history department; and a grand fireworks display on Alumni Weekend in the spring of 1993.[13]

However, the premier intellectual event of the celebration was a colloquium in January of 1992, entitled "Educating the Whole Person," featuring guest lecturers Ernest Boyer, Robert Brustein, and Gilbert Meilaender, who addressed that main topic. The event was sponsored by the three main endowments for public events that Roanoke had established: the Henry H. Fowler Public Affairs Lecture Series, the Center for Church and Society, and the Donald C. Jordan Humanities Endowment.[14]

Ernest Boyer was a distinguished figure in the academic world. He had been the United States Commissioner of Education, and at the time of his

12. Unpublished address to the Roanoke College Community Christmas Celebration, December 13, 2003, 1, 5.
13. Keller, *Prologue*, 55.
14. "Colloquium '92: Educating the Whole Person," a publication by Roanoke College for the 150th anniversary of its founding. The following synopses of each lecture are taken from that document.

lecture was president of the Carnegie Foundation for the Advancement of Teaching and a senior fellow of the Woodrow Wilson School at Princeton University. His lecture, "The Importance of General Education," addressed the intellectual dimension of educating the whole person. Lamenting the tendency at that time for colleges to rely on a distribution system—the individual student picks and chooses courses from required general areas—for their general education, Boyer called for colleges to forge a common core of learning that would draw all students and faculty together into a community of inquiry. He wished for a renewal of general education.

It is noteworthy that Roanoke College had just installed a new general-education curriculum that did feature a good deal of that common core of learning. Later called the "Centers of Distinction Curriculum," it possessed far more coherence than had the distribution system that preceded it. The college had modeled its new general education program after the honors program it had established in the mid-1980s. Brought on line in 1989 as Gring arrived, it was in full force by the time of Boyer's lecture.

A second major lecture, "The Options of Multiculturalism," dealt with the aesthetic realm. The lecture, given by Robert Brustein, artistic director of the American Repertory Theatre and professor of English at Harvard University, was prescient in its anticipation of a separatist kind of multiculturalism that eventually resulted in the identity politics so prevalent in the decades thereafter. After celebrating the individual and ethnic diversity of the benign sort of multiculturalism that emphasized equality of opportunity for all, he sharply criticized the approach to multiculturalism that separated people into defensive "tribes," who had their own set of norms, characteristics, and beliefs. Such a multiculturalism, he said, undermined any chance for a core of common learning.

A third lecture, entitled "Forming Both Heart and Mind: The Role of the Church-related College," and addressing the spiritual and moral dimensions of educating the whole person, was given by Christian ethicist Gilbert Meilaender of Valparaiso University. He began by identifying two approaches to the moral life: the virtue-oriented model in which the moral agent is deeply socialized into a tradition, and the "critical reflection" model, in which students are taught the principles and applications of the moral life according to various religious and philosophical perspectives. Meilander went on to argue that the first approach—"forming the heart"—happens in religious communities and families, whereas the second—"forming the mind"—happens in the classroom. In a church-related college, he argued, the teaching of ethical reflection should not be neutral, surveying various options without tipping one way or the other. Rather, the teaching of ethics in a church-related college like Roanoke should emphasize the teaching of ethics from a Christian perspective. It should make Christian ethics alluring and persuasive without being coercive or denigrating other views.

His commended approach fit what Roanoke was doing in its new general-education curriculum in a course entitled "Values and the Responsible Life." That course, usually offered in the junior year, did survey religious and philosophical ethics, but it featured Christian faith and morality as a central thrust. The adoption of this course renewed the theme in the historic mission of the college that emphasized a Christian basis for moral responsibility and service. However, Meilaender concluded his lecture by commending two requirements for church-related colleges that Roanoke would not be likely to fulfill. First, he argued that the board, administration, and faculty must be in regular conversation about how the Christian view of life might be promoted, not only in religion courses but in other places in the curriculum. It should sustain a public conversation about how this Christian base might be cultivated. Further, he argued that a serious church-related college will aim at some formation of the heart as well as the mind. In order to transmit a moral and religious tradition, it would have to maintain, via "hiring for mission," a critical mass of faculty who were deeply embedded in the sponsoring religious tradition, which in this case was Lutheranism. Only then would a Lutheran ethos be visible and alluring to those already in the tradition and those possibly drawn to it. (In this chapter's conclusion I shall return to the challenges Meilaender made in this lecture—and Roanoke's responses to them.)

It is worth noting that the adoption of the "Values and the Responsible Life" course into the required general-education curriculum was controversial because it was to be included in the prescribed curriculum of the whole college, not simply in a curriculum-within-a-curriculum that involved only a small group of faculty and students, as did the honors curriculum. The secularist wing of the faculty resisted the effort to reintroduce a required religion-philosophy course, something the college had not had for twenty years. "Coerced religion" was anathema to them, along with their estimation that the course was a version of "Sunday school." The director of general education, who also suspected that "proselytization" was illegitimately going on, monitored the course intently. One might respond to that suspicion by saying that, if you make the Christian way of life seem alluring, as the religion and philosophy faculty were doing, you could not guarantee that no students would adopt it for their own. To counter the charges that proselytizing and low-level "Sunday school" teaching were going on, the dean encouraged members of the religion and philosophy department, who taught the course, to open it up to professors from other disciplines. However, those faculty members would need training in the religious and philosophical materials presented in the course; and, after several summer training sessions, only a few professors from outside the religion and philosophy department deigned to teach the course because of the considerable intellectual challenge it presented to professors and students alike. After several years of attempts to "spread the burden," complaints about the course died down and the department continued carrying the burden of teaching the course to all students. Over the years the original consensus on a common core of readings in all sections gradually eroded, though the major Western philosophical and religious pillars of the responsible life were nevertheless incorporated into the course.

Curriculum

In the preceding chapter I detailed the curricula initiated by the honors program in 1986 and by the general-education program in 1989. Both were fresh and coherent curricula forged by the Roanoke faculty of the mid-1980s, with the support and encouragement of Dean Gerald Gibson, who himself was a strong proponent of the liberal arts. The curricula also represented a strengthening of Roanoke's historic commitment to the Christian faith as an important base for the responsible life. Of course, as time went on, changes were made to each; but both survived for nearly twenty years.[15] The whole of Gring's presidential stint was characterized by his strong commitment to these two curricula.

Several initiatives increased faculty-student interaction. Independent study projects were encouraged, more internships were arranged, and a Summer Scholar program was begun. To strengthen international education, the dean hired a full-time director to help the faculty fill the May Term with many travel courses. The new director also promoted programs to invite international students to Roanoke. Such programs attracted students

15. Gradually, the interdisciplinary character of the honors program was abandoned. Ironically, it shifted to a more rigorous version of the general-education curriculum, which had originally copied some features of the pioneering honors program. However, the honors program was expanded and continued to provide excellent educational opportunities to some of Roanoke's best students.

from twenty-four countries. Student quality was enhanced by way of an innovative strategy that used competitive exams for merit-based student scholarships. Average SAT scores increased, and retention also increased: by 2004 there were over 1,900 full-time students. Applications grew to 2,900 for 485 freshmen slots. Advancing on all these fronts helped the college's case for being awarded a Phi Beta Kappa chapter.

Faculty and Board

Gring's emphasis on "revenue neutrality" meant that there was not much growth in the number of tenure-track faculty during his time: in fourteen years the number grew from ninety to only about one hundred. However, the percentage of full-time faculty holding terminal degrees rose from 84 percent in 1992 to 95 percent in 2004, the last year of Gring's administration. Furthermore, retirees were replaced. The new arrivals on the faculty did not have to be cajoled by Dean Gibson into doing research; most were keen on participating in the scholarly life. Their contributions to their fields of inquiry began to mount.

As the student body grew, and Gring resisted opening new positions on the faculty, the college relied more and more on adjunct teachers to cover the needed courses. Behind the scenes, though, Gring was diligently cultivating donors for endowed chairs (endeavors that were to be realized by later presidents) to supplement the two that had already been established, the Jordan-Trexler Professor of Religion and the Fishwick Professor of English.

The Fishwick Chair was filled in 1989 by Robert Denham, who came to Roanoke from Emory and Henry College. Denham was one of the world's authorities on Northrup Frye, the Canadian literary critic; he was also a formidable Christian intellectual whose erudition added to the reputation of Christian scholars who performed in the secular disciplines. The Jordan-Trexler Chair was inhabited in 1999–2000 by Paul Hinlicky, newly arrived from a six-year stint in Slovakia, where he taught Christian theology on the Lutheran Divinity Faculty of Comenius University in Bratislava. I relinquished that endowed chair and the chairmanship of the religion and philosophy department in that year, when I was appointed senior Lilly fellow at Valparaiso University for my sabbatical year, 1999–2000.

A major change for the faculty had occurred earlier in the spring of 1993, when Dean Gerald Gibson left his position at Roanoke for the presidency of Maryville College in Tennessee.[16] As I have noted earlier, Gibson was the initiator of and catalyst for many new programs at the college. Many think of the 1980s—his heyday under Norman Fintel—as a golden age of faculty creativity and advancement. His successor, Kenneth Garren, a mathematics professor and associate dean, was "a master of detail who got along well with the college's faculty."[17] He kept the academic momentum going in the 1990s, but he was somewhat bound by "revenue neutrality." Garren, like Gibson before him, left his role at Roanoke to become the president of a nearby college, in his case, Lynchburg College. Following Garren in the dean's office was John Day, a Catholic who had earned a Harvard PhD in English. Day had been an associate dean at St. Olaf College, and many in the faculty expected a return to the more creative days of Gibson. They were disappointed, however, by Day's commitment to a "consensus" decision-making approach, which many interpreted as too hesitant and time-consuming.

Since faculty recruitment had been delegated to the departments, faculty members were hired mostly on the basis of departmental needs. Though academic deans continued to interview finalists, the deans' concern was whether or not the prospective faculty members were committed to liberal arts education. Even a mild query about church membership was eliminated.[18] Little attention was paid to prospective members' fit with the historical purposes of the college—that is, forming on Christian grounds young people from all social strata for responsible service to community,

16. Soon after Gring's arrival, a bevy of senior faculty complained to him that Gibson was turning the college into a "research institution" by requiring the faculty to engage in scholarly activity for tenure and promotion. Gring told the group to convey their concerns directly to the dean, which they did under highly uncomfortable circumstances. That action divided much of the faculty sharply between those who supported the dean's efforts to encourage scholarship and those who felt he was changing the nature of the college. Gring tried to moderate the conflict by proposing that the emphasis on research at Roanoke College was "research or scholarship on behalf of teaching." Gibson interpreted Gring's actions as a lack of support, which he felt hampered him in administrative decision-making from the early 1990s until his departure from the college. Soon thereafter he sought administrative work elsewhere.

17. Keller, *Prologue*, 66.

18. This hesitance on the part of the deans was reinforced by the human resources administrator, who told department chairs that, in their recruiting, they could only inquire about the candidates' competence in their field of expertise, not about their religious convictions, family life, or philosophy of life and education. This made it far more difficult to recruit whole persons to educate whole students. It further retarded "hiring for mission." Of course, many department chairs refused to bend to such narrow constraints and did conduct more comprehensive interviews.

country, and world. Yet, by happenstance—and in rare cases by intention—serious Christians did find their way onto the faculty of the college. They provided much support to the efforts of those seeking to strengthen those traditional Christian themes.

The academic leadership of the faculty, the department chairs, tended to be on the secularist side of things. Rare were those who held that a significant concern in hiring of faculty members was the candidates' support for the Christian element in the college's history and mission. By my estimate, at least half of the dean's council of department chairpersons were hostile to such a consideration in hiring, the other half generally apathetic. So there was little chance for the religious element to be strengthened through "hiring for mission"; indeed, such a concern was not even discussed. The secularist bent of the academic leadership was to be dramatically revealed in the conflict over the Lilly grant, which I will examine shortly.

Gring quietly continued Fintel's efforts to appoint Lutheran laypersons of means to the board of trustees, and to continue the tradition of including the bishop of the Virginia Synod and a prestigious Lutheran pastor or two in that body. Those laypersons were to become major benefactors of the college. However, though the Lutheran/Christian presence on the board was quietly strengthened, the board—as was its earlier habit—did not discuss the religious element in the college identity and mission. Formal representation of the Evangelical Lutheran Church in America on the board was sporadic and did not stimulate such a discussion. Therefore, the board left that concern to the administration and faculty members, both of which found the subject uncomfortable.

The "Republican" Heritage of the College

From its inception, a major theme in Roanoke College's identity and mission has had to do with forming citizens from all walks of life for the benefit of the country. The theme had lately been expressed in new language: the words "responsibility," "service," "ethical leadership," and "community" had taken the place of the old-fashioned words "virtue," "duty," "benevolence," and "republic." Rhetoric in this vein has been a staple in the college's mission statement and in the utterances of its presidents. Indeed, it is probably a rare college or university that does not justify its existence in similar terms. The more serious question is whether or not the school realizes its own rhetoric in academic and service programs.

The Gring years brought a steady increase in these areas. In the academic realm, "Values and the Responsible Life" was a required course that students took in their junior year during the entirety of Gring's administration. That course not only emphasized responsible service to one's fellow human beings but also the religious and philosophical bases that supported such service. The Christian foundation was emphasized, but other bases were not excluded. Certainly other departments encouraged service to the community, nation, and world—political science and education among them. And individual professors modeled that service.

The Fowler Program gained momentum, often offering joint programs with the Center for Church and Society that encouraged students, faculty, and the community at large to attend to the great public issues that were before the country and world. The Fowler Program was able to host former US Presidents (Ford, Carter) and other government officials who spoke to large crowds. Academic figures such as Yale law professor Stephen Carter lectured on virtue in public life.

Following the success of the spring 1985 joint program on "The USA and Germany—Signals of Danger and Hope," the Fowler Program and the center offered programs on the relationships of the United States with Korea (1996) and the United States with the United Kingdom (1998). The fall of communism in 1989 evoked a number of public events reflecting on that historic set of events. The two endowments jointly offered "Faith, Reason, and the American Enlightenment" in 2001, which featured Roanoke faculty from a number of departments. The Fowler Program and the center put on a major symposium in 2003 on "Religion and Politics in the Middle East," featuring Benazir Bhutto, Dennis Ross, and Stephen Cohen.

The Washington Semester, sponsored by the Lutheran College Washington Consortium, offered Roanoke students the chance to take two courses on public affairs and two internships in government service during their time in Washington. These academic and co-curricular efforts at promoting public understanding and service were supplemented by programs that involved both academic and practical involvement. The Co-Curricular and Service initiative appeared in 1999–2000; it was a two-course sequence required of all new and transfer students that promoted "involvement in community service and co-curricular activities."[19] Fifteen hours of co-curricular and service activities were required to earn a passing grade.

Straight service activities for students were emphasized by Chaplain

19. *Roanoke College Academic Catalogue*, 1999–2000, 55.

Henrickson, beginning in 1989, with his spring-break trip to Columbia, South Carolina, to build a Habitat for Humanity house. This annual trip continued throughout the Gring years. The chaplain's office also began co-ordinating other community service activities so that, by 2003, a full-time director of the Center for Community Service was hired to organize and manage myriad activities. Service activities thus had an aura of religious motivation about them. Roanoke was taking seriously its commitment to serve communities both near and far. President Dreher would have heartily endorsed this effort at "benevolence."

The Christian Heritage of the College

Ethos

With the expansion of the honors program and a general elevation of student quality, made possible by creative admissions programs, student life became more receptive to serious academic accomplishment. College choral programs continued to grow, which not only attracted music students but also offered a strong religious component in choral concerts. An annual Advent lessons and carols service at St. Andrew's Catholic Church in downtown Roanoke drew thousands to two consecutive sessions. A chapter of the Fellowship of Christian Athletes emerged among the successful Roanoke College teams.

About 20 percent of the student body identified as Catholics, while the no preference/no response percentile went from 14 to 22 percent. Self-identified Lutherans were about 8 percent of the student body, in a state (Virginia) where fewer than 1 percent of the inhabitants were Lutheran. The chaplain was busy enough to require a full-time assistant. Besides leading modestly attended services and discussion groups, he exercised a "ministry of presence," meaning that he was ready and available to those in need among the students and faculty. His strategy was to "be in relationship in a trustworthy way, and then talk about Jesus." The chaplain oversaw the campus work of pastors and leaders from various denominational groups, including that of a local priest who celebrated the Mass for the Catholic students on Sunday afternoons.

When asked to characterize the religious tenor of the student body, Chaplain Henrickson replied: "It's like our society, broken into subcultures. There are many nominal Christians, but it is a bit odd to be a serious one." He estimated that one-third of the student body had a sense of Christian identity and vocation, one-third could articulate what the Christian faith was about but were casual in living it, while the remaining third could describe it only vaguely and were uninterested in practicing it.[20]

Student life became more wholesome as personnel in the student affairs office expanded and became more professional. Large parties with alcohol were pushed off-campus, which was a mixed blessing. The good part was that students could find dorms in which they could sleep and study without disturbance. The downside was that the parties were completely unregulated, and the Salem community had to bear more of the student shenanigans.

The Religion and Philosophy Department

In an era when the Christian vision and ethos were no longer the organizing principles of the college, the religion and philosophy department was a crucial agency in carrying on the Christian thread of the college's historical sense of mission.[21] It was up to the task, partly because of the strong appointments that were made to replace retiring members of the department.

Gerald McDermott arrived at Roanoake in 1989, the same year David Gring became president. His new position in church history and world religions was granted by Gerald Gibson in the last years of the Fintel administration. McDermott came to Roanoke as a low-church Baptist evangelical and exited in 2015 as a high-church Anglican. Born into the Roman Catholic tradition and schooled in an elite Jesuit school, he soon lost enthusiasm for those Christian roots, only to be "converted" into evangelical Christianity

20. Conversation with Chaplain Paul Henrickson (Roanoke tenure, 1983–2013), Jan. 28, 2015.

21. The last time the language of "Christian college" was used to describe Roanoke was by Perry Kendig, early in his presidency (1963–75). At that time the college mission statement was more robust, and the "Christian republican" mission of the college was assumed. But that was soon to change because the historic mission of the college became vaguer and the new goal of the college—to become a nationally recognized liberal arts college—came to the fore. The college then proceeded in its hiring practices more according to the latter purpose than the former. It did not abandon the historic mission, but it continued the Christian republican themes as voices in the conversation. Roanoke became what I have termed an "intentional pluralist" church-related college, in which it guaranteed a voice at the table for both the Christian and the republican (service) themes. But neither were likely to become the organizing paradigm once again. See my typology of church-related colleges in the appendix; see also the intentional pluralist strategy in the conclusion.

during his days at the University of Chicago. He and his wife, Jean, lived in a Christian commune among "Jesus people" of the 1970s. After a stint as the principal of a Christian school in Moorhead, Minnesota, he took a PhD in American religious history at the University of Iowa. His thesis, entitled "One Holy and Happy Society," was on Jonathan Edwards's social ethic. His expertise in the life and thought of Edwards grew exponentially, and he became an international authority on the great eighteenth-century theologian.

McDermott became an effective and innovative teacher, an activist for evangelical causes at the college and in the community, and an increasingly prolific author. Because of his evangelical fervor, he drew many evangelical students, pastors, and community people into his orbit. He brought an evangelical presence to the college and the department that it had lacked for many years. But his activism, of course, also generated distaste for such overt evangelicalism among a portion of the faculty.

In 1990, longtime philosopher Roy Bent retired, and Hans Zorn took his place. Zorn fit well in the tradition of Roanoke College philosophers who traditionally had strong religious interests and taught courses laden with them—philosophy of religion, early and medieval Western philosophy, and metaphysics. He also taught sections of business ethics that were well-subscribed by business and economics majors. He was an observant Lutheran who came out of the Lutheran Church–Missouri Synod tradition.

In 1995, former dean Freeman Sleeper retired, and Jennifer Berenson Maclean, a Harvard PhD, was hired to fill his position in biblical studies. Trained by the famed New Testament scholar Helmut Koester, she brought a strong historical-critical approach to her teaching and research. She was also accompanied by her then husband, Ian Maclean, a South African who had also earned a PhD at Harvard and whose training was varied and rich. Both took up teaching with vigor, and Jennifer Maclean began publishing work she had begun as a graduate student.

When I went on sabbatical in 1999–2000 and subsequently left the endowed Jordan-Trexler Chair of Religion, as well as a tenured place on the faculty the following year, Paul Hinlicky was recruited to fill that chair and teach Christian theology.[22] Hinlicky had grown up in the conservative Slovak

22. I anticipated that I would leave full-time teaching after my sabbatical in 1999–2000. I was concerned that the Jordan-Trexler Chair would be occupied by a strong Lutheran public intellectual. I had been following Hinlicky's career for some time and decided that he would be the best person to succeed me. I even visited Bratislava several times to confirm my

Lutheran District of the Lutheran Church–Missouri Synod, in which his father was a pastor. Educated in the Missouri Synod system, he was caught in the middle of the church strife in that denomination during the mid-1970s. He was ordained into the Slovak Synod of the Lutheran Church in America and then completed his PhD at Union Theological Seminary in New York. He was employed in the Church and Society office of the LCA and edited *The Lutheran Forum* while he pastored a congregation and unsuccessfully sought a job in American Lutheran seminaries. He left the United States to teach at the Lutheran seminary of the Comenius University in Bratislava, Slovakia, where he had a highly influential teaching and writing role in a church and seminary that was newly freed from communist oppression and control. Because of his expertise and freshness of approach, he trained many PhD students, several of whom he later invited to teach at Roanoke College. Hinlicky brought a level of theological erudition to the teaching of Lutheranism that the college had never possessed before. Further, he began publishing books and articles with a flourish rivaled only by McDermott. Together, the two of them published more books during Gring's administration than did author-professors from any other department. Hinlicky's stature as a productive theologian soon brought him recognition in synodical, church-wide, and international circles.

Ned Wisnefske chaired the religion and philosophy department after my departure, and he continued his teaching, especially in the honors program. He published two books during this time. Though I left full-time teaching in 1999, I continued to teach on an adjunct basis while administering the Center for Religion and Society. I published five books during the Gring administration, and also wrote on issues of religion and society in many public venues.[23]

By the end of the century, the department had approximately forty majors—a good number of students taking them as second majors—and was offering such a variety of courses that they could have easily been mistaken for those of a seminary or graduate school of religion. Courses in the world religions were generally taught by believers in those traditions. The department professors were the mainstay of the "Values and Responsible Life"

---

judgment. Dean Kenneth Garren and I expedited the search process and brought Hinlicky to Roanoke College right when I was leaving for my sabbatical.

23. While serving as senior fellow in the Lilly Fellows program at Valparaiso University during my sabbatical year of 1999–2000, I wrote *Quality with Soul: How Six Premier Colleges and Universities Keep Faith with Their Religious Traditions* (Grand Rapids: Eerdmans, 2001). This brought together my thoughts about Christian higher education, of which this present volume itself is a continuing part.

course in the general-education program, as well as the "Formative Visions" course in the honors program.

In the 1980s and 1990s, two departmental majors were offered—one in religion and one a combined religion/philosophy—as well as two corresponding minors. After a new position in philosophy was filled by a promising young philosopher, Brent Adkins, in 2002, both religion (renamed "theology") and philosophy had separate majors and corresponding minors. Philosophy then sharply expanded its offerings and acquired student majors of its own.

In Gring's time, the religion and philosophy department became "one of the finest in the institution," and its members gained the college a reputation throughout the country and world by their lecturing and writing.[24] Internally, the members had a strong influence on the intellectual life of the college by offering their Christian insights in a number of venues. The department was stronger than it had ever been, and it befitted a college with the Christian heritage as one of its major identifying themes. Furthermore, the department was poised to gain even more strength when it would shortly receive three more endowed chairs to bolster Lutheran studies. Like his presidential predecessors, David Gring, as well as the director of church relations, was working behind the scenes to cultivate the donors for these prospective endowed chairs. But the donors would not have been attracted to offer such gifts to the department had not it already seemed to them to be a trustworthy carrier of the Christian vision at Roanoke College.

The Center for Religion and Society

In 2001, the Center for Church and Society became the Center for Religion and Society.[25] In the preceding chapter I enumerated the main purposes of the center: sponsoring public lectures; pioneering needed new courses; supporting cross-cultural educational ventures; and continuing-education events for clergy and laity. During the Gring years, the first and fourth purposes continued, while the second and third diminished. Though an important course on the Holocaust was pioneered during that period, the religion

24. Keller, *Prologue*, 38.

25. During the late 1990s, several Jewish donors had supported pioneering courses in Holocaust studies and had explored other activities that could be supported by the center, e.g., a center for conflict resolution. In order to include this Jewish presence, we thought it proper to expand the name of the center: "Religion" was more inclusive than "Church."

and philosophy department and the honors program elaborated so many new courses that it was unnecessary for the center to continue generating new ones. The third purpose—enhancing cross-cultural experience—was displaced by a far larger program of international travel and study that was sponsored by the college and guided by its full-time director of international studies.

The diminishment of those two purposes, however, did not mean less activity for the center, which proceeded to add new initiatives to its work. (I will turn to those in a moment.) The first purpose listed above—bringing speakers to the college on issues confronting the church and society—continued at the pace of about four events per year, including those done in conjunction with the Fowler Program. (Those events are far too numerous to list here.)[26] A select number of those topics—religion and evolution, the American Enlightenment, the fall of communism, and challenges facing faith-based organizations—were aired on public television and radio as well as on campus.

The original fourth purpose of the center—continuing education for the clergy and laity—proceeded in local churches, on campus, and in the annual Power in the Spirit Conference that was jointly sponsored by the Virginia Synod, the office of church relations of Roanoke College, and the Center for Religion and Society. As director of the center, I served on the planning committee for the Power in the Spirit Conference, which drew up to three hundred persons for its summer event. The center recruited and paid the keynote speaker for each of those conferences.

The Gring years brought new initiatives by the center. One of the most significant was an ongoing conversation among interested faculty and administrators about the nature and mission of a church-related college. These "faith and learning" breakfast meetings were held three times each term, and ten to twenty members and administrators attended regularly. The conversations centered on the burgeoning literature concerning the plight and promise of Christian higher education. Foremost in that literature were articles by James Burtchaell that were first published in the journal *First Things* in April of 1991, entitled "The Rise and Fall of the Christian College," which traced the trajectory of Vanderbilt University from the early vision of its founders as the Protestant equivalent of Notre Dame to its complete secularization.

---

26. The center's link on the college website has a listing of many of the programs, replete with audio and visual recordings: http://www.roanoke.edu/a-z/benne_center_for _religion_and_society.

Burtchaell followed this up in 1998 with a huge study of the secularization process in seventeen colleges and universities. He boldly entitled the book *The Dying of the Light: The Disengagement of Colleges and Universities from Their Christian Churches.*[27] The topic of the ongoing Roanoke conversation was: Is this happening here? If so, what can we do to retard or reverse it?

These conversations resulted in two further initiatives, both supported by President Gring and both important in strengthening the Christian heritage of the college. The first was membership in the Lilly Network of Church-Related Colleges and Universities: this membership entailed a significant fee, but Roanoke was an early joiner (1996). The network holds conferences, attended by representatives of its member schools, that probe the challenges of Christian higher education. Representatives from Roanoke attend each year and bring back constructive ideas about how to increase the commitment to the religious element in its mission.

A second spinoff of the "faith and learning group" was the establishment of a series of Faith and Reason gatherings that commenced in 2003, the last year of Gring's administration. In these gatherings, which continue to this day, faculty members and top-level administrators, including the president, are asked to reflect on how their faith impacts their work at the college—in the areas of teaching, research, treatment of students, and administrative work. There are no constraints on what "faith" means or about what effects their faith has, if any, on their work. This series provides the opportunity and challenge for faculty members to relate their religious convictions to their intellectual life on campus.[28] The lectures, held four (now three) times each academic year, are followed by a fine dinner in the president's dining room of the college's Colket Student Center. Over dessert, the assembled audience—between twenty and forty—carry on a lively conversation in response to the lecture. Over the years, at least half of the faculty members have contributed to or attended those lectures at one time or another.

Another major initiative that began during the Gring years, with his support, was the annual Crumley Lecture. James Crumley was a 1948 graduate of Roanoke College who went on to a long and distinguished career in the Lutheran Church in America, culminating in his becoming the president

27. *The Dying of the Light: The Disengagement of Colleges and Universities from Their Christian Churches* (Grand Rapids: Eerdmans, 1998).

28. The invitation to speak is often greeted with both enthusiasm and trepidation on the part of faculty—enthusiasm because they are rarely asked to speak about their deepest convictions, and trepidation because there is little in their training that prepares them for the task of relating their faith to their intellectual life.

(and then presiding bishop) of that church from 1978 to 1987. His friends gave a considerable gift to the college in his honor, which provided an endowment for an annual lecture; this series began in 1999 and continues to the present time. The lecturer is always an outstanding layperson—generally a Lutheran—who reflects on how his or her faith is expressed in his/her vocation. It has featured business executives, scientists, journalists, professors, judges, artists, and choral directors, among others. It draws an audience of distinguished laypersons from the featured professions as well as an array of Virginia Lutherans for the lecture and a celebrative dinner, at which the director of the Center for Religion and Society often gives a report on its activities. In later years that lecture has been opened to a wider audience of students and members of the community, and on occasion it fills the four hundred seats of Olin Theater.

Yet a further initiative of the center was the establishment of the Blakely Evangelical Studies program. Thomas Blakely was a prominent Salem citizen and Baptist churchman who bequeathed an endowment for the program. Since Professor Gerald McDermott had evangelical credentials, the program came under his direction. He used its resources to invite many evangelical speakers to campus, as well as to support his lecture trips to many countries around the world—Cuba, Hungary, Poland, and Slovakia—in addition to the United States.

A final new launch for the center was its Slovak program. Directed by Paul Hinlicky, who had just arrived from his teaching stint in Slovakia, the program helped fund Slovak students who came to Roanoke College to study; it also made it possible for newly minted Slovak PhDs to teach at the college. In addition, it supported the efforts of several Roanoke College professors to teach at the Lutheran seminary of the Comenius University in Bratislava. In addition, the center has published two books on religion and society in Slovak, edited by one of those recent PhDs, Michal Valco. The connection between the college and the Slovak Lutheran church continues to be a fruitful one.

Triumphs and Tragedies in the Last Years of the Gring Administration

The three planks in Roanoke College's mission—the informal one of *gaining national recognition* and the two classic ones of *forming responsible citizens* on the basis of the *Christian moral vision*—gained incrementally in the 1990s and into the new century. Gring was a sturdy supporter of all three. The 2002 Plan, finished in 1993, incorporated ways of strengthening all three as the college moved into the twenty-first century. Its theme, "Challenging Students to Make a Difference," incorporated those themes into its plan for the future.

The steadiness of forward momentum was accelerated when, in August 2003, the college was accepted for membership in Phi Beta Kappa, a goal for which it had striven for fifty years. Its twenty-four PBK members among the faculty and staff celebrated the occasion in the spring of 2004, just as Gring was departing the college.[29] A good deal of the credit for the college's finally achieving that goal goes to Gring, who "nibbled around the edges" of the important criteria the college needed to fulfill in order to achieve membership in that prestigious club.[30] Furthermore, it was no accident that *U.S. News and World Report* had moved its ranking of Roanoke from one of the best regional colleges to one of the best liberal arts colleges in the nation. Roanoke had made it into the charmed circle of the best 120 liberal arts colleges in America and had earned a Phi Beta Kappa chapter. It was indeed a triumph that all the constituencies of Roanoke College could savor.

That "nibbling around the edges" involved some rather noteworthy accomplishments by the Gring administration. The endowment was raised from $25 million to $83 million as the result of a successful campaign. Debt was reduced to a paltry $4 million. A new student center, a new fitness center, a renovated historic courthouse, completion of the expansion of the Fintel library, planning for new dorms and athletic facilities, and a new entrance to the college were tributes to his work in raising funds.

Another step forward had to do with the revision of the college's statement of purpose, which for all intents and purposes had dropped from the consciousness of most members of the college community. Both Fintel and Gring noted that there was little attention paid to the statement and that it had lost its guidance capacity. Part of the problem was that it had not been revised for twenty years, which an accrediting agency noted as it pressed for renewed attention to the statement. In 1999–2000 the faculty took up the task of articulating that statement anew, which was in many ways a reiteration of the classic themes of the college, with some important additions and changes. The new statement read as follows:

29. Keller, *Prologue*, 70.
30. The phrase was used by Gring in an interview (March 12, 2015) to describe his role in getting Phi Beta Kappa to the college.

Roanoke College is dedicated to educating men and women in high standards of scholarship to prepare them for responsible lives of learning, service, and leadership. In pursuing this goal, the College is committed to an integrative approach to education that strives to balance intellectual, ethical, spiritual, and personal growth.

The College pursues its mission through an innovative curriculum that includes a cohesive core of liberal arts as well as specialized, career-oriented programs of study. Students are encouraged to develop habits of mind, aesthetic appreciation, and cultural awareness needed to thrive in a global society. Moreover, the College provides opportunities to take part in community service, to engage in ethical and social issues, to participate in religious life, and to further their physical and social well-being.

The College supports its mission by ensuring excellent teaching, providing for communal activities and residential life, and maintaining an attractive campus in the Blue Ridge Mountains. Founded by Lutherans in 1842, Roanoke College welcomes and reflects a variety of religious traditions. The College honors its Christian heritage and its partnership with the Lutheran church by nurturing a dialogue between faith and reason. In keeping with its history and mission, the College strives to be a diverse community, nationally and internationally, and is committed to seeking new ways to serve its students and community.[31]

Besides the obvious effort to include the concerns of all the major divisions of the college, the new statement is noteworthy in expanding both the moral and the religious elements in the college's purposes. The republican tradition—supplying virtuous students from all walks of life for service to the community, country, and world—is noticeably present. The college's religious tradition—the Christian tradition broadly defined—is also visible. "Spiritual growth," "engaging in moral and social issues," "participating in religious life," "honoring its Christian heritage and partnership with the Lutheran church," and especially "nurturing a dialogue between faith and reason" are stronger signals of the college's religious heritage than those in the earlier statement, written in the late 1960s. A portion of this advance could be attributed to the work of the "faith and learning" group throughout the 1990s, as well as to the arrival of "postmodern" younger faculty members, who were less enamored of the Enlightenment's emphasis on reason alone as the way to wisdom than were the older faculty. It was also

31. *Roanoke College Academic Catalogue* (2000–2003), 3.

aided by a faculty workshop in 1995, including administrators and board members, entitled "Honoring Our Christian Heritage," featuring Martin Marty, distinguished Lutheran church historian from the University of Chicago Divinity School.

While there were skirmishes about many planks in the college's platform—some faculty members successfully lobbied for "spiritual" rather than "religious" in its first paragraph—it was the commitment to "nurturing a dialogue between faith and reason" that really provoked a battle when it was proposed. The phrase, of course, came right out of the extended discussion in the "faith and learning group" of the importance of that kind of dialogue in a church-related college. After heated discussion, the faculty divided exactly evenly in a vote. The moderator of the faculty, a devout Catholic, broke the tie; but she was uneasy with such a close result, and she brought the issue up again for another vote at the next faculty meeting. This time the new provision passed handily. This was an enormous gain for those who wanted the college to strengthen its relationship to its Christian heritage, especially to its intellectual dimension. But the strife in the faculty over this new plank was a harbinger of the strife to come, to which I will soon turn.

Gring's later years as president were not all rosy. The disturbing attack of September 11, 2001, became an occasion for more serious reflection on the identity and mission of the college. After that traumatic event, Gring called his cabinet and several leading professors to discuss what sort of plan for the new century was needed. In addition to a renewed attention to the academic program and college facilities, a major concern had to do with the "soul" of the college. Even though the college had recently revisited and strengthened its statement of purpose, the group felt that more ought to be done. One faculty member opined that Roanoke did not have a "core identity." Another said the college had to become more distinctive. A board member added that "Roanoke had no clear vision for our future."[32]

This quest for a sharper sense of mission came right at the same time (early 2000s) that the Lilly Foundation was inviting applications from liberal arts colleges around the country for two hundred $2 million grants. The grants were offered as part of Lilly's grand initiative, entitled "Theological Exploration of Vocation," to strengthen the religious element in colleges that wanted to take up that cause. For Roanoke, this was not just a wonderful opportunity to build on the momentum of strengthening the college's Christian identity that had been generated in the 1990s; now an even greater opportu-

32. Keller, *Prologue*, 75.

nity emerged to re-center the college's basic identity and mission around the grand Lutheran concept of vocation, a teaching that not only incorporated the service dimension of its mission but also a profound religious basis for that service. Such a re-centering would certainly add distinctiveness and clarity to the college's identity and mission.

When I was just returning from a year-long sabbatical, President Gring asked me to head up a committee to write a proposal for a planning grant to apply for the large grant that was being offered. I was already involved in Lilly programs—the Lilly Fellows program and the Lilly Network of Church-related Colleges and Universities—so I was a natural candidate to take up the task. Our committee wrote a proposal for the planning grant in late 2000, and it was accepted by the Lilly office. A Central Planning Committee was then organized to draw up the application for the main grant, which included the president, the chaplain, the director of church relations, the chair of the religion and philosophy department, four faculty members who had been involved in programs of the Center for Religion and Society, a board member, and several students.

The group worked diligently for months following the acquisition of the planning grant. It came up with a robust proposal that was offered to the faculty in a meeting in August 2001, just before the September 11 attacks. The planning committee gave reports to flesh out the recommendations of the proposal, which involved curricular change, and then opened the meeting to discussion. A concerted, relentless attack on the proposal then followed for the rest of the morning. It was reported that the secularist wing of the faculty, led by a group of openly secularist department chairs, had done their homework and had carefully planned their assault.[33]

---

33. I had written an article in *The Christian Century* in the spring of 2001 entitled "Reconnecting a College with Its Christian Heritage," in which I recounted the gains Roanoke College had made in the 1980s and 1990s in strengthening the Christian element in the college's identity and mission, similar to what I have written in this chapter. One of the secularist leaders copied the article and distributed it to the network that was intent on torpedoing the proposal. Toward the end of the article I mentioned that the college was attempting to get a Lilly grant to make vocation an organizing principle in the life of the college. I brashly predicted that we would get the grant and that it would enable the proposed program to "be implemented in the curriculum." That overly confident statement was brought to the attention of the faculty and scathingly criticized as presumptuous and dangerous, a threat to academic freedom and faculty control. Other arguments were marshaled, too, one against the proposal to recruit more Lutheran students. One of the secularist department chairs contemptuously allowed that those "dear little Lutheran angels will no doubt make great contributions in our classes."

Beyond the members of the Central Planning Committee, few spoke in favor of the proposal. Many faculty members were silenced by the vigor of the resistance. Junior faculty members who might have been supportive were often in departments chaired by vehement opponents and were thus intimidated. The noncommitted middle of the faculty tended to side with the opponents because they wanted things to stay as they were. To their minds, any strengthening of the college's relationship to its Christian heritage was likely to be oppressive. Though no vote was taken, the secularists had clearly won the day.

Gring, shocked by this "unfortunate eruption of antireligious paranoia," decided that the dissenters had to be taken seriously.[34] He asked the new interim dean of the faculty to revise the proposal after meeting with the dissenters.[35] The final proposal sent to the Lilly Foundation was very different from the first. Many bold proposals were revised or eliminated. Qualifiers were attached. The selection committee for the Lilly initiative found the proposal to be "ambivalent," and it turned the proposal down.[36] The hope to move Christian vocation to a central organizing principle of the college was dashed.

34. Gring's actual description of that morning's travails in an interview with the author (March 12, 2015).

35. This episode resulted in many painful hours of reflection on my part. At first I was angry with Gring for not supporting the original proposal in spite of the protest. But perhaps he foresaw too much conflict down the road when the college would try to implement the central proposals. Perhaps it was wiser to risk losing the grant than to risk continuing conflict and opposition in the faculty. For my part, I saw many mistakes in hindsight. The first grand error can be attributed to hubris: I thought we had triumphed over the secularists and they were in retreat. I underestimated their strength and resolve while overestimating what we had done in the 1980s and 1990s to advance the Christian cause. I should have noted that the split in the faculty over the clause in the new statement of purpose that mentioned "nurturing a dialogue between faith and reason" was a sign that we had not "won" over the secularists. In my complacence I had not organized support from the general faculty for the proposal. The second mistake was that our proposal had many curricular implications that frightened and angered the faculty. When I studied the successful proposals of those colleges that won grants, I noticed that few had proposed curricular changes for their colleges; rather, they located most of the Lilly initiatives in the noncurricular areas of college life. Faculties are jealous of their control over curricula, and I should have anticipated that. Finally, I should have insisted that Gring assess the final proposal more intensely before we submitted it to the faculty. He was a man with good judgment, and he might have detected the mistakes we made had he been encouraged to pay closer attention to the proposal.

36. When news of the rejection of the proposal by Lilly became known, a celebration by the "winners" was reported to have taken place.

Conclusion

The subtitle used at the beginning of this chapter to describe the work of David Gring was "incrementalist par excellence." That seems to fit perfectly. Not given to soaring rhetoric, imaginative visions, or bold actions, Gring was rather a president who provided the wherewithal for the college, made up of a whole set of actors, to move incrementally toward its goals.[37] The informal—but heavily supported—goal of becoming a highly ranked college was certainly moved forward. While getting its longed-for chapter of Phi Beta Kappa, the college moved from a highly ranked regional liberal arts college to one ranked in the top 120 in the nation. Without Gring's "nibbling around the edges," these goals would not have not been realized.

The college's historic goal of responsible service to the world was rhetorically and materially supported by Gring in his years as president. The Fowler Program, the Center for Community Service, and many other service projects were supported firmly and generously. The same can be said for his work and support for the "religious element" in the college's historic mission. He helped push the new initiatives of the department, the Center for Religion and Society, and its several new programs forward. He continued to cultivate donors for three new chairs in Lutheran studies. Significantly, he was instrumental in providing the wherewithal for a renewed burst of college creativity by leaving it in the best financial condition it had ever been in. It had minimal debt and maximal resources. Its endowment had soared. Certainly this was the work of an "incrementalist" in the best sense of the word.

On the other hand, incrementalists can sometimes overlook needed initiatives. For example, Gilbert Meilaender's summons to the college in his address at the sesquicentennial celebration went unheeded. In that lecture he argued that, in order for the college to have a strong relationship to its Christian heritage, it needed the board, administration, and faculty to engage in serious and continuous discussion about what that relationship meant and how it was going to be sustained. Sadly, such a discussion emerged only sporadically and anxiously, sometimes leading to conflict. However, not attending to that relationship was worse; it became increasingly marginalized, a concern of low importance. Nor was the faculty selected according to the new statement of purpose of the college. Hiring for mission came in a distant second behind hiring for the needs of each department. This guaranteed a

---

37. One of his colleagues caught his style this way: "David does not like to propose. He prefers to analyze and carry out what others suggest" (quoted in Keller, *Prologue*, 61).

fractured and fractious faculty that could not agree on much besides becoming a nationally ranked college.

These lapses were not initiated by President Gring; they were part of the college's practices that extended back several administrations. Crucial elements of the college's identity and mission were assumed, not intentionally addressed. And that "assuming" had become something of a habit that few wanted to interrupt. Gring acquiesced to that habit.

Furthermore, the Lilly debacle led many to wonder whether the "soul"—the central religious meaning of the college—could ever be creatively addressed. When Gring surprisingly resigned in the fall of 2003, the college was ready to call someone who could do just that. It turned to a charismatic young academic dean from the same college from which Gring came. Perhaps she could supply the needed gifts to address the challenge of "soul."

9

SABINE O'HARA (2004–2007)

An Abbreviated Search for Soul

When David Gring left Roanoke College in the spring of 2004, the college was in the best financial condition it had ever been in during its long existence. He had even insisted on a contingency fund to help the next president through any possible downturn in the college's fortunes. Debt was minimal. Ambitious building plans were underway for new dorms and a new entrance to the college. Work on a strategic plan had begun. Roanoke had moved toward Gring's goal of becoming a "college of significant distinction."

Yet, there was a bit of malaise clinging to all the success. It had to do with purpose, mission, identity, substance, or—in the language of this study—"soul." What was the unifying purpose of the college? What was the purpose of all this striving for recognition?[1] Had the college won the Lilly Foundation grant and enacted the proposal of the Central Planning Committee, the historic purpose of the college—to form young people from all walks of life in an ethic of responsibility based on Christian values—would have had a chance to inject substance into the rather empty goals of "recognition" and "distinction." What I have referred to as "Christian republicanism" throughout this book would have had a chance to return as the central theme in the college's identity and mission. Moreover, that central theme would have been given a Lutheran construal, since "vocation" was a key teaching of the Reformation.

---

1. This yearning for purpose or mission seemed to be a secular equivalent to the biblical question: "What good is it for a man to gain the whole world but lose his soul?" (Mark 8:36).

Though the school did not follow that route to "soul," it did not mean that there was no desire for more unity of purpose, more shared commitment to substantive goals. So when a presidential search committee began its hunt for a new president, it was on the lookout for someone who could provide that unifying vision. That someone was forty-eight-year-old Sabine Ursula Maier O'Hara, the academic vice president and dean at Concordia College in Moorhead, Minnesota, the same college from which Roanoke had selected its preceding president, David Gring. A thirteen-member search committee, representing the various constituencies of the college, pored over sixty nominations and applications and interviewed seven finalists, of whom they invited three to campus to meet with faculty, students, trustees, and staff. As George Keller exulted: "One person, Dr. O'Hara, stood out like a peony among the petunias."[2]

That was a colorful yet apt portrayal of how O'Hara came off to those various constituencies in her interviews at the college. In her presentations she exuded confidence, organization, articulateness, bold analysis, persuasiveness, imagination, and even glamor. She seemed to possess in spades what was not on David Gring's list of top strengths. She compellingly analyzed the current academic scene as being characterized by "silos" of independent and unconnected departments. She argued that the answer to the fragmentation of learning was more integrative learning, more interdisciplinary work, more discourse across campus.[3]

Besides the promise of being able to articulate a brilliant unifying vision for the college, other factors provided wind at her back. She was the first woman candidate for the presidency of the college; she was much more at home with academic jargon than were the two preceding presidents; she had impressive intellectual facility and a list of publications under her name. She was an environmental economist in an era that was beginning to take up environmentalism as a sacred cause. She had a record of academic and administrative performance in prestigious colleges and universities. She was young and vigorous. She was progressive in a school that was becoming more liberal with each faculty appointment. She won the position handily.

2. George Keller, *Prologue to Prominence—A Half Century of Roanoke College, 1951–2003* (Minneapolis: Lutheran University Press, 2005), 82.

3. This description comes from my recollection of her interview with faculty groups. She said what many of us wanted to hear. Though the fairly well integrated general-education and honors curricula forged in the mid-1980s were still in place, they had gradually lost the faculty's enthusiastic engagement and were fraying around the edges. After all, the curricula were nearly twenty years old, close to the end of the shelf life for such constructions.

The Milieu of 2004–2007

There was an apocalyptic whiff in the air. The United States had invaded Iraq in 2003 to topple Saddam Hussein, but the situation on the ground was not going well, though there was still enough confidence in George W. Bush by the electorate to reelect him to a second term in 2004. Terrorist episodes rattled the nerves of the world, and the Department of Homeland Security was established. A horrendous earthquake in Southeast Asia produced a tsunami that killed over 200,000 people in fourteen countries. Hurricane Katrina devastated New Orleans. A United Nations summit met in Montreal to address climate change. Human embryos were cloned by Korean scientists. The last months of O'Hara's time at Roanoke were sobered by the shocking murders on the Virginia Tech campus, only thirty miles from Roanoke.

But these disturbing features were accompanied by more positive developments. Facebook and Twitter came into being, along with the expansion and development of other high-tech information systems. Apple brought out its first iPhone in early 2007. The mapping of the human genome was completed. The economy was in an expansive mode, fueled by the expanding housing bubble—which was soon to burst.

Culturally, the country became more socially liberal by the year. A good deal of that had to do with the relentless momentum of the sexual revolution, in which one of the few criteria of acceptable behavior was consent. Sexual expression was increasingly liberated from traditional constraints, as sex was uncoupled from permanent commitment and procreation. Pornography flourished on the internet. Gay marriage as a cause was making headway: Massachusetts became the first state to legislate it in 2004. A dark side of the revolution was a lower marriage rate, especially among the working and lower classes, resulting in higher rates of illegitimacy. "Hook-up parties" were gaining momentum on college campuses, with their predictable destructive results.

On the other hand, new constraints were imposed by a culture that emphasized diversity and inclusiveness. Environmentalism—driven by fears first of global warming and then of climate change—imposed sharp limits on dissent from the "consensus" on climate change. "Sustainability" took on quasi-religious characteristics and began to be embodied in policies that subsidized approved energy sources (wind, solar) and penalized others (fossil fuels in general). Colleges and universities jumped on the bandwagon.

While on the surface one would think that the mantras touting diversity and inclusiveness would open doors for vigorous debate, the opposite actually occurred. Any perceived offenses to approved "victim groups" were resoundingly punished. "Political correctness" became a feared governing principle for those who departed from the elite consensus on many matters. Even public figures were felled by transgressions against the alleged consensus. Yet American institutions benefited from the increasing presence of minorities.

Intellectually, "postmodernism" became the rage. It emphasized the "social location" of all knowledge, which meant that claims to universal truth or shared meanings were met with great skepticism. Knowledge was perspectival. Radical forms of postmodernism denied any transcultural or even transpersonal truths. More moderate forms emphasized that we are not only in history, but history is in us. Our rationality is conditioned by the historical epoch and civilizational stream we inhabit. That realization makes it difficult to gain consensus on first principles in political and academic life, which lends a dark edge to the drive for "diversity" and "inclusiveness."

The Formation of Sabine Maier O'Hara

What had given Sabine O'Hara, the tenth president of Roanoke College, the right preparation to take up the challenges presented by the setting just depicted, as well as to guide a well-positioned and well-financed college toward a more substantive set of goals? First on the list was that she was German-born and -trained. Born in 1956 in a Germany still recovering from World War II, Sabine Maier had a strong work ethic trained in her by her father, a small business owner, and her very busy mother.[4] The oldest child in the family of five, with two siblings (a brother and a sister), she experienced a strong feeling of domestic solidarity, had a sense of obligation to take responsibility in the family and school, and developed a love of music.

Her grandmother was the most influential person for her as a child. She

---

4. The autobiographical data in this section come from an unpublished manuscript of a talk entitled "Revisiting Adam Smith," which Sabine O'Hara gave on March 17, 2005, at a Faith and Reason Lecture sponsored by the Center for Religion and Society. Lecturers in this series are asked to relate their faith commitments to their life as professors and administrators at the college. Often the invited lecturers take the occasion to reflect on the religious factor in their lives rather than talk about its role in their current work. That was the case when the new president, Sabine O'Hara, was asked to give one of the lectures. The happy result is that many facts about and interpretations of her life were given by the new president herself.

"was a strong woman who read her Bible every day, sang through the hymnal with me from the front to the back and back to the front, took me to church, Sunday school, her women's group, the bazaar group, and taught me to knit, sew, cook, and iron, and she knew every plant there was."[5]

Young Sabine excelled in elementary school and the *gymnasium* (the German equivalent of a college-prep, liberal arts high school), so there was little doubt that she would be the first of her family to go off to the university. That university happened to be Göttingen, where she studied biology for two years. Shortly thereafter she discovered economics, which was to be her main field of academic interest. Even more to the point, she discovered environmental economics, a new field in which she soon earned an assistantship and then a PhD, the first woman to do so at Göttingen.

During her time in that doctoral program, she had a chance to visit Peru, where she was alerted to the vast differences between her affluent Germany and the poverty of a Third-World country. She was angered by the role the Catholic Church played in "keeping people submissive and dependent."[6] She also did research on the dioxin scandal, which had erupted in the Hamburg area. This experience pushed her deeper into the field of environmental economics and ethics. Another significant event happened during that period: she met her future husband, Philip O'Hara, at a church choir rehearsal. Philip was an ordained pastor in the American United Methodist Church who was teaching in the German public school system. They were married in March of 1983 and later became parents of three sons.[7]

Soon after they were married, the two simultaneously experienced a remarkable dream. They dreamt that they should go to the United States to open themselves to new and different challenges. "To me, a German academic whose understanding of faith was defined by social responsibility and not by personal faith, this was a very disturbing experience. It was one of the strangest and most inspiring experiences I have ever had."[8] It seemed to be a call from God.

In an amazingly short time, Philip was invited (in 1984) to accept a call to a parish in Enosburg Falls, Vermont. There Sabine participated in parish life

---

5. O'Hara, "Revisiting," 1.

6. O'Hara, "Revisiting," 3.

7. Much later in their time in the United States, Philip had a stroke that affected his mental processes. Though he had earlier completed a PhD in New Testament at Vanderbilt Divinity School, he was unable to teach at Roanoke. But he was a strong, ever-present support for his wife. After they left Roanoke College, he suffered another serious stroke that ultimately led to his death in 2013. His wife stood by him in all this adversity.

8. O'Hara, "Revisiting," 4.

and took up an ambitious reading program while she improved her English-language skills. She discovered a religious base for her ethic of responsibility by reading widely in feminist, liberation, and ecological theology. She was inspired by the World Council of Churches' and the Lutheran World Federation's agendas of peace, justice, and the integrity of creation. She also took up a rereading of the work of Adam Smith, especially his *Theory of Moral Sentiments*, which indicated for her that productive and wholesome economic life had to operate within a culture of shared moral convictions. She was adding religious and ethical bases to her environmental economics.

In 1986, Philip moved to another parish in a suburb of Albany. Sabine accepted the position of director of public policy for the New York Council of Churches. That position provided the opportunity to advocate for the peace and justice agenda that had inspired her in her recent studies. It also provided the opportunity to work with various nongovernmental agencies and to represent the council in various summits and consultations at home and abroad. These activities brought her into contact with many individuals and agencies, and she networked with them for the next years.

Within two years, a professor from the Rensselaer Polytechnic Institute (RPI), who was impressed by her when both participated in a panel discussion, invited her to apply for a tenure-track position in economics at that institution. She won that position and spent five productive years (1993–99) in which she taught graduate and undergraduate students, wrote a book, and published twenty scholarly articles, all clustered around the subject of sustainable economic development. After only two years at RPI, she became director of its graduate studies in economics.

Having entered administrative work and having demonstrated scholarly expertise in environmental economics, O'Hara was invited by the president of Green Mountain College in Vermont to apply for the position of provost at that school. The college had just decided to focus its whole program on sustainability, becoming Vermont's premier environmental liberal arts college. She felt called to the position. Given Green Mountain's bold focus and her interest in precisely that focus, she decided to consider becoming a full-time administrator. "I think in connections, in structures, in directions. That's just how my mind works. I am very organized and can usually figure out how to move from the idea stage to the implementation stage. I knew I had to consider administration."[9] Consider she did, and she became provost at Green Mountain for three years.

9. O'Hara, "Revisiting," 8.

As a Lutheran, a rising star in environmental economics, a young but experienced administrator, and a highly accomplished interviewee, Sabine O'Hara was a prime candidate for the dean of the college and vice president for academic affairs at Concordia College in Moorhead, Minnesota. Facing a strong competitive field, she won that position. At Concordia she initiated many new ventures, but she had little time to see them through to completion before she became the tenth president of Roanoke College in the summer of 2004. She came with expectations by the search committee—similar to those laid on David Gring—that she would strengthen the Lutheran/Christian character of the college and sharpen and enliven its sense of mission.

Inaugural Address and Other Writings

Like David Gring before her, O'Hara chose to give her inaugural address in the fall of her arrival in 2004 rather than waiting to give it in spring commencement, as had been the pattern of earlier Roanoke College presidents. Again like Gring, she accommodated her rhetoric to her understanding of what animated Roanoke, which was quite different from what shaped the Concordia from which she had just come. She altered the robust religious rhetoric of her speeches at Concordia to better fit the spirit of Roanoke. Yet she often communicated her vision in religious terms, though muted.

This was true of her address to the staff of the college right after her arrival: she noted that she intended to restart the strategic planning process that Gring had initiated but had curtailed after he decided to leave the presidency. "In this competitive environment in higher education we simply can't be all things to all people; a strategic plan helps us focus our energy so that we can concentrate on who we are and how we are different from anyone else."[10]

---

10. O'Hara, "Firsts," unpublished manuscript for a set of opening remarks to a staff gathering at the college on August 10, 2004. The "firsts" of the title referred to her enumeration of how she became the first woman to do a number of important things—first in her family to go to university, first woman to complete an agricultural practicum in Germany, first woman to complete a PhD in environmental economics at Göttingen University, first female director of public policy for the New York Council of Churches, first woman in a tenure-track position in the economics department of RPI, and first female director of graduate studies in the economics department of RPI.

"Pathways to Prominence"

Her inaugural speech, which was the keynote address in a free-standing cel-ebratory event on October 14, 2004, took up the challenge she had set for herself to articulate "how we are different from anyone else." After announc-ing her title and offering eloquent thanks for the presence of so many friends from her past endeavors, she enumerated three "pathways to prominence" that would set the college apart from its competitors.[11] The three pathways were: a commitment to discourse; a commitment to service; and a commit-ment to innovation.

Noting that she had done much theoretical and practical work on dis-course, she defined that commitment as a "commitment to intellectual and civic nurture."[12] By that she meant a commitment to civil intellectual conver-sation among diverse partners across the campus that would gradually lead to shared truths and meanings. Such discourse would liberate the academic community from the "silos" that isolated one department from another. Discourse should take up the issues relevant to our society and the world: social, religious, economic, political, ethical, and aesthetic. In doing so, it would build a community that was willing to engage others, and thus would become a model for students. That kind of discourse was an essential part of the calling of academics.[13]

Her second "pathway to prominence" was a commitment to service, a theme well ingrained in the history and mission of Roanoke College. She en-visioned a college that went beyond training the young for individual success to shaping them to advance the common good. Such formation would lead to more meaningful and fulfilling lives and was in harmony with "our very

11. O'Hara, "Pathways to Prominence," unpublished manuscript of her inaugural ad-dress. The title had echoes of David Gring's inaugural address, "Marks of Significant Distinc-tion," as well as direct connections with George Keller's account of Roanoke's fifty years of successful striving for a Phi Beta Kappa chapter, entitled "Prologue to Prominence," which was soon to be published (2005).

12. O'Hara, "Pathways to Prominence," 2. O'Hara cited six of her writings to illustrate her expertise. Later in the speech she referred to herself several more times, and to other relevant scholarship of hers. This provided a very public signal of her intellectual prowess.

13. O'Hara instituted a "discourse award" during her time as president. In 2007 the award was bestowed on William Hill and me for our collaborations as directors of the Fowler Program and the Center for Religion and Society, respectively, and in inviting speakers to campus who took up issues from both religious and political perspectives. She honored these "conversations in the public square" as models of what she had in mind for public discourse.

roots as a church-related college."[14] She then enumerated the many service projects the college already sponsored. Further, service was not only *to* and *for* others, it was *with* others, as liberation theologians had taught. Such service meant immersion in the contexts in which one was serving; it was not paternalistic charity from above or outside.

It was in the explication of her third pathway, commitment to innovation, that she articulated the Lutheran/Christian element in the historic mission of the college. She argued that Luther himself defined the role of education as setting us free from blind surrender to old powers that hold us back. It "knocks a hole in them and wreaks havoc in the Devil's kingdom."[15] After noting that there is great respect for tradition in Luther's view, she emphasized his conviction that education is the "sacred ark" of civilization.

Maintaining this tension between innovation and preservation is a mark of a Lutheran church-related college, she argued, but Lutherans should overcome the tendency to allow reverence for tradition to win out over innovation. "We must honor our traditions yet must never allow them to turn into lifeless icons that hold us back and lock us into doctrinaire statements and beliefs."[16] Innovation requires resources, and that notion gave her the opportunity to announce a new endowed professorship in art history. She then announced a new undergraduate research program in which ten students would assist faculty in their research, an example, for her, of the kind of teamwork that would lead to more creative innovation.

She concluded her thirty-minute address with a quote from a distinguished Roanoke alumnus, Henry Fowler: "How fitting—instead of looking back with satisfaction—to look forward with anticipation, to dream boldly as our Roanoke College founders once did." Such bold dreaming, she declared, was owed to those who came before us and to those who will come after us. It would enable Roanoke to continue to prepare "students for responsible lives of learning, service, and leadership" (Roanoke College mission statement).

14. O'Hara, "Pathways to Prominence," 4.

15. O'Hara, "Pathways to Prominence," 5. It is a bit odd that she brought Luther's writings to bear on the subject of innovation, when she could have appealed to them more powerfully under the pathway to service. However, in her later writings, she explicitly appeals to his teaching on vocation to undergird the college's commitment to service.

16. O'Hara, "Pathways to Prominence," 6.

Other Talks and Writings

Sabine O'Hara was an accomplished and enthusiastic speaker before many different audiences, including the Roanoke faculty, whom she addressed in a series of talks on the Lutheran educational tradition. On those occasions she, like the presidents before her, repeated many of her favorite themes besides the ones in her inaugural address. One that came to the fore constantly was her distinction between *Erziehung* and *Bildung*. The first of those German words means "bringing up children right and educating them in the customs and traditions of civilized life, as well as the skills of trades."[17] *Erziehung* emphasizes basic civilizational training and what is popularly known as "vocational education." But Luther's teaching on the priesthood of all believers demanded that there be more than *Erziehung*: a certain gifted portion of the population must experience *Bildung*, which "refers to education in the Greek tradition of liberal learning. The priesthood of all believers needed articulate readers and writers, people knowledgeable in the languages, people who could read and interpret the Scriptures, free-thinking people trained in critical thinking and quantitative reasoning, familiar with history, the arts, music, and, of course, theology. In other words, education for Luther meant quite literally education to think liberally, to think freely, and to advance society."[18]

Another theme that recurred in her talks was education as intellectual debate and scholarship. She was fond of noting that Luther was a scholar who was rigorously trained for debate, for which he had ample opportunity in his reforming activities. Further, as a scholar, Luther knew that our knowledge was

17. O'Hara, "The Lutheran Educational Tradition," unpublished manuscript of a speech given to the Roanoke College faculty (March 2005), 1.

18. O'Hara, "The Lutheran Educational Tradition," 1. While it is true that Luther had a deep appreciation for the liberal arts, and ensconced them solidly within the gymnasium and the university, he did not connect them to the "priesthood of all believers" in the way that O'Hara assumed. The priesthood of all believers means that Christians can approach God directly through Christ and not through intermediaries such as their priest or through Mary or other saints. It does not mean that educated individuals can engage in private interpretation of the Bible, as O'Hara suggests. Luther developed his biblical commentaries and catechisms, and Lutherans developed their confessions (the Augsburg Confession and later the Book of Concord) precisely to teach a corporate, churchly interpretation of Scripture. The priesthood of all believers also means that Christians, in their daily callings, are called to be genuine priestly vehicles of love and care for fellow Christians and also for non-Christians. Instead of ordained priests being intermediaries of the people to God and to other fellow Christians, lay Christians themselves were called directly to those roles. In this latter sense, O'Hara rightly emphasized "freedom for."

always partial, subject to revision, and always prone to error. Therefore, scholars had to engage in discourse; they had to advance knowledge by free inquiry.

Yet another favorite theme involved her interpretation of Luther's great treatise of 1520 on "The Freedom of the Christian." She summed up his famous paradoxical statement—"A Christian is a perfectly free Lord of all, subject to none; and at the same time a Christian is a perfectly dutiful servant of all, subject to all"—as "freedom from" and "freedom for."

> God's grace is freely given and thus we are perfectly free and subject to no one but God. Yet it is out of this understanding of freedom that we serve our neighbor and are subject to all. Freedom is clearly freedom from—freedom from fear, freedom from oppression, freedom from limiting mindsets of traditions, customs and superstitions; but it is also freedom for—freedom for service to others, for the community, for the advancement of the common good. The German word for job is *Beruf*, which literally means to be called, and it is an expression of Luther's freedom for. Our word "vocation" best expresses this understanding of calling. . . .
>
> Only when it finds its expression in service is freedom truly realized. This is not a contradiction, but a tension within which we live. And tension is not bad, it simply is. We live within the tension between the two kingdoms: the kingdom on the left, which is the here and now of the messiness of human affairs; the kingdom on the right is God's world to come and the breaking in of God's reign even now. We don't need to resolve this tension and determine which side overrides the other. We simply live in this dialectic and tension. What an intellectual tradition![19]

Commentary

There had never been a president in Roanoke College's history who offered an overt Lutheran rationale for the college's mission as a church-related liberal arts college. Bittle and Dreher were not committed enough to Lutheran teachings to do so, while later presidents—from Morehead on—strangely did not offer such a rationale even if they were able to. (There is no doubt that Morehead, as a Lutheran theologian, could have done so, but he chose

---

19. O'Hara, "The Lutheran Educational Tradition," 1. Like her faulty interpretation of the priesthood of all believers, O'Hara's interpretation of the freedom of the Christian has serious problems, which will be addressed later.

not to.) Sabine O'Hara rose to the occasion and offered a robust Lutheran/ Christian basis for the college's liberal arts education devoted to service. She cited many Lutheran themes in providing that rationale: the priesthood of all believers, Christian freedom, the two-kingdoms distinction, vocation, the importance of scholarly competence, the partiality of human knowledge, and open inquiry toward truth.

Furthermore, her commitment to public discourse was meant to overcome the departmental sequestration of knowledge and expertise. She wanted the college to engage in the kind of conversation that would set the college off from the compartmentalization of knowledge that characterized much of American higher education, including the liberal arts colleges that were faltering in their commitment to their special calling. This unifying process would be strengthened by placing it on the foundation of the Lutheran educational tradition.

In her emphasis on innovation, she identified herself clearly as a "progressive Lutheran." She constantly warned about some of the traditionalist tendencies in Lutheranism. Instead, she emphasized the dynamic qualities that were present in Luther's life and work. This freed her to press liberal causes, particularly those having to do with sustainability. Her sense of mission, and the way she could articulate it, was something of a dream come true for many. The thirst for a charismatic leader who could unify the college around a vision that provided a Christian basis for service in the world seemed to be satisfied, at least in her rhetoric. She not only talked of responsibility and leadership, but she also offered concrete religious grounds for them; and those religious grounds were not only instrumental to moral ends, but were intrinsically important in their own right.

However, the flaw in her interpretation of Christian freedom (noted in footnote 18 above) proved to have fateful consequences when the college soon got down to articulating its guiding principles under the rubric "Freedom with Purpose." In short, her interpretation had Christian freedom without Christ.[20] True, she mentioned the grace of God that makes us free, but the point of that grace in Luther's thought is that it is embodied in the

---

20. It is fascinating how sparely Jesus is mentioned in the rhetoric of Roanoke College presidents after the fulsome reference to him by Bittle. This seems to be part of Roanoke's aversion to being too "confessional" or specific about its religious commitments, a way to emphasize its nonsectarian character. It also was part of the growing bashfulness about mentioning specifically Christian bases for its programs. However, such reluctance runs the risk of falling into a vague Unitarianism. Oddly, though O'Hara was very specific about Lutheran defining themes, she did not mention the redemptive work of Christ, which is definitely central to Lutheran teaching.

incarnate, crucified, and risen Christ. He is the one who sets us free from sin, death, and the devil. Therefore, nothing can interfere with the faithful Christian's eternal destiny. The Christian is free from anything that would try to do that; the Christian is a free lord of all.

Shortly after her mention of the grace of God, she quickly intimated that it is liberal education that sets us free from "fear, oppression, limiting mindsets, traditions, customs, and superstitions." While the role of grace and the role of liberal arts were mixed and muddled in her exposition, the college's later interpretation of "freedom from" in its guiding principles clearly identified it with the liberating capacities of the liberal arts. This, of course, would be anathema to Luther, who would denounce such a claim as changing the gospel (Christ sets us free) into law (the human work of a liberal arts education sets us free). Furthermore, it would claim that liberal education saves us, not Christ.

After that muddle, however, she got Christian freedom right. The grace of God in Christ sets us free from sin, death, and the devil—*for service to our neighbor.* She was clear and insistent on that. In spite of these shortcomings, O'Hara was on the path of re-centering the college on its historic mission and, as a huge bonus, providing a Lutheran/Christian rationale for that mission.

Renewed Efforts to Sharpen Identity and Mission

Sensing the college's lack of a coherent and unifying vision, as did the two presidents preceding her, O'Hara immediately began encouraging the college community to elaborate a clearer vision, sense of mission, and set of principles and purposes. A strategic plan would soon follow that elaboration. She also noted that the old "Centers of Distinction" curriculum was now nearly twenty years old and fading fast in terms of support by the faculty and impact on the students. Since these three tasks were so closely related, she soon set initiatives in motion to tackle them.

The initial step in the first task was performed under her direct leadership. A short "vision statement" was articulated that included the newfound goal of the college to be nationally recognized. It reads:

> Roanoke College is committed to being a leading national liberal arts college, a model of experiential learning, and a community committed to open discourse and civil debate as ways of learning and as preparation for service in the world.

The second step was to adapt a brief mission statement lifted from Roanoke's classic statement of purpose, which had this as its first paragraph:

> Roanoke College is dedicated to educating men and women in high standards of scholarship to prepare them for responsible lives of learning, service, and leadership. In pursuing this goal, the College is committed to an integrative approach to education that strives to balance intellectual, ethical, spiritual, and personal growth.

That first paragraph was tailored down to become the college's new mission statement:

> Roanoke develops students as whole persons and prepares them for responsible lives of learning, service, and leadership by promoting their intellectual, ethical, spiritual, and personal growth.

Both the vision and mission statements remain as the current self-identification of the college. The rest of the old statement of purpose was edited to become the new statement of purpose:

> Roanoke College pursues its mission through an innovative curriculum that combines a core program in the liberal arts, major fields of study in the natural sciences, the social sciences, and the humanities and fine arts, along with career-oriented, specialized programs of study. Founded by Lutherans in 1842, Roanoke College welcomes and reflects a variety of religious traditions. The College honors its Christian heritage and its partnership with the Lutheran church by nurturing a dialogue between faith and reason. In keeping with its history and mission, the College strives to be a diverse community, nationally and internationally. Central to achieving the purposes of the College is a strong commitment to liberal education and its vision of human freedom leading to service within the human community. The College's learning goals, therefore, focus upon developing both a student's confident sense of freedom in the world and a sense of purpose in using that freedom. Through these goals the College strives to produce resourceful, informed, and responsible citizens prepared for productive careers and for leadership in community.

The hard-won clause inserted in the revision of 2000 was retained: that is, the college honored "its Christian heritage and partnership with the Lutheran church by nurturing a dialogue between faith and reason." Soon thereafter, the theme of "human freedom leading to service within the human community" was introduced and repeated. This new combination of themes—the freedom wrought by liberal education leading to purposeful service—was certainly a reaffirmation of a classic emphasis of the college. The purpose statement was then elaborated in great detail in a section on "Freedom with Purpose," which provided a rationale—both philosophical and principled—for liberal arts education at Roanoke College.

This third ambitious step of defining purpose was taken up by the nine-person Task Force on Goals for Liberal Learning at Roanoke College, which was appointed by President O'Hara. It was convened by Jeffrey Sandborg, choir director and professor of music, and included the chaplain, two staff members, and five other faculty members. The new Fishwick Professor of English, Robert Schultz, was one of the faculty members, and he became the major drafter of the new rationale for liberal arts at Roanoke. The task force worked well and vigorously together and came up with "Freedom with Purpose" within the year.[21] This, as well as the new vision, mission, and purpose statements, were voted on that year by the faculty and board and became official documents of the college. Those documents, especially "Freedom with Purpose," were to become the launching pad for a strategic plan; they were also supposed to become the guiding set of principles for the new curriculum that a committee was soon formed to plan. These latter two tasks—the strategic plan and the new curriculum—that O'Hara took up at the beginning of her administration did not see completion until several years after her departure.

The lengthy elaboration of "Freedom with Purpose" is important to duplicate, since it represents O'Hara's and the college's major effort to provide the college with a clearer sense of mission, one that is in effect to the present day.

A LIBERAL ARTS EDUCATION AT ROANOKE COLLEGE

Philosophy

Education in the liberal arts is education for liberation. The term "liberal arts" derives from the Latin artes liberales *and means, literally, the subjects of study appropriate to free persons. And the verb "to edu-*

---

21. Assessment offered by Jeffrey Sandborg, in interview with the author (Dec. 2, 2015).

cate" means, in its Latin root, "to lead." A liberal arts education, then, is one that leads out from small worlds into larger ones.

It leads us out from small, safe worlds into larger, more interesting ones by training in us a dissatisfaction with partial knowledge, with sloganeering, and with fixed ideologies. It instills in us instead an appreciation for the true complexity of things and a lifelong commitment to learning. A mind so trained respects facts, employs apt methods, and engages in creative problem solving. It examines alternatives; it does not fear tension or paradox. It welcomes the stubborn "misfit" fact that cracks open a too-small view and releases us into a wider play of thought. And it encounters this liberating openness in the vision of artists; in the venturesome thought of philosophers, theologians, and mathematicians; in the observation and experimentation of scientists; in the insights of social scientists; and in the experience of living in community.

A liberal arts education at a small, residential college frees us from isolation within ourselves into a community of learners and sharers, a community of discovery and collaboration in which we can grow as individuals in constructive engagement with others.

A liberal arts education frees us from a reliance upon received opinion into an achieved personal authority by training the skills of critical thought, sound research, and informed and reasoned debate. At Roanoke College this freedom grows out of a tradition of debating societies within a community of open discourse.

A liberal arts education frees us from entrapment within the conventions of our present place and time into a wider perspective that comprehends our own legacies, the breadth of human history, and the variety of human cultures. To support this work, Roanoke College commits itself to the work of building a diverse and tolerant college community.

A liberal arts education frees us from superficiality and distraction into the satisfactions of knowledge in depth, in which depth of learning leads to useful understanding—and to pleasure, wonder, and awe. At the same time, a liberal education frees us from mere specialization into a wider dialogue, in which depth of knowledge is shared and debated to clarify distinctions, to discover patterns, and to integrate human knowledge into an ever larger and more adequate view.

A liberal arts education engages ethics and questions of ultimate meaning. It does not offer pat moral answers. Instead, it provides the basis of all moral behavior—it helps us to imagine the reality of other lives. In matters of ethical living, it does not limit itself to the human, social world, but includes thoughtful consideration of our place within the natural world. At Roanoke College these inquiries are informed, in part, by a tradition of Lutheran education that encourages a dialogue between faith and learning.

Education in the liberal arts frees us from purposelessness into productive careers and lives of service, in which our work to discover what is good, true, and beautiful leads on to work for good in the world.

The effects of a liberal arts education—an education for liberation—are a love of learning, an openness within the vastness of what we do not know, and a desire to use what we do know in ethical living, engaged citizenship, and service for the general good. The broad aim of such an education, therefore, is to produce resourceful, informed, and responsible citizens.

Principles

At Roanoke College a liberal arts education prepares students for lives of freedom with purpose. The college aims to produce resourceful, informed, and responsible citizens prepared for productive careers and for leadership in community, with an understanding of community appropriate to American diversity and to the increasingly global experience of the 21st century.

1. *Traditionally, the liberal arts are the skills of freedom. A liberal arts education at Roanoke College aims to produce **resourceful citizens** by developing these skills and habits of mind, including:*

   - *the ability to read, listen, and observe carefully*
   - *the ability to access information from disparate sources, to assess it appropriately, and to develop information into useful knowledge*
   - *the ability to think critically, analytically, and creatively; to apply apt methods; to reason with rigor; and to use effective problem-solving skills*
   - *the ability to use writing as a tool of thought and to communicate effectively in a variety of written and oral forms*
   - *the ability to construct, understand, and evaluate arguments that use quantitative reasoning*

- *the ability to understand scientific discovery and to appraise it wisely; the ability to make judicious use of new technologies*
- *the ability to work independently and collaboratively and to participate in experiential learning.*

2. *Knowledge is essential to freedom. A liberal arts education at Roanoke College aims to produce **citizens informed** by:*

- *the cardinal achievements of human imagination as expressed in the arts and humanities, in the sciences, and in the social sciences*
- *depth of knowledge in at least one academic field of study, complemented by a breadth of experience across the traditional divisions of knowledge sufficient to enable integrative learning and thinking*
- *knowledge of the histories, values, and achievements of both western and non-western cultures in depth sufficient for the appreciation of disparate values and perspectives; this knowledge includes the cultural insight gained through language study*
- *knowledge of the values and histories that gave rise to liberal democracy in the United States and an understanding of contemporary issues from a variety of perspectives.*

3. *Freedom, according to Martin Luther, includes both "freedom from" varieties of oppression and "freedom for" service in community. A liberal arts education at Roanoke College aims to produce **responsible citizens** by cultivating in its students:*

- *a commitment to academic integrity and intellectual freedom*
- *a life-long commitment to learning and to using that learning in active engagement with others*
- *a sense of responsibility in which individual identity is honored within a diverse community characterized by mutual understanding and respect*
- *a commitment to engage in contemplation and reflection as a prelude to action, to make principled and ethical decisions, and to participate in deliberative public discourse*
- *a commitment to health in its largest sense: the physical and emotional well-being of self within a community that balances intellectual, ethical, spiritual, and personal growth*
- *a willingness to understand and respond to the needs and challenges*

of our time, both as individuals and as members of wide, inclusive communities
- *a desire to contribute to the common good at Roanoke College, in the Roanoke Valley, and beyond.*

A number of observations can be made about these important new statements of mission. First, there had never been such a thoughtful and detailed rationale for a liberal arts education at Roanoke since the fulsome reflections on the liberal arts by the founding president, David Bittle, who spent a good deal of his lengthy inaugural address spelling out such a rationale.

Second, this was a strong effort to place at least one theme in the college's historic sense of mission—"responsible citizenship"—at the forefront of its purposes after it had been edged out by the somewhat empty goal of "recognition." Three extended discussions of the aims of a liberal arts education concluded in citizenship: "resourceful, knowledgeable, and responsible." Indeed, one could argue that they were more than overlapping; they were repetitive. Two or three discussions could well have been devoted to other callings that students were being prepared to enter: work, marriage and family life, and the church. Nevertheless, purpose as citizenship had made a strong reentry in the college's consciousness.

Third, there was a somewhat veiled assumption that students need liberating from all the traditions that had shaped them, that these traditions were intrinsically limiting and deforming. But this seemed to have included the wholesome traditions—religious, cultural, ethnic—into which many parents had formed their children. Rather than deepening, expanding, and critically appropriating the traditions from which students come, the philosophy of "Freedom with Purpose" seems to aim at removing their residue in order to rebuild the student anew via a liberal arts curriculum presided over by the Roanoke faculty.

Fourth, there was this issue: Who or what provides the moral base that leads to the responsible citizen? Historically, the college always affirmed that Christianity—but never solely Christianity—offered such a foundation. It provided a rich intellectual and moral tradition from which the college could draw for its efforts to form students morally. O'Hara seemed to endorse that basis. However, "Freedom with Purpose" was very circumspect about naming such a basis for moral formation. It hinted that the Lutheran emphasis on the dialogue between faith and learning is important, as well as its emphasis on service. But O'Hara's confusing interpretation of Luther's famous paradox of "freedom from" and "freedom for" was repeated in the philosophy and principles of "Freedom for Purpose." In those formulations, the grace of God in Christ does not free humans from sin and death; rather, the liberal arts free them from "varieties of oppression." Indeed, the bases from which moral formation must proceed are mainly a set of processes and formal categories used in a liberal arts education. No specific moral or intellectual traditions are named. So, while there is much to admire in "Freedom with Purpose," it emphasizes service and citizenship (purpose) while downplaying any of the substantive foundations for purpose.[22] This deficit had a considerable effect on the new curriculum, which was developed later.

Curriculum

In the meantime, the old general-education "Centers of Distinction" curriculum underwent some variations as it struggled to retain a coherent approach to liberal arts education. The "Values and Responsible Life" course continued to be a required third-year course in the general-education curriculum. Its teachers were under less discipline to work with a common core of readings, and thus the bases for the responsible life were more varied, though Christian bases were generally included. Moreover, more of the courses were taught by regular—rather than adjunct—faculty, since there were more hires in the religion and philosophy department. A first-year

22. Why did this new account of the philosophy and principles of a liberal arts education take such a turn? One reason is that the task force simply followed O'Hara's lead, misinterpretation of Luther and all. That mistaken route may have been prevented had there been a Lutheran theologian on the task force (there were none). Such a person may well have insisted that the Christian basis for moral formation be more clearly named. Or one might have hoped that Robert Schultz, the Fishwick Professor of English, who had recently come to Roanoke from Luther College, would have detected the problem with O'Hara's interpretation of Luther, as well as the circumspection about naming the Christian faith as a shaping vision for the college. However, like many before him, Schultz sensed that Roanoke was quite a different church-related college than was Luther, where "Christianity was more integrated into every facet of the life of the college" (Robert Schultz interview, Nov. 10, 2015). So he did not press either issue. Furthermore, there was the general tendency in the school, of which the task force was representative, to "assume" such a base rather than articulate it. Given the increasing presence of "secular progressives" (those who distrust religiously based moral values exercised publicly) on the faculty, such a public articulation may have seemed unfitting and perhaps embarrassing. It may have made it more difficult to pass the faculty.

required co-curricular course had the students involved in intellectual and artistic events on-campus and community service off-campus.

The honors program was revised from its interdisciplinary approach to make it a more challenging and disciplined version of the "Centers of Distinction" curriculum. It was expanded to enroll about forty first-year and transfer students, about double those selected in the old program. The equivalent of the "Values and Responsible Life" course was called the "Values Practicum" in the honors program. It was taught by Ned Wisnefske and emphasized moral reasoning more than the regular general-education course did.

Faculty and Board

The board continued to have Lutheran representation: a half dozen wealthy and generous Lutheran laymen, the bishop of the Virginia Synod, James Mauney, and a prominent Lutheran pastor from Richmond, Christopher Price, a 1975 graduate of the college. It was chaired by a committed Lutheran layman, Robert Wortmann. The Christian presence on the board was strengthened by the addition of Carol Swain, a 1983 graduate of the college who had risen from an impoverished background to a position as professor on the Vanderbilt Law School faculty after she had earned a PhD at Princeton. During her time on the board, Swain became a strong spokesperson in support of the Christian character of the college.[23]

The faculty continued to expand during the O'Hara years, increasing from 125 full-time faculty to 135. In the early 2000s, the faculty had already begun to expand after the 1990s decade of "revenue neutrality." Of the fourteen department chairs, only one or two were likely to have entertained any "affirmative action" strategies for Lutherans, thus assuring that there would be little effort to shore up Lutheran presence in the faculty. However, Robert Schultz began a new venture called the "Lutheran Writers Project," which organized gatherings at which Lutheran writers in the creative writing field were featured and honored. This program continues as an ongoing demonstration of how Lutheran aesthetic sensibilities are expressed in literature. Both Robert Denham and Schultz were formidable Christian intellectuals who brought their

---

23. Dr. Swain served for only one term, leaving because she felt she had little influence on the board. It seems that her direct, aggressive support of a stronger role for the Christian heritage in the life of the college transgressed the traditional low-key approach of the board in which that heritage was "assumed," not articulated or discussed.

considerable insights to bear in that field. And other Christians continued to move into faculty positions—either by happenstance or providence.

The "Republican" Heritage of the College

As I noted in the preceding chapter, the plank in the college mission that emphasized service to church and world had been transformed from descriptors such as "republican virtue" or "benevolence" into a vocabulary using words such as "responsible life," "service," and "ethical growth." There was much encouragement of students to engage in service activities in the first-year co-curricular programs of both the general-education and the honors programs; "service learning" was beginning to become an integral part of a number of courses in various majors.

But the flagship program for understanding the public world in which we live, as well as for encouraging commitment to public service, was the Fowler Program. Besides the regular classroom teaching of the Fowler-endowed professor of public affairs, William Hill, it offered three other programs to enhance that republican heritage: the Fowler Public Speaker Lecture Program, the Fowler Legacy Program, and the Fowler Student Paper Competition.

The Public Speaker Lecture Program, sometimes in cooperation with the Center for Religion and Society and the Jordan Endowment, brought many distinguished public intellectuals to the college to speak on contemporary issues, such as civil rights, the future of American liberalism and conservatism, the meaning of the 2004 and 2006 elections, global strategy in the twenty-first century, and so forth. The Fowler Legacy Program enabled up to twenty students to participate in the Washington Semester or travel abroad to study specific issues. The student paper competition awarded cash grants to students who wrote compelling papers on current challenges in society.

The Center for Community Service had become busy enough to hire a full-time director in 2003, which enabled it to steer more students toward service in antipoverty, housing, and education initiatives. The chaplain continued to lead Habitat for Humanity building projects on student breaks. All in all, it is safe to say that the college kept faith with its missional commitment of service to the world. A good deal of the actual service was fueled by the Christian motivation of students and faculty alike, even though those motivational grounds were often not enunciated publicly. President O'Hara supported that variety of initiatives with enthusiasm.

The Christian Heritage of the College

Ethos

The O'Hara years featured much continuity with the Gring years with regard to the "way of life" on campus. Serious religious participation by student and faculty in on-campus religious life was a distinctly minority phenomenon. Student religious organizations included a small portion of students, though InterVarsity, an evangelical student organization, made its appearance on the campus with considerable strength, enlisting evangelical and mainline Protestants alike. Full-time InterVarsity leaders enabled the organization to flourish.

There was a strong effort to get more students living on campus, not only for a more wholesome student ethos but also to diminish the negative feedback from the Salem community when students lived in residential areas. Most alcohol-fueled parties took place off campus, and thus a reasonable level of peace and calm prevailed on campus.

Chaplain Henrickson continued his "ministry of presence," praying at faculty meetings, preaching at baccalaureate ceremonies, offering solace and counseling to students and faculty who found themselves in difficult situations, conducting "Theology on Tap" conversations for students at a local bar, and presiding at Christian worship services spread throughout the week.

The Religion and Philosophy Department

Chaired first by Ned Wisnefske and then by philosopher Hans Zorn during the O'Hara years, the department was reviewed by an external panel that more or less said, "Keep up the good work."[24] It enjoyed an addition in the arrival of a promising young Muslim scholar, Caner Dagli, who taught courses in Islam and other world religions. Marwood Larson-Harris came on as a teaching associate in religion to teach the "Values" courses and world religions. Strong teaching continued by Wisnefske, Hinlicky, and McDermott, supplemented by the work of adjunct professors (of which I was one). McDermott published widely—four books on various topics during the O'Hara presidency—while Hinlicky was gearing up to publish a flurry of scholarly books.

The department's opportunity to establish a second endowed chair helped to ensure a Lutheran/Christian voice at the college permanently.

---

24. Ned Wisnefske's annual report to the dean (2004–05), 1.

A trio of sisters—Virginia Kirkwood, Margaret Tise, and Jesse Heffner, all Marion College graduates—honored their pastor father, Marshall Tise, by endowing the Marshall Tise Chair in Lutheran Studies. That chair was offered to systematic theologian Paul Hinlicky, while the Jordan-Trexler Chair in Religion was passed to Ned Wisnefske. This gave muscle to the strategy that President Gring had adopted during his administration: to gather Lutheran money to endow specifically Lutheran/Christian positions at the college, so that, regardless of the waxing and waning of budgets and faculty opinion, those positions—the professorships, the chaplaincy, and scholarships—would endure through the years.

The department continued to teach the "Values and Responsible Life" course, which ensured that all students would be challenged with visions of the moral life, including both religious and philosophical bases for it. Besides dealing with the foundations of the moral life, the course also required students to relate those foundational principles to issues of the day. The honors program featured something similar: a senior capstone course called "Contemporary Challenges." The department continued to stimulate campus-wide discussion of intellectual issues by inviting scholars from other departments to present their research in various symposia.

A new philosopher, Monica Vilhauer, was added to the department to join Brent Atkins, who had arrived in 2002, and Hans Zorn, who had come in 1990. The two new philosophers represented something of a departure for Roanoke philosophers. Neither infused their courses with religious concerns, though both focused on ethics. Zorn continued in the traditional mode.

During the 2004–07 period, the department began offering majors in religion, philosophy, and theology, and a high of fourteen majors in religion graduated in 2004–05. The total number of majors granted by the department remained relatively the same, though divided among the new majors.

The Center for Religion and Society

Though I had retired from full-time teaching in 2000, I continued to administer the center, to teach courses as a senior lecturer, and to maintain a schedule of lecturing and writing. The preceding chapter describes the many initiatives of the center itself. The public lectures, the Faith and Reason Lecture/Dinners, the Crumley Lectures, the Slovak scholar program, and the Blakely evangelical programs continued during the O'Hara years. A new initiative sponsored by the center was a monthly bishop's forum, at which members of the religion and philosophy department, the chaplain, and the bishop of the Virginia Synod and his staff met to discuss writings that members of the group found unusually interesting and relevant. In addition, a new series sponsored by the Fowler Program and the Center for Religion and Society involved lectures on the meaning of national elections. Starting with the election of 2004, and continuing every other year up to the present, a conservative and a liberal observer have offered their reflections to large crowds, often noting the religious dimension of elections. The two endowments also sponsored a set of lectures on the future of religious and political conservatism and liberalism in America, also to well-attended gatherings.

The most stellar event ever sponsored solely by the center happened in the spring of 2007, when world-renowned New Testament scholar Bishop N. T. Wright of England lectured on "The Resurrection of the Son of God" to a crowd of nearly three thousand packed into Bast Gym on a Friday evening. Bishop Wright also spoke at other venues at the college and at churches in the Roanoke Valley. It was highly unusual for someone of that "star power" to stay as a guest of the center over an extended weekend. The bishop made a great impact.

Concluding Reflections on O'Hara's Brief Sojourn

Though Sabine O'Hara had many goals upon her arrival at Roanoke, the primary one was certainly to sharpen the identity and mission of the college. That was what was hoped for by the college community when she came, and that is what she delivered. She presented her immediate revisions of the mission, vision, and purpose statements of the college to its various constituencies in an effort to make them think about what the college was all about. Her forming of, and support for, the Task Force on Goals for Liberal Learning pressed the college to grapple seriously with its identity and mission in a way that it had probably never done before. Her own ideas, elaborated in her inaugural address, her talks to the faculty, and her other writings, found their way into the work of the task force. The detailed "philosophy" and "principles" articulated by the task force then crucially became the guidelines for a strategic plan and the development of a new curriculum. As one appreciative member of the task force said, "She set the college on a clear course that bore valuable fruits beyond her time at the college."[25]

25. Interview with Robert Schultz (Nov. 10, 2015).

Yet, that accomplishment had a strong element of ambiguity. While it definitely strengthened the "service" motif of the historic commitments of the college with its "Freedom with Purpose" emphasis, it was much less clear and bold about a Christian base for that commitment. She certainly mentioned elements of the Lutheran rationale for education for service, as well as the intellectual dialogue between faith and reason; but the main agent of formation for purposeful service seemed to be the liberating processes of a liberal arts education itself.[26] The process of liberating students from their "narrow worlds" seemed to provide the ethical base for the responsible life by itself. Forthright affirmation of the role of substantive Christian belief and moral teaching in the formation of students seemed to be something of an embarrassment. Or perhaps the role of Christian belief and moral teaching was assumed. Nevertheless, this reluctance was soon to be illustrated in the new curriculum that was aborning.

O'Hara also made a vigorous start in the strategic planning process, but that was not completed in her time at Roanoke, for reasons that I shall soon note. But other projects were initiated or completed: four new residence halls were completed, the first student housing built since 1968; two classroom buildings were renovated; a new artificial turf stadium, the Donald Kerr Stadium, was constructed; the Goode-Pasfield Center for Learning and Teaching was created; two new endowed professorships were created, the Cassullo Professorship in Art History and the Tise Professor of Lutheran Studies (mentioned above). The admissions office set records for both the number of applications and incoming students; the college reached a new record of 1,900 students; at her last commencement in the spring of 2007, President O'Hara handed diplomas to 410 graduates, also a new record.

Until O'Hara's presidency, Roanoke College presidents had averaged tenures of nearly fifteen and a half years—seventeen if one does not count the one-year presidency of Thomas Dosh (the second president). I have entitled this chapter "An Abbreviated Search for Soul" because the flame

---

26. To be fair, this notion of liberation through education—what O'Hara termed *Bildung*—is part of the Lutheran tradition shaped by Luther and Melanchthon in their reformation of education in Germany. Both believed that such a liberal arts education (*Bildung*) could indeed imbue students with a "civil righteousness" that made them enlightened people and good citizens. This liberation was not about salvation but rather about civic virtue. While both thought that instruction in the Christian faith ought to be part of that *Bildung*, one could become a good person without it. There was such a trust in reason and historical experience that in the long run it tended to diminish the role of Christian instruction in *Bildung*. A similar process seemed to be going on at Roanoke College.

that burned brightly at the beginning of O'Hara's quest for clarity and integration in 2004 had been extinguished by 2007, a very short period of time compared to other presidencies.

The college account of O'Hara's early departure was typically bland: "After completing nearly three years leading the college, O'Hara announced that she had accomplished her key objectives and was ready to move on."[27] O'Hara herself said: "I came to Roanoke to accomplish these key objectives, and now that I have accomplished them, it is time for someone else to lead the college through the implementation of the identified initiatives and goals."[28]

Of course, that was not the whole story. Conflict erupted early in O'Hara's administration, first with the vice presidents and later with the lower administrators, and finally with the faculty. By the end of her second year, the turbulence was widespread, and an alarmed board took note; by the end of her third, O'Hara resigned. Underneath it all seemed to be a clash of management cultures and a huge difference in perception of what had to be done at Roanoke. Regarding management cultures, Roanoke vice presidents were used to a lot of autonomy in their own bailiwicks and much discussion before college-wide decisions were taken. O'Hara's penchant was more interventionist, abrupt, and authoritative than the vice presidents were accustomed to. But the difference in perception about what had to be done at the college by the president was even sharper and more decisive. In 2004, the veteran leaders at Roanoke believed they had just come off a string of successes and were looking to the new president to improve things further by building on previous successes. O'Hara had quite a different interpretation of the college she had come to in 2004: in her view, it had many serious deficiencies that required a wholesale makeover. She believed that a major renovation was in store under her leadership. These were significant differences in interpretation, and they led to serious conflict.

In the end, what many had hoped would become a long tenure was very brief, at least according to earlier Roanoke patterns. There was also an element of tragedy in the story: a highly competent and well-meaning person made missteps in an institutional context that was alien to her, and that inevitably brought great troubles to her and the college. Thus ended one of the shortest, but certainly not the least productive, of the Roanoke presidencies.

---

27. From the Roanoke College website's vignette of each Roanoke College president.
28. Evangelical Lutheran Church in America News Service, March 28, 2007.

10

MICHAEL MAXEY (2007–)

A Steady Hand on the Rudder

On a bright May morning in 2007, a standing-room-only crowd representing every constituency of Roanoke College was crammed into Antrim Chapel. After three stormy years as president, Sabine O'Hara had resigned in April. The crowd, having heard credible rumors that Michael Maxey would be appointed interim president, waited expectantly for an announcement to that effect by the president of the board of trustees, Robert Wortmann. The presence of the whole Maxey family confirmed that expectation. But Wortmann's announcement surpassed the expectations of that assembly: he announced that the board had unanimously voted to ask Maxey to be the permanent president—and that he had accepted. The chapel erupted in a standing ovation. There were many hugs and cheers of joy. After Maxey responded with his usual grace and humility, the crowd disbanded with great anticipation that the uncertainty and conflict of the last three years were past and that the college could look forward to a much calmer future.[1]

Maxey had already served for more than twenty years at the college and had earned the respect and admiration of the college community for his integrity, competence, and congeniality. He was very much a known quantity: there would be no unpleasant surprises coming from him. And so began a

---

1. Maxey responded to his appointment with a rousing rhetorical flourish, entitled "I Believe in Roanoke College." In this unpublished speech he praises all the constituencies whose contributions made such belief possible. Notable was his affirmation of belief in "liberal learning with its commitment to educating resourceful, informed, and responsible citizens," and "in Lutheran higher education with its respect for individuals and its devotion to academic freedom" (quotes he used were from the new "Goals for Liberal Learning").

presidency that extends to the present day. Since it is not yet complete, it is not amenable to conclusive assessment. Indeed, my first inclination, in writing this book, was to handle the Maxey years as an epilogue. But much has happened in the nine years of his administration, and it is important to give the reader an up-to-date glimpse of Roanoke College at the time of its 175th birthday. Therefore, in this chapter I will stick to the format of the earlier ones, but I will not engage in the kind of assessment that I offered at the conclusion of each preceding chapter.

Challenges of the Years 2007–2017

If he had had a choice, Maxey perhaps would not have chosen the milieu in which he was called to serve. Not long after he was sworn in, the most severe financial crisis since the Great Depression hit. The stock market plunged, and the Roanoke College endowment shrank. Some big banks collapsed, while others were bailed out; oil prices soared, while the value of homes collapsed, putting many new owners in an "underwater" position (i.e., they owed far more on their homes than those homes were currently worth). The recession spread across oceans and around the world.

Even after the worst had hit, the recovery was one of the slowest since World War II. After 2005, the economy never grew more than 3 percent per year. This had major effects: many workers dropped out of the work force permanently; the middle class struggled with paltry growth in income; indeed, many claim that the middle class shrank in the slow-growth years following the recession. But their fate was not nearly as difficult as that of the poor and working classes, who had fewer job opportunities as the economy shifted from its industrial base to a high-tech one. Globalization introduced cheap products from abroad that made many domestic factories noncompetitive. Whole industries virtually disappeared. Furthermore, high rates of illegal immigration led to competition for jobs at the lower end of the economy. But even more seriously, the marriage-and-family cultures of the lower classes disintegrated, which led to widespread illegitimacy, with its attendant woes for children raised in single-parent families.

Meanwhile, those in the high-tech sectors of the economy were richly compensated, adding to a growing inequality between the wealthy and the poor. The highly educated quickly recovered from the recession. They flourished amid an economy that did not offer enough opportunity to the rest of the society. Its fragility prompted the government to expand the safety net, with ambiguous effects: on the one hand, cushioning the effects of the stagnant economy, but on the other hand, increasing dependency.

The revolution set off in the realm of electronic communication during the 1990s accelerated after 2000. The internet and its attendant computers became available to nearly everyone. But the truly revolutionary innovation was the iPhone, first introduced by Apple in 2007: it has become, along with other phones like it, omnipresent among all segments of the population, but especially among young adults. While these instruments have certainly increased the extent and pace of communications, they have had ambiguous effects on people themselves. Some commentators claim that they encourage people to avoid face-to-face human contact, which then leads to weakness in social interaction and to the inability to focus attention. The amount of time spent on mobile devices—as well as the number of times daily they "needed" to be checked—is alarming. The social effects of instantaneous and ubiquitous communication, over time, remain unknown.

The electronic revolution also set off major changes in education. On-line education has been developed and adapted by many private and public institutions. This development quickly challenged traditional residential educational ventures, which had become more expensive, partly because of the availability of student loans. Liberal arts colleges were particularly squeezed, and they often reinvented themselves to become more attuned to parents' demands that their children be immediately employable upon graduation. Education was thus pushed in a utilitarian direction.

The economic turbulence in 2007 and 2008 had enormous effects on the presidential race of 2008. John McCain, an aging Vietnam war hero and longtime senator, was caught in a perfect storm of severe economic instability. That, combined with the war weariness of the country's involvement in two expensive Middle East wars, made it possible for a young, charismatic, but inexperienced senator from Illinois, Barack Obama, to become the first African American President in American history. His campaign promised hope and change. His Democratic Party swept to power in the Senate and House in 2008 and held its majorities in 2012. That enabled the President to enact his signature Affordable Care Act, albeit with not one vote from the opposition party. The bitter fight over the transformation of the American health-care system, as well as intense disagreement over the dramatic shift in foreign policy under Obama, led to a sharply polarized country. That division was reflected in the loss of both the Senate and the House by the Democrats in the midterm elections of 2014. The near paralysis that resulted from divided government led the Obama administration to rely on its executive powers, whose regulatory interventions were hotly contested in Congress and the courts.

The culture of this period extended and intensified the impulses of the early 2000s. The liberationist motifs gained further momentum. Academia continued to exercise the "hermeneutics of suspicion" on all inherited patterns, which in its view were distorted by racism and sexism. In this view, the individual should be set free from such constraints—and to a great extent he or she was. This was most true in the realm of sexual identity and behavior. Premarital sex became even more accepted. Homosexual activity was mainstreamed and legitimated, ultimately finding its culmination in the widespread acceptance and legalization of gay marriage. Sexual identities proliferated, as campaigns addressed the "T" in the LGBT agenda: the transgendered claimed liberation for those who wanted to be freed from their given biological makeup. Such developments led to great conflict within mainline Protestant denominations, resulting in splits. In 2009, the Evangelical Lutheran Church in America, the church formally connected with Roanoke College, experienced another division—after an earlier one in the first years of the twenty-first century. Like other mainline Protestant churches, its membership dropped drastically.

But this "deregulation" of sexual identity and behavior soon ran into serious conundrums. The supposed harmlessness of sexual desire was something of an illusion. The principle of consent, which became the only regulative moral principle, didn't seem clear or solid enough to deal with such liberated desire. It was not so easily tamed. Colleges and universities soon were convulsed by charges that young men violated consent in a widespread "culture of rape." But consent was hard to legally define and ascertain when both parties were under the influence of alcohol or drugs. Many of those accused turned the tables on the accuser. Schools attempted to address these problems with complicated rules, mostly prompted by federal instructions that were imposed on all who took federal aid of any kind.

However, it seemed that the "expressive individualism" set free by liberation from the constraints of traditional culture was a project only for the strongest. Most people wanted a connection to something beyond themselves; but there was no common culture to fall back on, and those who needed cultural guidance floundered and often needed therapeutic interventions of various types. Rates of depression among the young were elevated.

Such individuals often fled then to groups who promised a thicker identity than they had been given. They identified with groups whose members felt aggrieved in some way and demanded more "diversity" and "inclusion." Paradoxically, "identity politics" gained traction at the same time as individualism did. Fragile individual identities were absorbed into hypersensitive groups who were on the lookout for "micro-aggressions" and "triggers" that could rouse their ire. The faculty and administrations of schools that had encouraged both the individualism and identity politics often bore the brunt of that ire.

The elites who were in charge of the "commanding heights" of the culture—academia, the media, government bureaucracies, entertainment—were increasingly peopled by "secular progressives." They emphasized the importance of tolerance toward diverse lifestyles and adopted an openminded, pragmatic approach to life's challenges. They tended to live according to conventional norms but were chary of defending them for fear they would appear intolerant. They had weak connections to religious traditions, were basically optimistic about the society that was under their direction, and were distrustful of the public expression of religiously based moral values, especially if those values conflicted with the new canons of the sexual revolution. This provoked tension with those of traditional religious cultures who attempted to express their resistance politically, which, in turn, exacerbated the polarization of the political sphere.

Such tensions also arose concerning elite enforcement of certain "politically correct" convictions about climate change and its attendant remedies, the "social construction" of sexual identity, the extent of racism in American society, and the necessity and extent of "diversity" and "inclusion." Tolerance was not freely extended to those who disagreed with those convictions. The general nervousness of the culture was further stimulated by instances of domestic terrorism perpetrated by radical Islamists at home and abroad. Middle Eastern turmoil generated by clashes within Islam resulted in millions of refugees from the affected lands. Some were brought to the United States, touching off a debate about the wisdom of such practices.

All in all, the period from 2007 to 2017 was an unsettled time that was characterized by division and tension. Yet the country did not fall into violent contention, and democratic practices continued to survive. Many families still nurtured wonderful young people. But it was not an easy time to become president of a liberal arts college, as Michael Maxey did in the spring of 2007. What prepared him for the daunting task ahead?

The Formation of Michael Maxey

Michael Creed Maxey was born on December 7, 1951, in the small southern Virginia mill town of Bassett. His parents, Jesse Creed Maxey and Doris Pegron Maxey, both enjoyed large families that lived nearby. These extended families met often and left a powerful impact on young Michael. They were moderate Southern Baptists who worshiped regularly and practiced their faith vigorously. When racial change engulfed the region in the 1960s, Michael's maternal grandmother told him emphatically that "black people are God's children and should be treated justly." Michael heard that loud and clear.[2]

His father owned two five-and-dime stores, and the whole family—Michael, his mother, and his younger brother and sister—often pitched in to help in that operation, especially at Christmastime. Besides running the stores, the elder Maxey worked as a Railway Express agent and spent much time shipping furniture from the local factories. Before her marriage to Jesse Maxey, Michael's mother worked as a Western Union operator, a vocation that was exceedingly rare for women of that time. A very devout Christian, she wanted Michael to become a preacher, and she encouraged his involvement in many Baptist activities as he grew up. Doris Maxey died of cancer at age sixty-seven in 1989, but the elder Maxey still lives independently in Bassett.

After grade school and high school in Bassett, Michael went off to Wake Forest University in the fall of 1970, intending to become a medical missionary. Wake Forest at that time was still connected strongly to the Baptist tradition and had a firm supportive atmosphere for young, aspiring Christians. It also had a strong identity and sense of mission devoted to Christian service, which was impressed on Michael. During his college years he worked in nearby Baptist churches and ministries, where a number of "negative-type" preachers soured him on becoming a medical missionary. So he became a history major instead, graduating in 1974.

He wanted to continue his education at Wake Forest, but this time he chose graduate training in counseling, for which he received a master's degree in education.[3] He spent a year in Venice, Italy, as an interlude between

2. All this information about Michael Maxey was gleaned from an interview with him, January 15, 2016.

3. As part of his training in counseling, he practiced the use of the Rorschach test in analyzing the psychology and intelligence of those he interviewed. (In the Rorschach test, an interviewee was asked to interpret the shape made by a blob of ink on absorbent paper.) He

graduate study and work. During his graduate studies at Wake Forest, he worked as a resident head in a dorm, which prepared him to move to Averett College, where he was head resident and assistant to the dean of students. There he met Terri Petree, a young Baptist woman from Richmond who was working at Averett as an admissions counselor. They married in 1978 and then spent the next summer together working at a Baptist camp, which, Michael said, was "the best summer of my life" up to that time.

Newly married, the pair went off to the University of New Hampshire, where Michael completed a certificate in advanced graduate study in counseling in fifteen months. During that time he worked at a pastoral counseling center in the university town of Durham. Terri worked as a coordinator for the student union while her husband studied. After completing his certificate, Michael worked in the dean's office and then the education department as head of academic advising for four years. Both wanted to return to Virginia after years of cold winters and absence from their families; so Terri took a job in admissions at Ferrum College in southwestern Virginia, while Michael looked for opportunities in both the business and academic worlds. A job in resource development, a field in which Maxey had never worked before, came open at Roanoke College, and he was encouraged to apply.[4] More inclined to look at familiar academic institutions (Wake Forest or Averett) for employment, he nonetheless scouted out Roanoke to overcome his reticence. Hearing testimony about the integrity and quality of Norman Fintel's leadership at Roanoke, he applied for the job in a field for which he had little preparation. After a rigorous set of interviews he was hired, and he began at Roanoke in January 1985.

He showed so much leadership ability in his successful resource development activities during his first five years at the college that he received a number of offers from other colleges to leave Roanoke for another position elsewhere. In 1988, the elite Williams College tried unsuccessfully to recruit Maxey. Other offers followed. However, a visit from two of Roanoke's

---

chose to interview his mother as part of his practice. After going through the set of questions with her, he was impressed with her intelligence and said to her: "Mom, you are really smart." She simply nodded her head firmly, which to him meant that there was far more intellectual power in his mother than had been recognized.

4. One of his pastor friends once counseled him that he was too reticent to grasp opportunities that came up. This friend gave him a carving of a whale that had the figure of Jonah carved out of its belly. Maxey keeps the carving in his office to the present day. The biblical allusion reminds him to overcome his natural reticence when challenges present themselves (Maxey interview, Jan. 15, 2016).

greatest leaders from the past changed the trajectory of his life. Clarence Caldwell, revered community leader and retired business manager of the college, and Homer Bast, honored Roanoke administrator, coach, and professor (for whom the new gymnasium was named) got wind of these offers and appeared at his office in the fall of 1990. They put this claim on the young Maxey: "We want you to devote your career to Roanoke College." Coming from such worthies, the challenge seemed like a message from God himself, and Maxey took it to heart.[5]

After his success in resource development, Maxey was invited in 1989 to become director of admissions, even though, as before, he had no real experience in the area he was invited to lead. He overcame his hesitation and took the position, in which he performed remarkably well for the next fifteen years. Each year the number of applicants to the college increased. More significantly, the number of entering freshmen went from 429 in 1989 to 566 in 2007. There was a gradual increase in the number of yearly graduates during the Maxey years, culminating in a record 410 in 2007.[6] He became a quiet hero to the faculty, who knew their livelihood depended on his success. He was known for honesty in reporting the real situation in a field—admissions—where stretching the truth was a constant temptation. He became widely respected as a talented man of integrity by nearly everyone in the Roanoke College community.[7]

When the three-year O'Hara administration came to a turbulent end with her resignation in April 2007, Maxey was a natural candidate for interim president, since he had gained the trust of the community and had performed well in a number of important positions over twenty-two years at the college. He did not expect to be a candidate for president because he

5. Their summons and Maxey's response brings to mind the career of a much earlier professor of religion, Luther Augustine Fox (1843–1925), who also had many invitations to move to more prestigious positions. At the end of his life, Fox reflected: "Regardless of what I might have done elsewhere, I am glad my life has been devoted to Roanoke" (see p. 65, above). Perhaps Maxey will say something similar at his retirement.

6. Roanoke College Office of Institutional Research.

7. In the early 1990s, the Maxey family became members of College Lutheran Church after a good deal of reflection on their religious convictions. This move came years before he had any idea of becoming president of Roanoke, but had the happy effect of keeping alive the tradition that every Roanoke College president be a Lutheran and belong to College Lutheran Church. This was doubly important: it kept the presidency in Lutheran hands even though the board rules no longer required it; and it provided an opening for Maxey to become involved in Lutheran affairs at the local, regional, and national levels. He soon became a major player among the presidents of Lutheran colleges and universities.

did not have a PhD, which had become a prerequisite for candidacy for the presidential office of nearly every liberal arts college.[8]

When the president of the board, Robert Wortmann, came to his office in April, Maxey thought that Wortmann might ask him to serve as interim president. Wortmann's first words were: "We don't want you as interim; we want you as permanent president!" Unprepared for such a challenge, Maxey was astonished at the offer. He consulted Terri and his three sons, who all encouraged him to take the job—for which, naturally, he had no prior experience. He also remembered his Baptist mentor's counsel to overcome his reticence in taking on new challenges. But what was conclusive was a call from Christopher Price, distinguished Lutheran pastor and member of the board, who said: "This is your calling, Mike. Consent to it." And so he did. The announcement of his appointment was made public to the college in mid-May, to the relieved and joyous response of the entire Roanoke College community.

Asked to reflect on his journey up to that point in his life, Maxey saw, throughout his life, a pattern of doors opening to positions for which he had little preparation. Those doors, he thought, were part of God's calling him to step through them to add his contribution to the institutions he served, especially Roanoke College. His Baptist mentor gave him the courage to step forward and serve. Maxey's trajectory to the presidency of the college seemed a fitting capstone to the earlier request to devote his career to it.[9]

As he embarked on the top leadership role at the college, Maxey, like the three presidents that just preceded him, thought that the college lacked a clear sense of identity and mission. He attributed a good deal of this lack of clarity to its pragmatic spirit: the college leadership was interested in grappling with practical problems and tended to leave issues of identity and mission to the realm of tacit assumptions. He perceived that one of O'Hara's gifts in her three years as president had been to sharpen that sense by appointing the Task Force on Goals for Liberal Learning at Roanoke College. That task force then came up with an extensive rationale for the college's identity and mission, articulated in the document "Freedom with Purpose."[10] But that

8. The last president of Roanoke without a PhD was Charles Smith, who was elected in 1920.

9. One of the pair who visited him earlier to ask the young Maxey to devote his career to Roanoke College, Clarence Caldwell, had nominated him for the presidency in 2004. In 2007, Caldwell sent that same letter of nomination to the board. This time board members voted unanimously to make Maxey the next president.

10. The workings of that task force and the document it produced are recorded in the previous chapter.

was still just a document; it had to be embodied in a strategic plan and a curriculum.

In anticipation of being appointed interim president of the college—but before he was surprised by being called to become permanent president—Maxey had written a paper about the challenges that faced the college. Those he mentioned in the paper reflect some of the social dynamics I have just sketched above. He argued that the college faced demographic, technological, economic, and political challenges. Regarding demographics, he pointed out that the birthrate among the middle class was declining, thus limiting the number of precisely the kinds of young people who would tend to matriculate at Roanoke College. Furthermore, those from the burgeoning immigrant populations had not yet gained an appreciation for liberal arts colleges and could not afford them. The public universities were also facing a recruitment shortfall, so they became competitors with the liberal arts colleges for those students. Roanoke's recruitment pool was being contested.

Technologically, the college had to keep up with the constant changes in information technology. This meant large expenditures for hardware, software, and the technicians who could manage the new systems. Online education was just beginning at this point, but it would soon compete with residential learning. The college community had to adapt to these changes. For example, Fintel Library had to accommodate its resources to changes in the publication of books and journals, in student reading habits, and in the cataloguing and storage of information.

Economic challenges were daunting. The income of the middle class was stagnant, while the price of education was going up. Technological upgrades, new faculty, new dorms, and expanded facilities were not cheap. But the rising price of education was not due to those factors alone. The government stepped in with its many loan offers to students who needed help. Unsurprisingly, colleges took advantage of that opportunity to raise their prices in order to pay for the new accoutrements. Increasing student aid was also an instrument to help students pay for college. By 2014, the total cost of student aid surpassed the total cost of faculty salaries.[11] The whole process had another astounding effect: student debt surpassed total credit card debt in the United States.

Politically, Maxey thought that the government itself presented real dangers to liberal arts colleges by its various regulatory incursions. A serious example was the government's threat to rank colleges by their graduation

---

11. Maxey interview, January 15, 2016.

rates and the success of their graduates, measured in economic terms. Complicit in raising the price of education, the government now wanted to shape the colleges up by measuring them with one crude criterion. Maxey joined other presidents of liberal arts colleges—led by Lynchburg College President Kenneth Garren, former Roanoke academic dean under David Gring—to resist this incursion.

The Maxey Vision for Roanoke College

With all this in mind, Michael Maxey offered his vision for Roanoke College at his inauguration ceremony on October 27, 2007. In contrast to the three presidents before him, Maxey was appointed from within and had no need to "size up" the college in preparation for his speech. He *knew* what the college was all about.

Before moving to his "three views," Maxey addressed three important subjects. First, he emphasized the solemnity of the occasion: it "celebrates the community beliefs that bind us together."[12] He knew what those beliefs were, and he intended to affirm them. Second, he noted that Roanoke College had gotten better annually. It had made impressive progress, though he believed that progress had not yet been fully recognized. This was something of an antidote to O'Hara's conviction that the college needed a major makeover. Third, he spent generous time expressing his gratitude to his family and to the many constituencies of the college.

The three views he took up in the address were one "up close," one from "a greater distance," and one of "envisioning our future," the last one being an exercise of the imagination. The close-at-hand view enumerated the obvious gains made by the college: its improvement in its physical appearance; its movement from recognition as a regional to a national liberal arts college; its growth in the number (2,000) and diversity of its student body; its award of a Phi Beta Kappa chapter; its commitment to incremental change; and its giving prominence to human relationships. "People matter here."

The view "from a greater distance" included the lovely environment of the college. It also pointed to the fact that educating the young was a process that, over time, will influence the world. Maxey quoted Robert

---

12. Michael Maxey, unpublished manuscript of his inaugural address, 1. Hereafter, page references to this manuscript appear in parentheses within the text.

Frost: "College is where young people are having it out with themselves about God and man and sociology and poetry." Maxey followed with: "At our heart is the firm belief that helping young people 'have it out' with life's great questions ultimately helps society" (10). He followed that thought by citing Bittle's originating commitment to educate the whole person: "A person of learning, without moral principle, is only prepared to injure society." Such an education emphasized both breadth and depth in learning, the former provided by a new curriculum under development and informed by "Freedom with Purpose" that would shape "resourceful, informed, and responsible citizens."[13] The depth would be provided by its majors.

A final element in the long view was the college's relationship with the Lutheran church. Noting that Martin Luther was a professor and that the Reformation was born in a classroom, Maxey affirmed that "Lutherans encourage respect for individuals, academic freedom, consideration of life's ultimate questions, and questioning authority. . . . Lutherans give us more than room to breathe, they give us breath" (15).

The third view of the college involved envisioning a future. For Maxey this included enhanced learning experiences that embraced both research and service-learning for students. Faculty members were to be offered resources to improve teaching and support research, both of which would be strengthened by the three new professorships that he announced. Two of those professorships were endowed by Charles and Helen Schumann for the religion and philosophy department: one in Lutheran theology and one in Christian ethics. The college's endowment had to be increased dramatically to enable it to support economic and other kinds of diversity among its students. "Roanoke does not seek standing as an elitist place," Maxey said (18). He continued: "We will align our curriculum and offerings with our value system," which to him meant supporting a new curricular proposal to help students grapple with "the essential questions of life" (18).

Maxey then went on to enumerate the renovations planned for a number of buildings and concluded with an inspiring visionary statement by John F. Kennedy, who promised the nation to place a man on the moon by the end of the decade. Maxey finished by claiming that "the same level of aspiration and drive live here. We will dream. We will focus. We will work. We will arrive. And together we will enjoy the view" (21).

13. This was a reference to the new statement of principles recently articulated under O'Hara's administration.

Commentary

It is fascinating how Maxey reiterated the three themes in Roanoke's historic sense of mission, its Christian "republicanism": moral formation for citizenship and service; a formation founded on religious bases of ultimate concern; and its education open to all sectors of society. He recalled for the Roanoke community Bittle's emphasis on moral formation and educating the whole person, and how that reinforced these themes. He also conveyed a genuine sense of gratitude to those who had helped him along the way; after being on the scene for many years, he was in the position to know who had brought him to that present moment.

While it is significant that Maxey affirmed the college's relationship to the Lutheran tradition as an important element in its mission, his defining of what Lutheranism stands for was rather generic and thin: respect for individuals, questioning authority, academic freedom, and consideration of life's ultimate questions.[14] No mention of vocation, the importance of grace, or faith and learning engagement—which were right in the college's statement of purpose.[15] Nor was there any mention of strengthening that relationship, though the newly endowed chairs in the religion and philosophy department were, in fact, intended to do just that.

One irony stood out in his depiction of Lutheranism's gifts to the college. After saying that Lutherans "give us room to breathe," he claimed that "they give us breath." But this was said at a time when observant Lutherans on the faculty and in the administration were a dying breed. Outside of the religion and philosophy department, the observant Lutherans on the faculty and administration were few indeed, perhaps fewer than a half dozen, and their numbers were not being monitored or intentionally replenished.

All in all, the address struck themes steeped in the Roanoke tradition and promised continued attention to them, and those promises were made by a new president who was familiar and trusted by the whole college community. The address was comforting, if not bold.

14. This depiction of Lutheranism's gift to academic life as freedom brings to mind the remark of a student from the college who was invited to a Lutheran faculty conference sponsored by a Lutheran fraternal organization. Asked what he thought was his most important learning about Lutheran higher education that he gained at the conference, he replied: "The great strength of Lutheran colleges is that you can believe whatever you want."

15. Nor was there any mention of Jesus, which meant that the last mention of Jesus in an inaugural address was in 1975, when Norman Fintel was installed.

Other Writings

Maxey gave a stronger affirmation of the role of the Lutheran tradition in the college's life at the installation of Christopher Bowen, the new chaplain called to the college in the fall of 2013 (after the thirty-year tenure of the newly retired Paul Henrickson). Bowen was called to the college from a large parish in the Tidewater of Virginia. He was youthful—he arrived with a wife and a young family—and ready to take up a chaplaincy that, though solid and respected, needed new initiatives.

In his brief remarks Maxey strongly affirmed the Lutheran heritage of the college: "For me, [the Lutheran heritage] is central and as relevant today as it was in 1842. I believe in Lutheran, liberal arts, residential higher education. It is a personal conviction for me and it is an institutional intention for us. It makes us vital. And it makes us relevant in wonderful, powerful, life-changing ways."[16]

He went on to elaborate the "four legs" of Lutheran education "that define our identity at Roanoke College. They inspire my own actions as president here, and they influence our ideals as a college." The first leg was grace: "I believe God's grace is one of the most important ideas we have to share at Roanoke College. It was certainly the most important attraction to me when I joined College Lutheran Church."[17] The second was the Lutheran love of learning, and the third was "welcoming all while proclaiming our Lutheran center. We are Lutheran at our core and inclusive in our community life together." The fourth—and to his mind the most important—was the Lutheran concept of calling, or vocation. That Lutheran teaching was particularly meaningful to him as president of the college, and he saw it as central to the new chaplain's work: "It is compelling for our intentions for the ministry of our chaplain. Assisting students in their aims of finding meaning in life and answering ultimate questions about our relationships to God, to other people, and with the creation is our most noble work and it is desperately needed in the world."[18]

The difference between the reticence of his inaugural address and the robustness of his "Testimony of Faith" speech at the chaplain's installation

16. Maxey, "Testimony of Faith," unpublished manuscript of his remarks at the installation of Chaplain Bowen, 1.

17. Maxey, "Testimony," 1.

18. Maxey, "Testimony," 2. It is an irony that such a high evaluation of "vocation" by the president came after the faculty had denied its centrality in the controversy over the Lilly Grant. See the preceding chapter.

service is certainly noticeable. A good deal of the difference can be attributed to the audience. Those assembled for the inauguration were hugely diverse; those at the chaplain's installation were the inner circle of Christian believers. Maxey was "preaching to the choir." The rhetoric was certainly bold, claiming that the college was "Lutheran at our core." Perhaps that was more aspiration than description, but he wanted this talk to be illustrative of his own convictions about the college.[19]

In the previous three decades, presidents of Roanoke College have always given a welcome to the gathering at its annual Christmas dinner for faculty, staff, and their guests. It is a very large event, and attendees cover the spectrum from devout Baptist janitors to skeptical professors. In view of such a mixture, the college has been hesitant to attach the descriptor "Christian" to anything. Indeed, it calls the Christmas break the "Winter Break" and sends cards wishing recipients a "Happy Holiday Season."

But in his welcome at the first Christmas dinner of his administration, Maxey was quite explicit about the "Christmas season of the year when we come together or converge." Highlighting the theme of "convergence," Maxey quoted Teilhard de Chardin: "Remain true to yourself, but move ever upward toward greater consciousness and greater love. At the summit you will find yourselves united with all those who, from every direction, have made the same ascent. For everything that rises must converge." He praised everyone who has a part in helping students make that ascent. He said: "We hold this celebration at this moment and this season, in part, to remember the birth of a Savior to the world who calls us to humbly love others as we love ourselves. There is nothing hateful or exclusionary about the faith that holds that we are all God's children."[20]

The Strategic Plan

One of the first tasks Maxey took up after his inauguration was the formation of a strategic plan. He began by "listening to lots of people in an effort to restore 'normality' and get a good reading on what had to be done."[21] He also wanted to take seriously the new "Freedom with Purpose" statement that

19. Affirmed during the Maxey interview (Jan. 15, 2016).

20. Maxey, "Christmas Welcome," unpublished manuscript (Dec. 19, 2015). It is interesting that his affirmation of the faith that "we are all God's children" recalled what his grandmother had said to him many years before, during the struggle over integration in Virginia.

21. Maxey interview (Jan. 15, 2016).

had been developed in the first year of O'Hara's tenure. In taking it seriously, the college "will be one of the nation's top one hundred liberal arts colleges," which would indeed increase "its national prominence and reputation."[22] Various groups worked on the plan over a year and a half, and the statement was finished in 2009, the same year a new curriculum was installed.

Keying off "Freedom with Purpose," the plan embraced four themes. The first involved a strong commitment to the new liberal arts curriculum, "Intellectual Inquiry," which would advance the vision of "Freedom with Purpose." An important initiative was to "increase the number of students involved in research, artistic endeavors, independent study, study abroad, internships, service learning, and leadership experiences to the highest levels in Roanoke's history."[23] The first theme also included the intent to have students win more national awards and fellowships and to produce more students going to graduate schools.

The second theme committed the college to link academic, co-curricular, and residential experience. That involved building more residential dorms to get a higher percentage of students on campus and attempting to create an environment where intellect and character were developed more intentionally.[24] The third theme embraced a leadership role in the Roanoke Valley that involved enrichment of its cultural life and service to the community. The fourth led to efforts to increase "diversity" on campus, support faculty scholarship development, double the number of endowed professorships, and increase compensation "commensurate with our national standing."[25]

22. http://www.roanoke.edu/about/administration/strategic_plan 1–7. The following references are to that document.

23. http://www.roanoke.edu/about/administration/strategic_plan 1–7. This was taken quite seriously. A directorship of Experiential and Service Learning was established to increase both forms of learning, which were intended to be connected with courses in the student's major. By 2016, there were twenty-one courses involving community service, two hundred internships, and four hundred students involved in student/faculty research projects (interview with Richard Grant, the director, on Feb. 23, 2016).

24. Dorm space was increased; nearly three-quarters of the students lived on campus by 2015, and President Maxey and Chaplain Henrickson developed an orientation that included a "pledge to a way of life that embodies Roanoke's four pillars—academic excellence, commitment to community, service to others, and a life of personal distinction." Maxey sought some clear message for entering students that was as distinct as the ideals that engaged him when he was an entering student at Wake Forest University (Maxey interview, Jan. 15, 2016).

25. A number of endowed professorships were established, including—in the religion and philosophy department—the Schumann Chair in Christian Ethics. Given the slow recovery from recession, faculty remuneration did not increase markedly; but neither did it recede, as it did in many schools.

A fifth theme was "support for our ambitions," which included efforts to increase the graduation and retention rates, increase the size of the student body, conduct a major campaign to increase the endowment to $150 million by 2017, construct a new athletic and recreational center, renovate the science facilities, and "align reputation with reality."[26]

While this plan was not technically a strategic plan, it offered a set of goals to strive for, many of which have been realized. It set Roanoke on its regular path of incremental gains.

The New "Intellectual Inquiry" Curriculum

One of President O'Hara's goals at Roanoke had been to build a new curriculum guided by the "Freedom with Purpose" set of principles. The faculty was also ready to shape a new curriculum. The old "Centers of Distinction" curriculum had lost its allure and discipline for faculty and students alike. Dean John Day appointed Paul Hanstedt of the English Department to head up the process. Along with a group of faculty members interested in curricular renewal, Hanstedt attended a workshop on that topic offered by the American Association of Colleges and Universities. They were greatly exhilarated by their experience and resolved to work toward a new model of liberal arts education. Eschewing a top-down approach, the General Education Task Force involved over 50 percent of the faculty in committees that finally came up with five different models for the new curriculum. One idea dominated, and the task force proceeded to develop that model. It brought the fleshed-out model to the faculty in the spring of 2008, and the faculty passed it by a vote of 56–44. The proposal included a request that a full-time director of general education be hired to develop and then monitor the new curriculum, now called "Intellectual Inquiry," or simply INQ.

Some of the resistance to the new plan stemmed from the new model's rejection of a "content-based" approach to liberal arts education. The INQ curriculum was not built on the idea that all students should be exposed to a common base of knowledge, as well as to know the accepted content of each discipline by means of surveys of that field. Instead of "what every

26. Increases in the student body, retention, and graduation rates were difficult to realize for the reasons given early in the chapter. They remained rather stable, with a slight drop in student enrollment—to 2,025 full-time equivalents by 2016. However, the endowment rose to $137 million by 2016, and an impressive $35 million athletic and recreational center, the Cregger Center, was completed and dedicated in the fall of 2016.

educated person should know," the curriculum focused on "how every educated person should think." At each level of the curriculum, professors were
invited to teach on subjects that fascinated them and would likewise fasci-
nate students. There was no attempt to cover prescribed material in a field of
learning; but within each course, a certain "critical-thinking" approach was
to be nurtured. Students were encouraged to discern which questions were
worth asking and pursuing. They were to question inherited notions and ask
which authorities were reliable and which were not. They were to test their
own thinking by articulating their arguments in public speaking and writing
projects, which were then subject to critical review by their professors and
fellow students. Further, students were to absorb a "way-of-thinking" appropriate to the subject matter under investigation. In forming students into this
educative process, the curriculum was intended to instill certain skill sets
(reading, writing, speaking) and certain dispositions (curiosity, integrity,
compassion, perseverance). This approach then became the rationale for
each course in the general-education program (INQ), which persists to the
present day. The rationale for each set of INQ courses is spelled out carefully
and in great detail.[27]

The first-semester seminars (110) in the INQ curriculum offer a wide
variety of topics, of which the following are examples: "Who or What Is
God?" "Sink or Swim in College," "My New Identity," "Scientific Pursuit
of Happiness," "Strange Tales from the Bible," "Biology in Music." The goal
of each course is to introduce students to the "liberative" process of active
thinking and learning described above. A generous amount of written and
oral communication is required. There is no attempt to cover specific materials or topics or to relate them to each other, but each course is closely
monitored to make sure it covers the requirements of the INQ curricular
goals, which is true of all INQ courses.[28]

The second-semester course of the first year of the curriculum (120)
is of specific interest to the inquiry of this book because it takes the place
of the "Values and Responsible Life" course of the old curriculum in which
students were to encounter Christian and philosophical ethical claims. The

27. The educational philosophy that lies behind the INQ curriculum is enunciated in
the documents that govern the courses. Besides those documents, additional explanation of
the curriculum was generously offered by Paul Hanstedt, a key figure in the development of
the curriculum, and Gail Steehler, the current director of general education. Hanstedt has
become a consultant to many schools who seek to develop similar curricula.

28. Given the tremendous amount of care and scrutiny given each INQ course, it has
become clear that the director of general education has to be a full-time position.

general title under which all INQ 120 courses gather is "Living the Examined Life." Just as in the 110 course, professors are invited to build a course around a subject or question of their intense interest, while students are given the choice among these topics with the hope that they, too, will be intrigued by the topic. Each course uses the same process of "critical thinking"; furthermore, each course must use an ethical theme from an "ethical tradition" of the professor's own choice. Sample titles are: "Thinking Animals," "The Moral of Our Story," "The 1960s and American Values," "Ethics in Communication," "Life and Death in Medical Ethics," "Happiness and Goodness," "Origins of the Civil War," "The Robot, My Frenemy," and "Theologians under Hitler." While the religion and philosophy department offers perhaps a third of these courses, the wider faculty from many other departments offer the lion's share.

In most cases, professors draw on ethical themes that are implicit in the general store of cultural moral wisdom, such as the Golden Rule or utilitarian notions of the greatest good for the greatest number. A few proceed from systematic ethical systems (one or two from explicit Christian biblical or theological grounds) and a few more from philosophical perspectives— from the reflections of Socrates, Aristotle, or Spinoza, for example. Most assume commonsense moral intuitions when grappling with the issue they have selected. The honors curriculum, however, demands a more rigorous application of moral reasoning in its 120-level course.[29]

The 200-level courses proceed similarly. They fasten on a particular topic and use the methods of reasoning in each respective discipline to draw students into a specific way of thinking. Two-hundred-level courses include: INQ 240 ("Statistical Reasoning"); INQ 241 ("Mathematical Reasoning"); INQ 250 ("Scientific Reasoning, with lab"); INQ 251 ("Scientific Reasoning, without lab"); INQ 260 ("Social Scientific Reasoning"); INQ 270 ("Human Heritage I"); and INQ 271 ("Human Heritage II").

The 300-level courses focus on contemporary issues, and they encourage students to draw on their cumulative work in the INQ curriculum in order "to synthesize diverse disciplinary approaches in a collaborative investigation of a contemporary issue."[30] There are other requirements in the INQ curriculum:

29. The honors curriculum was expanded to include forty to fifty new students each year. It paralleled the old "Centers of Distinction" curriculum and now parallels the new INQ curriculum, with some additional intellectual experiences. Furthermore, the courses are expected to be more demanding.

30. This is a link to the documents that stipulate the requirements of each INQ course: http://www.roanoke.edu/inside/a-z_index/academic_affairs/faculty_information/course _proposals_and_syllabi.

foreign-language competence, a health-and-performance course, and an intensive learning course that is a student's sole course during an academic session.

Commentary

Few liberal arts curricula in American colleges have as clear a rationale and as careful a monitoring system as does the INQ curriculum at Roanoke College. The rationale exhibits keen intellectual inputs, and the monitoring features a careful scrutiny of each INQ course. It is clear that the college cares about its central offerings; moreover, only 15 percent of the courses are taught by adjuncts. INQ is widely accepted by the faculty and elicits much wider participation than did the old curriculum. Many professors feel freed from teaching survey courses and freed for teaching subjects in which they have real interest; moreover, those subjects elicit the interest of students more than survey courses do. There is also evidence that the curriculum is working. Students report that they are getting more usable skills from the curriculum, and outside evaluators are impressed with the Roanoke approach.[31]

A small number of the faculty, like many professors at other schools, think that abandoning a content-based curriculum was a mistake, even though both faculty and students seem to like the topical approach. Those faculty members believe that every educated person should have encountered common readings in their college years: great texts in literature, philosophy, and religion; historical surveys of American and world history; American constitutional readings; courses that delve into the methods and content of the social and natural sciences; and explorations of great artistic accomplishments. Many of the topical courses would appear to them to be trendy, random, scattered, and too "thinly sliced."

A surprising feature in the development, establishment, and scrutiny of the INQ curriculum was its rather weak formal connection to "Freedom with Purpose," which was the showpiece of the O'Hara years and a continuing beacon for the identity and mission of the college. Curriculum development did not key directly from "Freedom with Purpose." Yet, according to Paul Hanstedt, both the new statement of purpose and the INQ curriculum "came out of the same culture."[32]

It is that culture that seems problematic, especially concerning the Chris-

31. Interview with General Education Director Gail Steehler, February 23, 2016.
32. Hanstedt interview, Feb. 18, 2016.

tian heritage that has been one of the major sources for moral formation in the long history of the college. In the preceding chapter I noted that "Freedom with Purpose" remains completely formal and nearly silent about the religious or philosophical bases on which "purpose" is founded. The same tendency is true of the INQ curriculum. The second-semester 120 INQ course, "Leading the Examined Life," mentions only "ethical traditions" and does not stipulate that those traditions come from systematic and comprehensive visions of the moral life. Rather, the course is satisfied with ethical themes that are mostly gathered from the professor's moral intuitions, which may or may not be grounded in a recognizable moral theology or philosophy. It is not even assumed that biblical Christianity is one of the foundations for moral reflection, let alone that it is given an assured or prescribed place in the overall offerings. And few INQ 120 courses flow from biblical or theological grounds. The ones that do appear are not invited, but neither are they discouraged.[33]

I should point out that Christians can offer courses with such a foundation, but only a few do. Even professors in the religion and philosophy department seem reluctant. There are a number of reasons for that reluctance. One is that Roanoke College has always assumed that Christian perspectives will be expressed academically, even though it did not plan them. Over time, such assumptions tend to weaken. Another reason for reticence is the increasing domination of academia by "secular" progressives who see little relevance for religion in public life, including education. They distrust its impingement on public life, particularly religiously based moral convictions that do not cohere with notions of tolerance and "diversity," especially with those having to do with sexual matters. With such assumptions at play, Christian professors tend to keep their convictions private.

This general atmosphere, akin to the French notion of *laïcité,* which systematically excludes religious values from public life, operates in American higher education to some extent. It mistakes "separation of church and state" for "the separation of religion and public life." The latter has never been accepted in American political life, but it is increasingly accepted in academic life.[34]

---

33. When it was explained that the college made sure that the Christian faith was taught as one of the major bases for moral formation in the long history of the college, the general-education director noted that such a commitment was no longer the case. While the general-education committee was not hostile to the faith's being introduced in an INQ course, it did not assure that a sampling of such courses was present in its offerings. There would be no effort to enlist faculty to teach courses involving Christian faith and ethics.

34. In discourse outside the classroom, such separation seems to be practiced. When

Board and Faculty

The board of trustees continued along the lines that it had during the O'Hara years—but relieved of the stresses that were part of those years. It was a strong board of mostly successful businessmen and -women, though it was "diversified" by the addition of two black members, both graduates of the college. The daughter of retired President Norman Fintel, Peggy Fintel Horn ('78), was also added to the board. Though three Lutheran clergymen and several Lutheran laypersons, including the newly appointed Horn, continued to serve on the board, there was little systematic attention given to the religious element of the college. A $220 million campaign, "Roanoke Rising," was launched and soon strengthened by a $25 million gift from the Mulheren family, longtime benefactors of the college. The new $35 million athletic and fitness center (completed in August 2016 and dedicated on October 27, 2016) was named the Cregger Center after the new board chairman, Morris Cregger ('64), who had replaced Robert Wortmann in 2011 and had stepped forward with a large gift. The renovation and expansion of the two 1960s science buildings are next on the capital agenda.

The number of faculty members increased from 135 full-time equivalents in 2007 to 152 in 2016; those with terminal degrees in their discipline increased from 94 percent in 2007 to 96 percent in 2016. The faculty also enjoyed modest raises. No cutbacks occurred in those difficult economic times, but by 2015–16 there was a hiring freeze when the number of new students did not reach the requisite level. A new dean of academic affairs, Richard Smith, arrived in 2009 and soon began to appoint new department chairs who happened to be friendlier to the religious mission of the college than the former ones were; the department chairs were also rotated more frequently. Smith took seriously the college's statements of vision, mission, purpose, philosophy, and principles, and he insisted that the academic programs of the college flow from those articulations. The Lutheran composition of the faculty diminished further when the following longtime professors retired: William Hill from the public affairs department (though he continued to administer the Fowler Program); Benjamin Huddle and Vernon Miller from the chemistry department; and the author of the present volume, from the

the director of the Fintel Library at the college died unexpectedly, a memorial service was held at the library. Many speakers extolled his character and competence, but only the president mentioned that he was theologically educated and a committed Lutheran. It was as if that dimension of his life should remain private, even at his memorial in a church-related college.

religion and philosophy department. But all four carried on their service to the college in diverse ways.

Faculty continued to increase their scholarly activities and involvement in professional guilds. This phenomenon not only enhanced the external reputation of the college, but it also tended to draw faculty loyalty and attention to their academic guilds rather than to the college as a whole enterprise. Departmental involvement was strong, but overall participation in the public functions of the college suffered. The college operated more like a diffused university than a cohesive liberal arts college. However, regular faculty continued to offer most of the general-education and major courses of the college and to work intensively with students. In this sense, the liberal arts spirit continued. More faculty members offered to engage in research with their students: by 2016, the number of such projects rose to four hundred; moreover, by that time, professors supervised more than two hundred internships. So, as involvement in the corporate dimensions of college life diminished, attention to individual students and their specialized development increased. A contributing factor in these developments was the increasing demands of parents and students that had a utilitarian emphasis. Having research and internship experiences on their college dossiers certainly enhanced the chances of employment or getting into graduate school.

The "Republican" or Citizen Heritage of the College

As I noted in the preceding chapter, the college took seriously the "service" part of its mission by making the director of the community service center a full-time position. The center emphasized service in antipoverty, education, and housing initiatives. The chaplain continued to lead Habitat for Humanity projects on breaks in the school year, but in addition put first-year students to work on building a Habitat house as part of their orientation each fall. Further, the college established an associate dean for "student engagement," which included both service and experiential learning. By 2016, more than twenty classes had service learning as part of their requirements.

The Fowler Program carried on the lectures and colloquia listed in the preceding chapter. Its public-speaker lecture program continued to include a number of events in cooperation with the Center for Religion and Society, which I will list later.[35] But a number of distinguished speakers at stand-alone

35. The spring of 2012 signaled the end of a long period (1983–2012) of cooperation

events deserve to be mentioned: Alan Dershowitz, George Will, Sandra Day O'Connor, Doris Kearns Goodwin, Stephen Carter, Joseph Lieberman, and Robert George. Students and faculty were never bereft of intellectual stimulation on matters of public concern.

The Institute for Policy and Opinion Research continued to enrich the college's commitment to public life by providing a research arm that studied public opinion on matters of policy and governance. The Center for the Rule of Law, an independent organization housed on campus, had strong connections with various Roanoke personnel and faculty, who participated in its programs.

The Christian Heritage of the College

The Religion and Philosophy Department

During the time under discussion (from the beginning of Michael Maxey's presidency to the present), the religion and philosophy department experienced many highs and a number of significant challenges. First, the highs. The department reached a high of ten full-time professors in 2011–12; it also employed a number of adjunct professors. Among the tenure-track positions were the two new endowed professorships made possible by the Schumanns: the first was the Schumann Professor of Lutheran Theology, which was offered to Ned Wisnefske, who had been the Jordan-Trexler Professor of Religion; the second was the Schumann Chair in Christian Ethics, which was offered to James Peterson after an extended search. Peterson replaced me as the department's professor of Christian ethics and as the director of the Center for Religion and Society. The Jordan-Trexler chair was then offered to Gerald McDermott, who occupied it until his departure in the spring of 2015. This made four endowed professorships in the religion

---

between the director of the Fowler Program, William Hill, and yours truly, the director of the Center for Religion and Society—in planning and executing programs. The Fowler Program had a larger budget than the center did, but Hill was willing to invite religious perspectives on the issue or policy that was being addressed. That willingness demonstrated the relevance of religion to public life, something that was important for the college to model. Speakers on religion were usually less expensive than marquee public officials or intellectuals, but they were rarely inferior in preparation or the quality of their presentation. It was a fine example of cooperation that continues with the new director of the center (who started in 2012).

side of the department—the envy of other departments.[36] The department then offered majors and minors in religious studies, Christian studies, and philosophy.

The teaching and scholarly contributions of the department's faculty were impressive, to say the least. Excellent teaching, many speaking engagements at home and abroad, scores of journal articles, and a plethora of books issued from the members of this department. Never in its past had the department been so productive and reputed. Several authors rose to international fame in theological and philosophical circles.[37] Meanwhile, they also taught in the new INQ curriculum. All told, the teachers on the religion side of the department certainly provided a strong and cogent Christian voice on and off campus.

Given this stellar performance, it was perplexing that the department was faced with something of a dearth of majors and minors. The move toward more utilitarian majors that I mentioned earlier in the chapter was certainly one of the reasons, one that affected other departments in the humanities as well. Another was perhaps the faculty perceptions that the department's religion side was "too Christian," and "too orthodox Lutheran," and thus advisors did not steer students in its direction. Yet another might be that students from Christian backgrounds had just enough knowledge of their own tradition to inoculate them from desiring to learn more, and therefore turned their attention to study other religions and other subjects. Furthermore, outside evaluators observed that endowed professors teach only four courses per year, giving them insufficient exposure to the students. They also suggested that too many majors were offered.[38]

36. "Envy" was not just a figure of speech, but rather a negative reality. In the external program evaluation of the religion side of the department, the authors note that there was a negative faculty perception that only "orthodox Lutheran theology" was taught by those who occupied those chairs (Program Evaluation, Spring 2015, 3). But in point of fact, only one person explicitly taught Lutheran theology, and his work was hardly rigid or narrow. Because two of the endowed chairs carried "Lutheran" in their names, many faculty members seemed to believe that all professors in the department taught the same thing. This was one of the unintended consequences of endowing four chairs in a relatively small department.

37. In the period from 2007 to 2016, Paul Hinlicky published seven major works, including a 1,000-page text in systematic theology; Gerald McDermott published eight books and edited several more; philosopher Brent Adkins published four books, while his colleague in philosophy, Monica Vilhauer, published two. All were published by respected publishing houses.

38. The department did move toward offering one major in religious studies, which would include two different tracks: the study of non-Christian religions and Christian studies.

Another issue faced by the department was the puzzling feedback from the external evaluators who assessed both the religion and philosophy wings of the department. These program evaluations are required by the college periodically. In contrast to the evaluators who reported during the O'Hara administration that the department should "keep up the good work," the two sets of evaluators seemed to think that both wings should undergo dramatic change. The two who evaluated the religion wing criticized the emphasis on the normative teaching of Christianity and suggested that it turn in a "religious studies" direction.[39] It should not so overtly commend the Christian tradition (speak *for* it) but rather engage more in the "academic study of religion," in which they would speak *about* many religious traditions.

The philosophy side of the department likewise underwent sharp criticism. Though the religion and philosophy department had always been a combined department in which there was much overlap among the faculty and the courses they taught, the evaluators found such overlap objectionable. Philosophy and religion should be more strictly separated. Mixing them contaminated both, but it especially contaminated philosophy. Similarly, the historic Roanoke tradition of philosophers taking up religious issues and themes in their courses was met with reproach from the evaluators. Excepting perhaps the course in philosophy of religion, the philosophy courses should be resolutely secular, they said, bending in an *avant garde* direction. These two sets of outside evaluators seemed curiously intent on changing the historic direction of both wings of the department.

These reports stimulated a vigorous discussion within the department and the administration. However, after the dust had settled and three members of the department had left—for various reasons—a new situation emerged in which the religion and philosophy department could adopt some of the recommendations of the evaluators without moving in a dramatically different direction. Two of the members who left were junior professors, but the departure of the third, a department veteran, was something of a shock. After a twenty-six-year sojourn at Roanoke, Gerald McDermott left to assume the Anglican Chair at Beeson Divinity School. A powerful voice departed, leaving one of the endowed chairs, the Jordan-Trexler, vacant.[40]

---

39. The faulty perception that only "orthodox Lutheranism" was being taught in the religion side of the department was fueled by the age-old worry that any effort to commend the Christian tradition amounted to "proselytizing" and "coercion."

40. Before McDermott decided to take the position at Beeson, the occupants of the endowed chairs gathered to discuss the problems that might arise when those occupants departed or retired. They decided to take up a number of different tasks: to identify clearly

The Benne Center for Religion and Society

For thirty years (1982–2012) the center was, first, the Center for Church and Society, and then the Center for Religion and Society; but in the spring of 2012, it was renamed the Robert D. Benne Center because generous donors and the college itself decided to honor me, its founder. Those donors had established an ample endowment for the center. Before James Peterson became its director in the fall of 2012, I had five years (2007–12) of directing the center during the Maxey years.

During that time the programs of the center went on routinely, as described in earlier chapters: public lectures, sometimes in joint sponsorship with the Fowler Program; the annual Crumley Lecture, featuring Lutheran laypersons reflecting on their vocations; the four Faith and Reason Lecture/ Dinners per year; publishing the work of Slovak scholars; the quarterly Bishop's Forum; and the Virginia Synod's summer "Power in the Spirit" gathering. Many of these events were done in cooperation with other agencies of the college. In addition, I continued to lecture and publish under my title as director, and I continued to teach at the college in an adjunct capacity.

There were several events during those years that deserve mention. In the spring of 2008, Robert Seiple, former head of World Vision and then the United States Special Ambassador for International Religious Freedom, spoke on the subject "Religious Freedom around the World" at the annual Crumley Lecture. In the fall of 2008, the influential public intellectual Richard John Neuhaus gave his last public lecture before succumbing to cancer. Lecturing just before the election of 2008, Neuhaus spoke on "Moral Imperatives and Political Choices—A Christian Response" to a large crowd. Rather than offering direct political commentary Neuhaus plumbed the deeper moral issues facing the country. In the spring of 2011, the well-known writer Jody Bottum and John Meacham, then the editor of *Newsweek* magazine, offered reflections on American exceptionalism. The event was cosponsored by the Center for Religion and Society and the Fowler Program, as was a forum entitled "Lincoln's Moral Constitution," featuring Lincoln scholars Allen Guelzo and Gary Gallagher.

In the fall of 2012, I turned the reins of the center over to James Peterson,

---

the wishes of the donors of the chairs so that the college would be faithful to their wishes; to suggest to the president a process—led by the president—for replacing departing occupants of the chairs; and to arrange an orderly process of departure so that several vacancies would not come up at the same time.

who had come to Roanoke College as the Schumann Professor of Christian Ethics in the fall of 2011. Peterson came from McMaster University in Hamilton, Ontario, where he had held endowed professorships in both divinity and medicine. He was already well published in the field of Christian bioethics and was editor of the distinguished journal *Perspectives on Science and the Christian Faith*. Peterson came to the center with many new contacts for speakers and immediately brought fresh voices into its offerings. He started out with a huge success in the fall of 2012 by inviting the travel guru and Lutheran layman Rick Steves to give the Crumley Lecture on his sense of calling in the travel business. The college had to schedule two appearances for him at the four-hundred-seat Olin Theater to accommodate those who wanted to attend.

This event foreshadowed changes in the Crumley Lecture series. First, the college moved the event to the fall rather than the cluttered spring. Second, it was intentionally opened to the student body and the community in a public lecture that followed a dinner for invited guests from the surrounding Lutheran community and patrons of the college. Earlier, the lecture had been offered only to invited guests who attended a late-afternoon lecture and then a celebrative dinner. In the year following Steves's appearance, the fall of 2013, the Crumley series again featured a lecture that attracted a capacity crowd to the Olin Theater. Jennifer Wiseman, senior scientist of the Hubble Space Telescope, lectured on "What No One Has Ever Seen Before: Revelations of the Hubble Telescope." She spoke quite naturally of how her faith and work coincided. Again, students and members of the community alike had access to the lecture.

Other changes followed. The center's sponsorship of the Virginia Synod's "Power in the Spirit" summer gathering was ended because it did not fit the central mission of the Center for Religion and Society. The Faith and Reason lectures/dinners were reduced from four to three, but those lectures continued to draw a good portion of the faculty.

Peterson undertook a major new initiative when he began to offer lectures—mostly having to do with the interaction of religion and science—in cooperation with faculty members from the natural and social sciences. Those efforts by Peterson, coupled with invitations to lecture to members of heretofore uninvolved departments in the Faith and Reason sessions, began a gradual process of inviting more people into the engagement of faith (usually the Christian faith) and learning (many secular disciplines). By 2016, Peterson had worked out common projects with every department of the college. The intent of these initiatives was to encourage more faculty members not only to tolerate, but to welcome—and perhaps even expect—the efforts of Roanoke College professors to relate their faith to their callings at the college.

It was also in 2015–16 that Peterson began a new program with students, called the "Benne Fellowship Program." Students who were interested in the programs of the center applied to become Benne fellows. Three were selected from the array of applicants and were invited to all the events of the center, were offered small honoraria, and were given the opportunity to have ongoing conversations with the former and current directors of the center. In return, they were expected to perform modest service to support the cause of the center. In the first year, all three fellows were on the dean's list, and one was president of the student body. Each year three more will be selected.

Peterson expanded his role as professor and director to myriad engagements within the community, especially its hospitals, as an expert in bioethics. He carried on an extensive lecturing schedule in the United States, the United Kingdom, and Canada, and he has planned several new books.

Ethos

It would be unlikely that the way of life at Roanoke College would be very different from the general conditions of life described at the beginning of the chapter. Roanoke tracked American society nearly exactly: 72 percent of its students identified as Christians, but only about 20 percent actually participated vigorously in Christian activities and organizations on campus.[41] But the intense Christians on campus were a lively and respected subculture who were gathered into a number of religious organizations.[42] The new chap-

41. Interview with Rev. Chris Bowen, Feb. 18, 2016. Pastor Bowen is the Pickle Dean of the Chapel and chaplain to the Roanoke College community. He began his service during fall 2013 after having served a Lutheran church in the Tidewater area of Virginia.

42. A disturbing controversy erupted in the spring of 2015, when one of the leaders of the evangelical InterVarsity Christian Fellowship came out as gay and revealed that he was in a relationship with another man. He was asked to step down from the leadership position. The Student Government Association and college administrators took this move as discrimination on grounds of sexual orientation—which is against college rules—and defunded the organization. InterVarsity, however, contended that the young man was asked to resign because his conduct and beliefs violated its teachings that sex belonged only within marriage. InterVarsity was not banished from campus and continued to flourish as the largest Christian organization on campus. But lingering resentments continued to be directed at InterVarsity by a small number of students directly associated with the incident.

lain, Chris Bowen, brought vigor and imagination to that subculture, not only in his own programs but also in supporting other denominational and parachurch organizations. His "Theology on Tap"—an evening discussion of theological topics—drew about fifty students to conversations at a local pub. A small organization called "Discernment" gathered around efforts to clarify future lay and clerical vocations. The "RC Lutherans" (the new name for the Lutheran student organization) accounted for about thirty members, while the Catholic student organization had about the same. InterVarsity claimed about sixty in its fellowship. Other religious organizations, including the Jewish Hillel fellowship, had also organized and enlisted smaller numbers of students.

There were hopes that the college's 175th birthday, as well as the commemoration of the five hundredth anniversary of the Reformation in 2017, would bring about a renewed interest in the college's history and mission. One important symbol of that history was the erection of an impressive statue of Martin Luther in the Luther Plaza in front of the new Cregger Center. The statue was donated by the Schumann family, who had earlier endowed two chairs in the religion and philosophy department. Further, the college planned major programs honoring both anniversaries that it hoped would enlist wide participation of the whole community.

For most students, however, religious practice and belief were casual. Many did not know that Roanoke was a church-related college, and they had little interest in deepening their faith. Parties continued to be a major source of entertainment, with binge-drinking common. Sexual mishaps occurred too frequently, and the college, like many other schools, had its share of legal conflicts brought on by charges and countercharges of sexual assault.

Members of the faculty viewed the contemporary student generation as more fragile than those immediately past. The young had been raised in a fractured culture that was widely permissive but allowed only "one strike and you're out" punishment for violating the few remaining constraints. That culture insisted on tolerance for every subculture except those subcultures that believed in transcendent truth and moral values. There was little solid to fall back on. Students shaped by an affluent culture were led to believe that they should never suffer. Their self-esteem had been repeatedly endorsed, even in the absence of any accompanying accomplishments. So when they met challenges that made them uncomfortable, their lack of resilience led them to resort to counseling and various types of prescription remedies. Their overreliance on sophisticated phones further insolated them from real-world social interaction.[43] As one faculty member put it, "This generation is at one and the same time the most connected and the most isolated."

But that was certainly not the whole story. Many students were brought up with care and devotion, and they matched or surpassed the best ones of earlier years. Student accomplishments in the new joint research projects were impressive. There were many topflight students in the honors program, and Roanoke students won competitions for prestigious scholarships. The seriously religious were quite aware that they were in a minority that had to be strong in their faith and life. Many saw this as an advantage, and they exerted influence beyond their numbers.

Conclusion

It is not possible to offer a full conclusion to this chapter on the Maxey years because they are not over. However, it is important to attempt plausible interpretations of the college in its current incarnation, and of its possible futures, to which we now turn.

---

43. These impressions of the Roanoke student body were gathered from a sampling of faculty, administrators, and students. I make no claim for their social-scientific standing.

Two Rival Interpretations and the Way Ahead

As we come to the end of the long story of Roanoke College, it is important to offer an assessment of its current state, especially with regard to its "soul." Such an assessment could move in a number of different directions. I will propose two contrasting interpretations.

Interpretation 1: The Glass Is Nearly Empty

"Roanoke College is not and never has been a religious college," declared a faculty member who was irritated by the possibility that the college's application for a Lilly Grant on Vocation might be approved by the faculty in the early 2000s. The latter clause of his sentence is patently untrue, as this book has demonstrated; however, there is the ominous possibility that the first clause is plausible, given a certain kind of skeptical lens. Such a lens leads to the first interpretation: the religious element of the college is but a whiff of vapor in an empty bottle. There is no such thing as the "soul" of Roanoke College; if there ever was one, it departed many years ago.

What currently makes the college viable is its mix of reasonably good students who come to the lovely Roanoke Valley and meet up with a few good professors they like, as well as a coterie of friends whom they find congenial. They get a better-than-average education that includes valuable elements of liberal arts learning. This preparation garners them employment and they move on in life with good memories of professors, friends, and lively parties. The college provides a generic small-college experience that most young people like, an experience that is duplicated in hundreds of generic small colleges. Two cheers for Roanoke College.

There is a bow to "service" and "responsible leadership in a global society" as crucial values of the college, but most colleges make the same claims. Colleges have to justify the grand sums they extract from the government, the students, and their families. But there is little mention of the college's historical insistence that biblical Christianity is not only a basis for such values, but the best basis. The college is very bashful about any such claims, both in its formative principles and its curricular rationale.[1]

The college has heretofore been successful in recruiting students without any kind of religious pitch. It will not jeopardize its success by rashly putting forth a public religious façade.[2] When it orients its new students, the college gives little time to introduce them to its religious history and heritage. Nor does it hold up specifically Christian ideals—among others— to guide them in their lives on campus. It's true that the Christian heritage continues in some small corners of the curriculum and faculty, but one can avoid it if one wishes to. Religious students can find like-minded comrades in religious organizations, but the overall atmosphere of the college is decidedly secular.[3] Far more students sleep in on Sunday morning than go to local churches. The kind of religious presence at Roanoke, such as it is, is probably equaled on many secular campuses. Therefore, all the huffing and puffing in

1. This waning of the Christian rationale for service may partly be the result of the college's utilitarian view of the faith as an instrument of moral formation. Treading softly on the normative truth claims of the faith has meant that when some other rationale for service came along that was just as useful but less controversial, that rationale could easily move in as the instrument of moral formation. In this era, "civic humanism" is a likely alternative to the Christian, since it is widely used and "inclusive." "Giving back" is a more common and tolerable moral base than "Christian service to the neighbor."

2. Intensely religious students report that nothing is said about the religious element in the recruitment approach of the college until the student mentions that he or she is interested in that dimension. Then the "religious welcome mat" comes out. Until that moment the college's religious heritage is veiled.

3. As in society as a whole, the increase in "nones" has become evident at the college. Institutional research indicated that in 2015–16, nearly 500 (485, or about one-quarter of the students) marked "no preference" or "no response" to the question of religious adherence. Such results did not necessarily mean that the students were antireligious; but it did indicate that they had no clear commitment to a religious tradition. There were only 139 Lutheran students; but there were 336 "minority" students, indicating which identity group was more important to recruit. http://www.roanoke.edu/inside/a-z_index/institutional_research/enrollment_statistics.

this book is of little avail.[4] The trajectory of secularization is relentless and soon to be completed. All one has to do is look at a more detailed picture.

The President and Board

The presidential rhetoric in recent inaugurals has trod very lightly on the college's Christian heritage, mainly because presidents have accurately perceived its rather anemic role in the college's various constituencies. When presidential rhetoric does soar in other contexts, it is often to small groups who like that sort of thing. Mostly, however, the presidential rhetoric is ignored by the faculty or entertained as a "grace note" in an otherwise secular message. It is a nice religious gloss on a basically secular enterprise.

Though recent presidents have indeed been sincere in their own rhetoric, there is little they can do about the situation. The board has a long and firmly held tradition of not talking about religion and politics. The Lutherans on the board are not likely to stir the pot. The next presidential appointment could easily go to a non-Lutheran, or even a non-Christian, as has happened in other eastern Lutheran colleges. The board has no strategy for keeping the Christian heritage alive at Roanoke.

The presidents' most important academic role has been to appoint the academic dean, and recent presidents have selected deans who are very unlikely to place the religious element of the college in their list of priorities. Affirmative action for Lutherans would be unthinkable, even though the Lutheran presence on the faculty is nearly extinct. A president meddling in the curriculum would be quickly resented. Neither presidents nor deans have involved themselves closely in hiring for mission, especially for the "Christian republican" part of the college's historic purpose. The hiring of the faculty is essentially left up to the departments, who make hiring decisions mainly on the basis of their own needs.

Faculty

Faculty members' fortunes—and loyalties—are closely connected with their department and their professional guild. Few have an interest in the larger

---

4. When I told one faculty member about my inquiry into the "soul" of the college in this book, he quipped: "It is no doubt a very short book."

narrative and purposes of the college. Indeed, the college no longer includes a serious account of its religious heritage in its orientation of new faculty. Any attempt to enlist faculty in strengthening the college's religious element would be met with resistance, as it was when the Lilly proposal was debated. They are content with the current arrangement as long as it does not affect them. Even that thin arrangement is weakening by the year.

The college has historically "assumed" that it would spontaneously gather faculty who supported its Christian republican mission. It has not intentionally "hired for mission," and it is purely accidental when it does hire Lutheran Christians.[5] Even more ominously, there are few in the faculty with intense convictions that the Christian heritage should not only be nurtured but also strengthened. For example, a discouraging response of one of the college's more serious Christians to the question "How is the Christian heritage of the college faring?" was: "Gosh, I haven't thought about that for a long time."

Most faculty members do not see any connection between the Lutheran heritage of the college and their own work. Even faculty members who are Christians often do not see any linkage: college education (public) and religion (private) inhabit two separate realms. Those who do see linkage are quiet about it, imposing censorship on themselves in the "secular progressive" atmosphere that dominates higher education today. In that atmosphere, religiously based arguments are unwelcome. When the few outspoken Christian conservatives express themselves, which is rare, they are met with disdain and are unlikely to be elected to any important faculty offices.[6]

Since "secular progressive" convictions are heavily dominant in the college, and they correlate strongly with liberal political propensities, political and cultural conservatives are few and far between. "Liberationist" views are heavily dominant in the humanities and social sciences. Though the "political correctness" associated with elite institutions is not as heavy at Roanoke as at some other colleges, there is the sense that conservatives should be

5. Like most Lutheran colleges, Roanoke keeps careful track of the number of minority faculty, but it has not counted the number of Lutherans or Christians for many years. That seems to indicate that their presence or absence is not crucial to the identity and mission of the college; or it could also mean that the college has just assumed that they were there. In either case, its inattention will not bode well for maintaining its Christian heritage.

6. One conservative Christian professor argued that no faculty members will be able to make the classical Christian argument for marriage and sexual ethics in the near future. Neither would they be hired in the first place if they held such beliefs publicly.

quiet if they are to be welcome. Conservative students find out quickly that they also need to keep their opinions private. The political and cultural conservatives who have administered some of the endowed programs—and who have tried to invite both conservatives and liberals—will be soon displaced by those who will find little room for conservative voices.

Curriculum

Though there is room for Christian-based courses in the INQ curriculum, they are neither assured nor even encouraged.[7] If they were absent, there would be no notice by those who attend to the curriculum. Indeed, there may be some distaste for more overtly Christian courses being offered, especially if they are doctrinally orthodox. Liberal theological perspectives are welcome when they agree with the "secular progressive" agenda.

The sampling of Christian-based courses currently present in the curriculum is sparse. It is dishonest to maintain that the college continues to honor the Christian heritage as even one important base for moral formation or for the "examined life." Only a few students select the courses that are offered.

Part of the problem is that the formal "Purposes and Principles" do not explicitly mention such a base, and thus it is not attended to. There is much more concern that global and multicultural issues be covered, as well as those concerns of the required triumvirate—gender, class, and race. When "moral reasoning" or "ethical traditions" are used in the INQ courses, they are left to the choice of the individual professor, and it is rare that a professor actually develops a systematic philosophical or religious base.

The "Republican" or Citizenship Heritage of the College

Like almost every other college, Roanoke promotes "service" heavily and effectively. But while earlier generations connected service with its Christian

---

7. The "Self-Study for Program Evaluation 2014–2015" (unpublished paper) has no mention of the Judeo-Christian tradition as a source for "ethical reasoning." Like other goals of the curriculum, the ethical goals are process-oriented rather than substantive in character. Seniors evaluating their experience in the INQ curriculum rated the contribution of the college to "developing or clarifying a personal code of values and ethics" lower than at peer institutions (p. 17). That may have something to do with students rarely encountering a course that had a systematic account of ethics from which to reason.

base, the current incarnation of the college says little about that base. It is true that the chaplains have gathered Christians to perform works of service, but even they are careful not to mention the moral base very often. In this era, such an allusion might be viewed as "noninclusive." Nevertheless, it is fair to say that the "citizenship" plank in the college mission has fared well. It is not mere rhetoric. But emphasis on this theme is increasingly disconnected from a Christian base. It is far more likely to rest on widely shared "civic humanism," which is also employed at secular schools. Christian motivation is the one that dare not speak its name.

The Religion and Philosophy Department

While the department—in both its religion and philosophy wings—is still quite strong, there are troubling signs for its future. One of the strongest teachers, scholars, and exponents of the Christian tradition, Gerald McDermott, left for a prestigious position at another school, and his endowed chair—the Jordan-Trexler—remains unfilled. Two more holders of endowed chairs are near retirement. Only one explicitly teaches Lutheran theology. There is some suspicion that one or more chairs could be moved to other departments. It may be that "religious studies" types will be offered those chairs, thus leaving no one to speak *for* the Lutheran/Christian tradition, but rather *about* it as one religious perspective among others.

There would be a good deal of background sentiment in the college to move in the direction of "religious studies," since the department has always been under suspicion for "proselytizing." As secular progressives have come to dominate the faculty, classical doctrinal Christianity has increasingly been interpreted as oppressive and hegemonic. It should be studied more as a museum piece than a live option in the contemporary world of "tolerance" and "inclusion." Teaching Christianity normatively is always under suspicion; never mind that feminists, multiculturalists, gays, and environmentalists can teach from heavily ideological perspectives without worry.

A glaring problem on the religion side of the department is that it lacks a biblical scholar, which is a bit shameful in a Lutheran-related college. Given the hiring freeze, it may be some time before that position is filled. The philosophy side still has one professor who teaches in the historic Roanoke mode: philosophical approaches to religious themes. But the move toward a purely secular philosophical orientation seems to have gathered momentum.[8] Indeed, the recent outside evaluators tried to push philosophy away from its religious preoccupation while they proposed that religion be diverted from its emphasis on Christian theology toward a more varied "religious studies" approach. Such may well be the direction of the future: a paucity of majors may lead to pressure on the department to become more "diverse" in order to market itself better.

Benne Center for Religion and Society

Though the center will continue reliably to pursue its mission of engaging Christian claims with those of the secular world, its programs admittedly operate in only a small corner of the college. The center reaches only about a quarter of the faculty in its Faith and Reason lectures/dinners, and it is questionable whether it can gather more. Presenters are unlikely to demonstrate sophisticated encounters of their faith with their work at the college; they are more likely to "tell their religious story." The center's programs do reach a good representation of students, faculty, and community members, but any lasting effect on their thinking is problematic. For the most part, the center's impact is limited.

Ethos

Religious life on campus for the last few decades has been a distinctly minority phenomenon, something existing on the periphery of college life. Moreover, the episode in which InterVarsity Christian Fellowship was defunded has left a lasting chill on religious organizations that belong to orthodox traditions.[9] Those organizations now avoid dealing with anything controversial, especially with regard to sexuality issues. They—along with other orthodox Christians on campus—are strongly discouraged from publicly expressing "incorrect" views; most accommodate to that atmosphere.

Many campuses that are completely secular would harbor as much religious expression as Roanoke. A sure mark that its Christian heritage is ba-

---

8. Christian students have reported discouragement of their faith perspective by professors of that persuasion.

9. See footnote 42 in the preceding chapter. One of the few conservative Christian organizations on campus was defunded.

sically irrelevant is that it is scarcely mentioned to prospective students and their parents when touring the campus. One guide, when asked by a parent whether the college had a religious connection, notoriously quipped, "Yes, but it doesn't make any difference."[10]

Interpretation II: The Glass Is Half Full

A far more positive—and equally plausible—interpretation of the presence of "Christian soul" at Roanoke would challenge the negativity of the first. If Roanoke is the kind of church-related college that gives its Christian heritage a guaranteed "voice at the table," then Roanoke's glass is at least half full. As an educational institution, it prizes intellectual excellence most highly. The intellectual distinction of the professors in the Christian studies wing of the religion and philosophy department is unsurpassed on campus. Not only do the professors put forward compelling Christian arguments in the classrooms and public arenas of the college, they project them beyond the college onto the national and world stage. Roanoke's religion faculty is one of the best of any small liberal arts college in the country. Four endowed chairs have enabled the college to recruit first-class Christian intellectuals. They have the broadest educations among the faculty, and they willingly engage other faculty on matters of mutual interest. Moreover, the other Christians on the faculty often have private dialogues with students about their faith and vocation. Christian students know this and find an ample supply of friendly counselors. Many students have had their faith deepened; there have even been conversions.

The recent presidents have stood firmly behind the building of just such a strong Christian intellectual presence on campus. From Fintel onward, they have worked at funding the four endowed chairs in the religion wing of the department; because of these efforts, it has far more than any other department.[11] There is a deep sense that the presidents are supportive of

10. Reported by a Lutheran clergyman who intentionally asked the guide about the college's church relationship.
11. The college has employed a wise strategy of raising money among Lutherans for programs and chairs specifically supportive of the religious functions of the college: the chaplaincy, endowed chairs, and scholarships. While direct support from the Evangelical Lutheran Church in America and from the Virginia Synod has diminished to a vanishing point, indirect support for these religious features of the college by wealthy Lutherans has been very significant. The resource development division and the presidents have diligently pursued this strategy.

efforts to maintain and even strengthen the Christian heritage of the college. Many other academic ventures would be pleased to have that kind of support. The Christian voice is unlikely to be diminished as long as that administrative weight stands behind it. Furthermore, the presidents have supported chaplains who are not ashamed of the faith and who preach and teach the Lutheran construal of the gospel unabashedly. There is no common-denominator approach to the faith either intellectually or pastorally. The "real thing" can be taught and caught at Roanoke College.

While the Lutheran members of the board may not be assertive in nurturing the "soul" of the college, they are definitely supportive of the efforts currently going on. Moreover, they would respond positively to further efforts to guard the Christian heritage of the college. The bishop of the Virginia Synod, plus the two distinguished pastors who serve on the board, are respected by other members and know what is at stake in the current challenges the college faces. The current bishop and the president of the college have a strong consultative relationship. Though recent academic deans have not been aggressive in furthering the religious mission of the college, they have been respectful of the intellectual firepower of the Christian academicians on campus, have admired the interdisciplinary nature of the faith-and-reason ventures, have held the college accountable to its statement of purpose and its principles, and have even suggested strongly that the speakers of the Benne Center be made available to a larger audience. There is no hostility to the "Christian" part of "Christian republicanism." Moreover, there are strong Christian voices among the current vice presidents who are attentive to religious concerns.

Faculty

By providence or blind luck, though not by plan, the presence of serious Christians among the faculty has increased in recent years. Oddly, in some departments where the leadership had been stridently secular, Christians have crept in "under the radar." While they are reluctant to relate their faith to their teaching in the classroom, they deal sensitively and pastorally with Christian students who want to connect their beliefs with their studies. They are willing to make such connections in their writings and in other venues such as the Faith and Reason lectures/dinners, which have no shortage of willing speakers.

Furthermore, a strong contingent of old-fashioned liberals on the faculty welcome the free interaction of competing ideas and thus are open to

Christian voices in the mix. They do not seek those voices, but they do not impede them either. Roanoke College is an unlikely place for "political correctness" to suppress invited speakers of a conservative Christian hue. There is an openness to Christian arguments if they do not claim special privilege; the fact that they are less frequently expressed is more a result of Christian self-censorship than of overt resistance.

Curriculum

As I have noted above, the INQ curriculum, unfortunately, makes no provision for Christian-based courses in the INQ 110 and 120 series, but neither does it proscribe them. As the religion side of the religion and philosophy department comes to full strength again, there will be more faculty members to supply such courses for the curriculum. And when such courses have been offered, they have been well-subscribed; so when they appear in the future, there will be a greater opportunity for professors to meet students earlier in their academic careers. Furthermore, a number of professors offer service-learning courses that operate from explicitly Christian motivations. No particular substantive view of the good life is privileged in the INQ curriculum, so the Judeo-Christian heritage has as good a chance as any to be expressed. It is up to committed faculty to take the initiative.

The Religion and Philosophy Department

After a time of turbulence set off by internal strife and the outside evaluators' "revolutionary" feedback, the dust has settled and the department has agreed that both Christian studies and the study of other religions ("religious studies") will coexist on the religion side of the department, offering one major with two emphases. This will encourage more single and double majors—as well as minors. The philosophy side of the department will continue its historic concern for religious themes while also taking secular philosophical interests seriously. There is a good chance that the two vacancies in this department will be filled by professors who are in line with the historic direction of the department. The remaining department members continue to provide impressive teaching and research.

From 2016 to 2018, the department will have a chance to influence campus intellectual and aesthetic culture as the college celebrates not only its

175th birthday but also the five hundredth anniversary of the Reformation. Department members will be deeply involved in the planning and execution of those celebrations. With regard to the former, there will be many lectures assessing the historical trajectory of the college: speakers will intensely examine its identity and mission over the years, giving vigorous attention to the presidents and their administrations as they have been portrayed in this volume. The "soul" of the college will be much discussed. During the same time, the college will be devoting many efforts to celebrate the ideas, the music, and the impact of the Reformation on Western history, including the role they have played at Roanoke College. The college has never had richer resources for commemorating these two great celebrations as it has currently in several of its departments, but especially in its religion and philosophy department. Perhaps this recollection of its primordial "soul" will have a lasting effect on its life.

The Benne Center for Religion and Society

With a relatively new director and an increasing endowment, the center will continue to flourish. It will have a chance to increase its impact by featuring programs attractive to the whole college and community, by increasing the number of Benne fellows, and by extending its conversations with all the academic departments in an even more vigorous way. The director will also strengthen connections with the hospitals and medical schools of the Roanoke Valley. The center will continue to be a steady beacon of Christian reflection at the college.

Ethos

"Where everyone is a Christian, no one is," was the insightful remark of Søren Kierkegaard about his nominally Christian Denmark. Throughout most of its history, Roanoke College rested on a culture that was at least nominally Christian. But in American society today, the growing distaste for orthodox Christianity has diminished the store of nominal Christians. They do not wish to be associated with "retrograde" notions. However, the positive side of this winnowing out is that serious Christians in America have become better defined and firmer in their beliefs. This has happened at Roanoke as well.

Christian organizations are probably more vigorous and committed now than they have been for some time. Even the tensions over the defunding of InterVarsity Christian Fellowship have been interpreted as a blessing by some members of that group. It has flourished *in spite of* the tensions. Other religious groups, including the Fellowship of Christian Athletes, are also lively. Christian students are very visible in leadership positions.

The chaplain, an unabashed Lutheran, reaches about two hundred students each week with various kinds of education and worship programs. He has worked hard to meet and minister to all the various constituencies of the college. He has strong support from the administration for his programs.

The Path Ahead

Which of the two interpretations one adopts—either the mostly empty glass or the half-full glass—depends, at least in part, on what one wishes to see. Those who expect to see a much more vigorous "soul" in the college would view its current status as pitiful. If it is so weak, their view is, why bother? Be honest and dissociate from its trivial connection to the Christian heritage. Those people would, surprisingly, be joined in their unhappy interpretation by a bevy of secularists who want to see the "soul" depart completely. "Roanoke is not and never has been a religious college," they would repeat. Both would heartily endorse the mostly empty interpretation.[12] But those who appreciate a milder dose of "soul," one that is not too aggressive or pervasive, will be content with what the college currently expresses, and they would likely endorse the half-full interpretation. They are content with the way things are. Those who want a stronger role for the faith in the life of the college might go either way: on bad days the first interpretation seems more accurate, whereas the second one holds true on good days.

I find myself in that third group. I wish for a stronger role for the Christian heritage—particularly its intellectual tradition—in the life of the college. On bad days, when the Christian heritage seems unwelcome in the public life of the college, I am despondent. On good days, when I see how much we have to build on, I am hopeful.

12. Oddly enough, such a confluence emerged in the 1970s, when there was an effort by a number of faculty members to disconnect the college from its relationship to the Lutheran Church. One faction was the "why bother" group, who were devout Christians; they were joined by skeptics, who wanted the same thing for very different reasons.

It is in that hope that I propose a strategy that is consistent with what I have termed "intentional pluralism."[13] By "intentional," I mean that the college purposely offers the Christian voice a "place at the table" in every facet of its life—academic, co-curricular, administrative, student. There already is such a voice, but it is more accidental than intentional. Furthermore, the representation is not complete or systematic. An effective strategy needs to be both comprehensive and disciplined. The point of such a strategy would be to have *open and unabashed Christian presence in every facet of the life of the college that would make Christian intellectual and moral commitments publicly relevant to the college.* This "witnessing" would have to be nimble and sophisticated. It would not claim special advantage in making its arguments or witness, but it would be open and public about it.

By "pluralism," I mean that the college should accept the fact that there are many religious and philosophical perspectives among its constituents. No one can, nor should, dominate—that is, provide the governing paradigm for the college.[14] All have an equal opportunity to argue for and express their visions. The only way the Christian vision is privileged is that it is guaranteed a place at the table, whereas other comprehensive visions are not, though they certainly can be represented there.

This "privileging" is both fitting and modest. It is fitting in the sense that the faith has had an important role in the college's life and mission from its founding to the present day. The college still has a strong relationship with the Virginia Synod and the Evangelical Lutheran Church in America. No other vision has played that historic role or had that institutional connection. It is fitting that the college maintain that role and connection in a significant way, both in its academic life and its ethos. But the "privileging" is also modest. The Christian vision and ethos constitute one of the bases for the college's commitment to liberal learning and service to the world. Other visions of life feed into the basic commitment to liberal learning in pursuit of the responsible life. Reciting the Christian teaching on this or that

13. See the listing of characteristics of the "intentional pluralist" school in the typology in the Appendix.

14. This is an acknowledgment that the college lacks a single organizing principle. What can give guidance is the commitment to the liberal arts—including a Christian component—as preparation for a responsible life of service. That is not far from what provides a substantive guiding principle for the college at this time. That, along with the desire to be recognized, seems to be the motivating commitment. Whether or not the college's current version of the liberal arts—"a critical way of thinking"—will be effective over the long run remains to be seen.

issue cannot simply trump other views. Arguments must prevail in open discussion in a pluralistic context. It is proper that the college not be called a "Christian college," even though it takes its Christian heritage seriously.

This "modest privileging" of the intentional pluralist strategy seems reasonable and nonthreatening. Most fair-minded persons would assent to it. Now, what would it look like? How would the college actualize it? Who would be responsible for carrying out the strategy? I will try to answer those questions in the following (concluding) pages. I will do so in a way that does not presuppose that the same personnel are in the positions in which they find themselves currently. Rather, it will offer something of an agenda for whoever comes into those offices.

The President

There is little doubt that the office of the president is where strategy begins. He or she must be convinced that strengthening the soul of the college, its Christian heritage, is of paramount importance, one of the top five ongoing concerns of the college. Therefore, it must be a subject of regular conversation and reflection. It cannot be relegated to the private sphere. Doing so would ensure its long-term irrelevance, especially in a society whose "commanding heights" project a distaste for public religion. The president need not be alone in moving forward with this strategy; a core of faculty members and administrators are strong believers in Christian higher education, and they can be assembled to understand and then strategize about how "intentional pluralism" might be instituted. There are task forces for many important concerns of the college. Most colleges now have offices or task forces to encourage "diversity." If "soul" is also important, there is every reason to assemble an office/task force that can help the president think about "soul" matters.

The next important task is to instigate a serious ongoing conversation with the board of trustees regarding this "intentional pluralism." Though the board is not accustomed to talking about these matters, it is imperative that it do so. Board members have to understand the strategy that the president proposes, and they need to support him in it. Above all, they have to appropriate it in such a way that, when the next presidential vacancy comes along, they will have a clear criterion for recruiting a new president. If such an understanding is lacking, the next president of Roanoke College could undo in one generation what it has taken many generations to build. There are certainly other leadership qualities that require attention in the recruiting process, but the ability and commitment to care for the "soul" has to be near the top of the list.

Board composition is also important. The tradition of having the bishop of the Virginia Synod and several distinguished pastors as members is an important one to continue. It might be wise to formalize that tradition. It is even more important to have devoted and accomplished Lutheran/Christian laypeople on the board who are committed to a strong version of Christian higher education. Such members are most likely to support "intentional pluralism."

The president should oversee a revision in the college's publicity and admissions material that would positively note its Christian republican convictions. Language can be found that would emphasize those convictions without conveying signals of exclusion of students from other religious traditions or from no religious tradition. A portrayal of a robust, pluralistic "conversation" about the "great questions of life" can be made quite attractive.

The Academic Dean

Next in importance is the selection of a dean who understands and supports the strategy. That should not be unduly controversial, because the college statement of purpose supports "nurturing a dialogue between faith and reason," among other themes that support the religious element in the college's identity and mission. Actualizing the strategy would entail the following steps:

1. Orienting both students and faculty to the grand narrative of the college, replete with its Christian heritage. For students, such an orientation would remind them of the college's history and its commitment to Christian values as a basis for a life well lived.[15] Faculty members would have a more disciplined orientation to that history and mission. New professors could be given copies of a reprinted *The First Hundred Years* by William Eisenberg for the inspiring story of the college's founding

---

15. The establishment of a student competition for writing an essay that honors the witness of President John Morehead contributes to this goal; but the students should be offered a more complete story of Morehead than they currently receive. His witness to the values of the college was magnificent, and it deserves more than a paragraph.

and early years. That could be supplemented with selections from later histories, including this volume. New faculty members should also engage in conversation with those veterans who themselves feel "placed" within its narrative. Continuing the work of the "ancestors" can be a strong motivator.

2. Organizing periodic faculty retreats that would rehearse and reflect on the identity and mission of the college. This would include a persuasive introduction of the "intentional pluralist" strategy to which the college was committed. Such retreats could also occasionally revisit the statements of purpose and principles to ground the faculty in the broad institutional thrust of the college. Part of that revisitation would be an explication and demonstration of what it means to engage in the "dialogue between faith and reason." It might also mean continued scrutiny of how the INQ curriculum includes the Christian voice in an intentional way.

3. Selecting department chairs who would be committed not only to the substantive purpose of the college but also to its "intentional pluralist" strategy. They would recruit new faculty not only in accordance with departmental needs, but they would also "hire for mission." Part of that mission would be to ensure that at least one member of the department is interested in engaging an active Christian faith with his or her secular discipline. This would involve a "soft" affirmative action for these kinds of reflective Christians in general and Lutherans in particular.[16] It would certainly not mean hard quotas or preferring piety over competence; but it would include in "diversity" concerns the need for a Christian voice in that diversity.[17]

4. Meeting with every finalist for tenured faculty positions to ensure that those candidates are in harmony with the substantive purposes of the

16. This would not be so outlandish because many departments already have such faculty, though most of this has happened coincidentally. Thus, some departments have had few exemplars of "faith-learning engagement," something to which the college commits itself. Further, it would be important gently to privilege Lutherans among the candidates. A Lutheran-related college without Lutherans is something of an absurdity. If the Lutheran vision and ethos are important to the college, they need to be incarnated in Lutherans who live out their faith. Likewise, it is crucially important that the president be an observant Lutheran Christian who understands the imperatives of Christian higher education and who would press "intentional pluralism" forward.

17. It would perhaps be helpful to include religious and political conservatives in the "diversity" basket. This would mitigate the increasing dominance of academic life by "secular progressives," who are tempted to enforce a stultifying conformity when they have supremacy.

college, including its commitment to cultivate a dialogue between faith and reason. Though not all faculty members would be expected to engage in such a dialogue themselves, they would be asked to support those who do and to be open to their concerns.[18]

The Cabinet

"Intentional pluralism" in the president's cabinet would be something of a redundancy because the Roanoke vice presidents have always had a strong representation of Christians, some of them Lutherans. But insisting that the work in each division be open to Christian values and perspectives is another matter, since training for the various divisions has been subject to a professionalization that in recent years has marginalized "religiously based" concerns. Professionals in student life, admissions, resource development, and academic affairs are often trained to reduce values to the lowest common denominator and to avoid offense by not sounding "sectarian" in their approach. In the process, however, they tend to privatize religious concerns. It is important to reflect on how "faith-learning engagement" takes place in these highly professionalized fields. For example, student-life personnel can find ways of witnessing to Christian values and perspectives when they talk to students about the college's expectations. The effort to arrive at student "covenants for living together" is already a step in that direction. Periodic conversations on such concerns would be wholesome indeed.

The Chaplain

An important prerogative for the president is to appoint a chaplain to the college. Roanoke has had a tradition of strong Lutheran chaplains who stand for the faith without being insensitive to those who are not Christian/Lutheran. In the past decades they have come up with imaginative programs and have ministered to the community in a very effective way. The endowment of the chaplaincy makes it a stable position at the college; however,

18. A friend who is a graduate of Calvin College but currently teaches at St. Olaf humorously distinguished between the two colleges with regard to the requirement that faculty do faith-learning engagement. "At Calvin," he said, "you have to do it whether it is good or awful; at St. Olaf you have to do it only if you can do it well."

perhaps it needs to be elevated to a cabinet position. Such a move would ensure that religious concerns will be entertained in the ongoing deliberations of the cabinet.

The chaplain might also reinstate a useful ongoing discussion that earlier took place in the Bishop's Forum, which was attended by members of the department of religion and philosophy, the bishop and his staff, and the chaplain. It seems important for an ongoing conversation among those three "offices" to take place, since they all are concerned with the health of the Christian soul of the college. Each of them makes important contributions to those concerns, and each needs to communicate regularly.

The Religion and Philosophy Department

The president and dean have the high duty of making sure the endowed chairs on the religion side of the department are filled with faculty who fulfill the general expectations of the donors of the endowments. The donors wanted a strong religion side of the department (the Jordan-Trexler Chair in Religion), a scholarly and appreciative account of Lutheran contributions to Christian theological, biblical, or historical studies (the Tise Chair in Lutheran Studies), an alluring presentation of Lutheran theology (the Schumann Chair of Lutheran Theology), and a robust study and commendation of Christian ethics (the Schumann Chair of Christian Ethics). Conscientious attention to the proper selection of endowed chairs will ensure a strong Lutheran/Christian voice in the department and the college.

The department itself must decide its direction, but, given the presence of these four endowed chairs, it would be fitting to continue a strong "theological" emphasis on the religion side of the department. Likewise, philosophical approaches to religious ideas and claims should continue in harmony with the historic emphasis of the philosophy side, while taking up major options in more secular philosophical concerns.

The Benne Center

The Benne Center for Religion and Society can continue to reach more segments of the academy and the community. Two new initiatives (which are not really new) need to be initiated. The first involves an organized, ongoing discussion by interested faculty members and administrators of the status and destiny of Christian higher education in America. This would parallel and support the president's task force on nurturing the soul of the college. This kind of ongoing discussion would keep alive and increase faculty interest in that task. There is a growing literature on Christian higher education that would greatly aid in keeping that conversation alive.

A second project to be initiated would be the "Front-burner Conversation," which was simply a brown-bag luncheon in which a faculty member explained his or her research projects to other interested faculty. Such a forum is much needed in the current era of "silos," in which disciplinary boundaries prevent interdisciplinary discussion. With such a program in place, the center could elevate the level of intellectual interchange within the college.

Ethos

The founding and expansion of the honors program of the college elevated the academic quality of the student body markedly. A similar program might elevate and expand the presence of student Christian leadership and scholarship at the college. Since the department of religion and philosophy now has plenty of endowed chairs, but too few majors and minors, a new scholarship program might be established to make greater use of the endowed chairs and increase the number of majors. Lutheran/Christian money might be raised by the resource and development division to gather a large scholarship endowment to support Christian student leadership on campus. If enough money could be raised to provide handsome scholarships—covering full tuition perhaps—for a half-dozen topflight students per year, the "leaven" and "salt" functions of Christian presence on campus could definitely enrich the student ethos. A national competition for such Lutheran/Christian students could be held, from whom a half dozen would be awarded scholarships. In addition to tuition, each student would be assigned a Christian faculty tutor who would work with that student over four years. A small stipend would go to faculty members for their work. The purpose of such a tutoring relationship would be the student's firm formation in the Lutheran/Christian intellectual and moral tradition. While at the college, these students might recapture an era in which the "best and brightest" were most likely serious Christians. After graduation, some of these students would go into the ordained ministry, some to academic pursuits in theology, and some into secular lay vocations. Such a focused program would fit well into the overall "intentional pluralist" strategy.

An Urgent Final Word

Absent a strategy approximating what I have suggested above, the half-filled glass (the positive interpretation) will most likely empty slowly. Whatever is left of "soul" will depart. Why? Because the winds of secularization are blowing through the halls of academia in America much like they are blowing through other sectors of the "commanding heights" of the culture. Christianity—especially in its classic or conservative form—is in sharp conflict with the "secular progressivism" that is increasingly regnant. Classic construals of the faith are being pushed out of the public sphere, including the sphere of higher education.

Liberal interpretations of Christianity will be tolerated as long as they accommodate themselves to the shibboleths of the progressive agenda. However, those liberal versions will give up many of the essentials of the faith to the Zeitgeist and thus render themselves both uncritical and uninteresting. So—why bother? Other religions are more interesting and lack the "baggage" of Christianity, at least in the sanitized form they are taught in most parts of the academy. This is the path taken by many institutions that were once connected with religious traditions. But no longer.

Classic Christianity carries an intellectual and moral tradition that has been publicly relevant to Roanoke College for many years. That tradition is grounded on certain convictions: that Jesus Christ is definitive and unique for human salvation; that the Bible is the written word of God; that Christians are to bring the gospel to all the world; that all humans are mired in sin, from which they must be liberated by the gospel; that they must repent and amend their lives according to the commandments of God; that Christians have multiple callings in the world in which they critically participate and serve their neighbor; that the church is one of those important callings; that the love of God in Christ is to be conveyed in those callings; that marriage is a divinely ordained institution around which Christian sexual ethics revolve; and that the earth is a creation of God, to be tended and stewarded, but not to be worshiped. Living out these truths is the key to human flourishing: it brings peace and joy. All these tenets are bounded by the realization that our own formulations of the faith are limited by our finitude and distorted by our sin. Humility is called for.

Such convictions animate millions of Christians today, including many at Roanoke College. But Roanoke College is not the church. It should not aim at conversion of its students. Nor should it aim at unanimity of faculty belief. Yet, those Christian convictions in their intellectual form have engaged in a lively give and take with other claims in the college's educational offerings over the course of its 175 years. They deserve to be represented.

Those convictions were the ones that fired the imagination of David Bittle, the founder of Roanoke College. He believed that they should provide the guidance system for the college, and he saw to it that they did. They have been reduced, over time, from *the* guidance system to *a* voice in a pluralistic conversation. Meanwhile, the college has grown in numbers and quality, if not in coherence. It still believes, with Bittle, that "the most momentous duty of one generation to another is its education," and it continues the "Christian republican" themes that he and all the other presidents held dear. After Bittle, however, the persistence of those themes was generally assumed, not articulated and intended. Throughout its life, the college relied on a friendly "Christian culture" that supplied its faculty and sustained its themes.[19] But those days have waned, perhaps never to return. In response to that new challenge, the college must resolutely care for its "soul." In doing so, it will keep faith with the living Christian tradition that bore and sustained it. It will heed the voice of its "ancestors."

---

19. The friendly religious cultures upon which Roanoke relied in its "assumptions" changed over the course of the years. At the beginning it was the spirited evangelicalism of the Second Great Awakening. Then it was an amalgam of Southern evangelicalism and northern "enlightened" evangelicalism. After the turn of the twentieth century, it relied on a generic American mainline Protestantism that persisted until very recently, when the amalgam of Christianity and American culture fractured. With the coming of a "cooler," if not hostile, attitude toward Christianity—especially in its classical, or orthodox, form—the college can no longer rest on such a culture.

Appendix

Four Types of Church-Related Colleges

Four types: orthodox, critical mass, intentional pluralist, accidental pluralist

Major divide: the Christian vision as the organizing paradigm for the orthodox and critical mass types (the first two) versus the organizing paradigm coming from secular sources for the intentional and accidental pluralist types (the last two)

Public relevance of Christian vision:

Orthodox: pervasive from a shared point of view
Critical mass: privileged voice in an ongoing conversation
Intentional pluralist: an assured voice in an ongoing conversation
Accidental pluralist: random or absent voice in an ongoing conversation

Public rhetoric:

Orthodox: unabashed invitation to fellow believers to an intentional Christian enterprise
Critical mass: straightforward presentation as a Christian school but including others
Intentional pluralist: presentation as a liberal arts school with a Christian heritage
Accidental pluralist: presentation as a secular school with scarcely an allusion to Christian heritage

Membership requirements:

Orthodox: near 100 percent; orthodoxy tests
Critical mass: critical mass in all facets
Intentional pluralist: intentional representation
Accidental pluralist: haphazard sprinkling

Religion/theology department:

Orthodox: large and privileged; theology
Critical mass: large flagship; theology
Intentional pluralist: small, mixed; some theology
Accidental pluralist: small; mostly religious studies

Religion/theology required courses:

Orthodox: all courses affected by shared religious perspective
Critical mass: two or three; dialogical effort in many other courses
Intentional pluralist: one course in general education
Accidental pluralist: choice in distribution or an elective

Chapel attendance:

Orthodox: required in large chapel at a protected time daily
Critical mass: voluntary at high quality services in large nave at a daily
  protected time
Intentional pluralist: voluntary at unprotected times; low attendance
Accidental pluralist: for the few on special occasions

Ethos:

Orthodox: overt piety of sponsoring tradition
Critical mass: dominant atmosphere of sponsoring tradition—rituals and
  habits
Intentional pluralist: open minority from sponsoring tradition find their
  private niche
Accidental pluralist: reclusive and unorganized minority from sponsoring
  tradition (dominantly secular atmosphere)

Support by church:

Orthodox: indispensable financial support; majority of students from
  sponsoring tradition

Critical mass: important direct and crucial indirect financial support; at least 50 percent of students from sponsoring tradition

Intentional pluralist: important focused indirect financial support; small minority of students from sponsoring tradition

Accidental pluralist: token indirect financial support; student numbers from sponsoring tradition no longer recorded

Governance:

Orthodox: owned and governed by church or its official representatives

Critical mass: majority of board from tradition; some official representatives

Intentional pluralist: minority of board from tradition by unofficial agreement

Accidental pluralist: token board membership from tradition; college or university is autonomously owned and governed

Index